Strategies for
Writing Successful Essays

Strategies for
Writing Successful Essays

Nell W. Meriwether

NTC Publishing Group
a division of NTC/CONTEMPORARY PUBLISHING GROUP
Lincolnwood, Illinios USA

Executive Editor: Marisa L. L'Heureux
Editor: Heidi L. Hedstrom
Cover and interior design: Annette Spadoni
Illustrator: Tony Walczak
Design Manager: Ophelia M. Chambliss
Production Manager: Margo Goia

Acknowledgments begin on page 211, which is to be considered as an extension of this copyright page.

Library of Congress Cataloging-in-Publication Data

Meriwether, Nell.
     Strategies for writing successful essays / Nell W. Meriwether
          p.   cm.
     Includes index.
     ISBN 0-8442-5992-6 (pbk.)
      1. English language—Rhetoric. 2. Report writing. I. Title.
     PE1408.M48   1997
     808.4—dc21   97-18518
                                                      CIP

ISBN: 0-8442-5992-6

Published by NTC Publishing Group,
a division of NTC/Contemporary Publishing Group, Inc.,
4255 West Touhy Avenue,
Lincolnwood (Chicago), Illinois 60646-1975 U.S.A.
© 1998 by NTC/Comtemporary Publishing Group, Inc.

9 ML 9 8 7 6 5 4 3 2

Contents

Chapter Six The Process Essay 71

Chapter Seven The Problem-Solution Essay 85

Chapter Eight The Definition Essay 99

Preface

Many students hear the word *essay* and cringe. They believe that "good" writers simply sit down, and the words just come to them: such writers are able to write excellent essays in one sitting. Small wonder that students who believe this find writing essays such a frustrating experience! The reality, as this book will show, is that nobody—or perhaps a rare individual indeed!—is able the first time to compose a correct, truly compelling essay, something that will intrigue and wow its readers. The truth is that writing is a three-step process of prewriting (selecting a topic and planning what you will say), drafting or writing (getting the first version of your essay on paper), and revising (making changes to improve content and correcting spelling and grammatical errors). This book will guide you through this three-step process; once you have learned to break writing down into these three steps, you will hopefully see that you, too, are capable of writing a "good" essay and that writing can be a pleasurable activity after all.

Organization of the Text

Strategies for Writing Successful Essays is divided into three parts. Part One, "The Process of Writing" comprises the first three chapters of the book, each of which details one of the steps in the three-step writing process. Chapter One outlines the criteria you should use in choosing a topic and discusses the necessity of determining the audience, purpose, and tone for your paper *before* you begin writing; it also introduces you to eight prewriting strategies that can help you explore your topic and prepare you for the second step in the writing process—drafting—the subject of Chapter Two.

Drafting, as you will learn in Chapter Two, entails writing your first version of your paper, concentrating on breaking it into three parts: introduction, body, and conclusion. Notice that I say *first* version of your paper. As said above, the writing process includes three steps, the last of which is revising, the topic of Chapter Three. Once you have revised your paper, according to the instructions outlined in Chapter Three, you will have a finished product, an essay that reflects thought, planning, and hard work.

You may be wondering what the remaining thirteen chapters of *Strategies for Writing Successful Essays* could possibly entail, since having read the first three chapters, you are already well-versed in the writing process. Note the word *essays* in the title; having provided you with the three-step model for writing, *Strategies for Writing Successful Essays* goes on to discuss *essays* themselves. Although there are many types of essays, they can be grouped into four general categories: *narration* (telling a story), *description* (creating a verbal picture of something through words), *exposition* (explaining something), and *persuasion* (taking a stand and trying to sway your reader to your way of thinking).

These types of essays are explored in Part Two, "Kinds of Essays." Chapters Four through Fourteen introduce you to the many types of essays, such as the Evaluation Essay, the Pro-Con Essay, and the Classification Essay, discussing how each type is suited to one of the four categories of writing. For example, say you have been assigned to write a descriptive essay. You will find that the character sketch, covered in Chapter Five, is well-suited to descriptive writing.

Part Three, "Writing Aids," builds upon what you have learned in Parts One and Two about the writing process and the various types of essays. Part Three discusses two additional topics that will benefit you in both your academic career and your life beyond school: writing essays in test situations (Chapter Fifteen) and developing a writing style that is both correct and uniquely yours (Chapter Sixteen).

Features of the Text

The following features are an integral part of this book and serve to emphasize the points made throughout the text:

- **Writing Strategies:** In Chapters Four through Fourteen you will find numerous strategies for approaching each of the three steps of the writing process; the strategies vary according to the type of essay being discussed.

- **Student and Published Models:** For each type of essay discussed in Chapters Four through Fourteen, there are two model essays—one by a student and one a published piece—that serve as excellent examples for you to emulate.

- **Activities:** In every chapter you will find activities that will enable you to apply what you have learned. Some activities ask you how a model essay fits a particular format, while others ask you to focus on a specific aspect of writing, such as your paper's audience.

- **Guidelines:** Specific guidelines are presented for writing each type of essay discussed in Chapters Four through Fourteen.

- **Checklists:** Checklists help you to approach each step of the writing process in a systematic way to produce prose that is clear and correct.

- **Possible Topics:** Each list of possible topics contains possibilities that would be appropriate for the type of essay assigned. Alternatively, the list acts as a springboard, helping you to explore the many topics about which you can write.

The goal of *Strategies for Writing Successful Essays* is to help you to write in any situation about any topic, be it describing a painting, explaining how to use the Internet, relating a perilous white-water rafting experience, or persuading people to adopt your opinion about a given issue. You can help this book achieve its goal by carefully reading through each chapter, analyzing the model essays, and following the writing strategies discussed throughout. Once you have finished reading *Strategies for Writing Successful Essays,* you will hopefully find essay writing to be a fun and worthwhile experience.

Good luck!

Strategies for Writing Successful Essays

The Process

In the past, instructors often expected students like you to come to the classroom and write on a given topic without prior thought on the subject. However, in recent years, the trend has changed. Recognition that writing is a process—not just a sitting-down-and-doing-it affair—is now the norm. Several steps are generally identified as the basic ones in the process; these include prewriting (selecting a topic and planning what you will say), drafting or writing (getting a first version of your essay down on paper), and revising (making changes to improve content, reading for errors, and proofreading).

Working through each of these steps can make anyone a better writer. In prewriting, for example, you take time to think about the topic and experiment with it before actually writing the essay. This prewriting stage helps to produce papers that are more focused and better organized. In the writing stage, you no longer need to consider what you say as the final version; it is a first attempt, something that you can improve on. Your revision, the third stage, is not just a rewrite of the essay but a look at the paper from many angles. One very effective revision technique is to get together with other students and peer evaluate the first draft, using a list of questions designed for the particular essay. Another technique is self-evaluating according to a procedure planned for the essay. Whatever is done in the revision process helps you to see errors you might not see without specific direction.

# of Writing

Not only is writing not a one-step process, quite often it is not even linear. For example, in the middle of drafting your essay, you may decide that it is necessary to go back to the first step and start over again with a different aspect of the topic. So in a way, the writing process is not really separate steps; it is a continually flowing process involving thought and trial and error. Nevertheless there are things you can do as you prewrite, draft, and revise that will make the process work better for you.

Steps in the Writing Process: Prewriting

This first chapter will focus on prewriting strategies. Prewriting allows you to think about the purpose for your writing as well as the audience for your paper and to work within that framework for the best results.

Selecting a Topic

The first thing you need to do before you begin writing is, of course, to find something to write about. Sometimes this problem will be solved for you—for example, when your instructor asks you to analyze the first three chapters of a book the class is reading. Often, however, the choice is left to you. You may know that you need to write a problem-solution essay about a community issue, but you yourself must select the issue. So where do you begin?

Throughout this book, we will be giving you suggestions on how to choose a topic for different kinds of essays, and we will also provide some topic ideas to get your thinking started. In addition, as you work through the prewriting strategies in the next section, you will realize that some of them can help you take a vague topic idea—forestry, for example—and work with it until you get a specific handle on it—for example, how selective burnoffs can improve the tree quality in the woods in your area.

In the meantime, here are some general recommendations. You should seriously consider choosing a topic that

- you are interested in and/or feel strongly about;
- you know about, preferably from firsthand experience, or that you can easily find out about;

- your audience will be interested in;
- you can write about in a three- or four-page essay.

Determining Audience, Purpose, and Tone

Before you can begin to plan an essay, you need to think seriously about whom you are writing for, what your purpose is in addressing that audience, and what tone or attitude about your subject—serious, indignant, happy, tongue-in-cheek, conversational, or humorous—you want to convey. Once you have a general idea of each of these, you can begin to plan out how to organize and develop your paper.

Knowing your audience is necessary to keep your focus in writing. It helps your reader feel that the essay was meant specifically for him or her to read, and it gives you as the writer a sense of direction or purpose. Knowing your audience also means understanding how much knowledge your audience already has of the subject matter, what terms need to be defined, whether the audience is biased toward certain ideas, and how simple or complex the writing needs to be.

The purpose and tone of your essay is also bound up in the audience. For example, if you are writing a persuasive paper, your purpose may be to convince a group of concerned citizens to agree with your position on a controversial issue. The information you put into your essay will make clear your viewpoint and stance on the issue. You will use terminology the audience will understand, and your tone—or attitude toward the subject—will reflect your serious purpose. On the other hand, if your purpose is to write a descriptive piece concerning the habits and habitats of polar bears for a wildlife magazine, you will choose words and arrange material to help the readers "see" what you are describing. The tone you use will probably be light and conversational, and holding and keeping the attention of your nature-oriented audience will be a deciding factor in how the piece will be written.

Using Prewriting Strategies

When you have a pretty clear idea about audience, purpose, and tone, you can go on to explore your topic through various prewriting strategies. These strategies can help you do several things. They can provide the means to narrow a topic that is too broad or expand on a too-narrow one, as well as focus in on the specifics that you will need to cover in your paper. They may also lead you to adjust your audience, purpose, and tone as you get a better idea of the material you have to work with. In addition, prewriting strategies can provide a rough organization for your essay. Once you get in the habit of prewriting, you will automatically make it a part of your writing, and it will come naturally.

Many strategies can be used in the prewriting step; some work better than others, depending on which kind of essay you are writing. In the chapters that follow, a different prewriting technique is given for each essay described. If, however, the one suggested doesn't work well for you, the following list has prewriting techniques that can be adapted to almost any essay form. You may find that your ideas lend themselves better to one of these techniques, and you may find it easier to organize your thoughts using it. The important thing is not to settle on one prewriting strategy to the exclusion of others. Try different kinds to see how they work for you.

The prewriting strategies that follow are given in alphabetical order, not in the order of the essay type or the order of difficulty. Experimenting with a variety of prewriting strategies will help you learn the ones that work best for you.

Brainstorming

Brainstorming is a prewriting technique often used for its simplicity. All it involves is choosing a topic and writing down everything that comes to mind about it. There are no rules to follow; just jot down words, phrases, or sentences about the topic as you think of them. Don't even worry about writing in order or censoring yourself for things that don't seem to fit together. After you have written a page or so of ideas, put your thoughts together in some order. These will help you decide on a thesis statement that will be the focus of your paper. (We will talk about thesis statements in Chapter Two.)

Here is what one student wrote when asked to brainstorm about a childhood memory.

Topic: Camping in the Wilderness

My first real camping trip—eleven years old

A long way from home/in another state

Had to cook our food outside, eat in tin pans, wash own utensils

Camped out in the wilderness

Got stung by bees all over my head when I reached for a limb

Cried and called home to tell Mom and Dad/afraid I was going to die

Dad is allergic/thought I might be too

Face and neck swelled up and hurt bad

Camp counselor gave me Benadryl and took me to emergency room

Bees swarmed on me like they were dive bombers

Weather turned cold overnight/not enough warm clothes/nearly froze

Camped out during Thanksgiving week—missed school

Had fun but boy was I glad to get home

Worked on merit badges

When he went back to group some of his ideas later, he came up with the following notes.

1. Got stung by bees—cried—afraid I was going to die since Dad is allergic—called home to tell Mom and Dad—hurt really bad—face and neck swelled up—camp counselor gave me Benadryl and took me in to town to the emergency room—bees swarmed over me like dive bombers

2. My first real camping trip—eleven years old—camp a long way from home in another state—camped out in wilderness during Thanksgiving week—got to miss school—turned cold overnight—nearly froze cause didn't think it would be so cold and didn't bring enough clothes

3. Had to cook our own meals—fun but not like home—ate in tin pans—had to wash own utensils—worked on merit badges—was glad to get home

These groupings made it clear that he had several different directions he might go with his essay, but he ultimately decided to concentrate on the incident with the bees.

Brainstorming is a good prewriting exercise to see what you might have to say about a general, half-formed topic. In addition, it opens your mind to thoughts and ideas you might not have considered before. Brainstorming works well in helping you to come up with specific ideas for almost any kind of essay. It is a strategy that can be worked on individually, as in the example above, or as a class exercise with everyone focusing on the same idea. For another example of brainstorming, see page 180.

Activity 1: Brainstorm a Topic

Write one of the following topics at the top of a piece of paper:

- extracurricular activities
- work and school
- my family
- exercise and health

After choosing a topic, begin writing down everything you can think of about it. Don't worry about order or whether you have complete sentences or correct punctuation. When you have covered a page or so with ideas, look back over them to see the angle you have used in gathering your thoughts. Group the ideas together so that you have three or four groups. Now share your results with a classmate who selected the same topic to see how similar or different your ideas are.

Classical Invention

Classical invention is a term taken from Aristotle's method of organization. Aristotle was one of the greatest thinkers in ancient Athens; his orations are still analyzed and admired because of their organization and eloquence.

Aristotle's method of oratory consisted of doing five things: (1) defining his subject, (2) making comparisons, (3) forming relationships, (4) projecting future possibilities or relating past events, and (5) giving a testimonial to clinch the effectiveness of the subject.

Aristotle's method of oratory can be used as a good prewriting technique. It involves dividing your thoughts into five categories: definition, comparison, relationship, circumstance, and testimony. Under each of the categories, you should write questions to help you focus in on the topic and see how much you can find out about it. Some of the questions may simply point you in a certain direction, and you may not even choose to answer them, but they will give you ideas for how to approach the topic.

To show how classical invention works as a prewriting strategy, the illustration below uses the subject "Honor," which you would write at the top of the page.

Topic: Honor

Steps	Possible Questions
Definition: Look in the dictionary and define the word *honor.*	• How has the word changed in meaning through the years? • What are some words that are similar in meaning to honor?
Comparison: Compare the word with other words that are similar, such as *respect, esteem, prestige, dignity,* or *integrity.* Then pose questions that suggest contrasting ideas.	• How is honor compared with esteem or respect? • Can honor be recognized as dignity or integrity? • What is the difference between honor and dishonesty? • How is honor contrasted with turncoat or disgrace?
Relationship: Question the connection between honor and other similar ideas, looking for a relationship between the cause and the effect of what happens.	• What causes one person to achieve honors while others do not? • What does it take to be thought of as honored? • Does it make a difference, for example, if one receives honors? • Is there any effect if one is honored by the president or the governor or some prestigious group?
Circumstance: Make up questions having to do with the circumstances or conditions associated with honor. Focus on *why.*	• What is the purpose of honoring people? • Why are some people honored while others are not?

Testimony: Make up questions about people who have received honors and about things that have been written about honor.

- What are the circumstances that cause some people to receive honors at events such as graduation exercises?
- Do honor graduates get better positions? Do they deserve the honors they receive?
- What has Mother Teresa of India been honored for?
- Why is John F. Kennedy still honored even though he was president for only part of a term?
- What made George Washington a symbol of honor?
- What do the Ten Commandments say about honoring parents?
- What is the honor code of various groups?

Classical invention is a prewriting exercise that demands thought, but it is well worth the effort to achieve the quality of writing shown in the finished product. Another example of classical invention is shown on page 104.

Activity 2: Use Classical Invention

Divide into groups, with five people in each group. Select one of the following words or another abstract term of your choice:

- democracy
- prejudice
- goals
- self-fulfillment
- loyalty

Have each person in the group write questions for one category in the chart similar to the questions shown in the sample chart. After the questions have been posed and discussed in your group, determine what would be a good angle to write from. Compare your ideas with other groups in the class that have chosen the same topic.

Clustering

Clustering is a prewriting technique that helps you to produce ideas by making associations or by breaking down a topic. With clustering, you create a diagram that helps you discover relationships among ideas. The procedures for clustering are simple:

- Write the subject at the top of the page.
- Quickly write down and circle all related ideas that come to mind.
- Draw lines connecting the ideas either to the subject or to one another.
- Keep associating and connecting as long as you can. The more ideas you have, the better.

An example of clustering is given below using the topic "Childhood Memories."

Topic: Childhood Memories

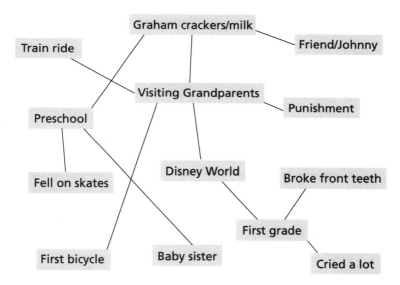

As shown in the example, some ideas relate easily, while with others the connection isn't as strong. The longer you keep trying to make associations, the more ideas you will come up with. As you see how the ideas are related, one overriding thought should emerge from each cluster that could later serve as a topic sentence for each paragraph of your essay.

Clustering can be used with almost any essay; for another example of clustering, see page 142.

Activity 3: Create a Cluster

Choose one of the following topics and write it on a piece of paper:

- things I learned from my brothers and/or sisters
- worries
- a memorable vacation
- learning to dance

Now begin writing down words or phrases that pertain to the topic. Circle all ideas that are related. Draw lines connecting the circled ideas either to the subject or to one another. Now recopy your clusters, grouping similar ideas together. You may want to share your results with a classmate who selected the same topic.

Freewriting

Freewriting is what the name implies—writing freely or with abandon. Sometimes it is used to zero in on a topic; at other times you may have a topic but not be sure that you have anything worthwhile to say about it. The only rule for freewriting is that almost anything goes! Punctuation is not important, nor are complete sentences or order of thoughts: the point is to get ideas down on paper.

Sometimes freewriting is done as the instructor times the class for two or three five- to ten-minute periods. After the first timing, you can tell by what you have written if you have anything to say about the subject. If not, as the instructor times the class a second or third time, write on a different topic or continue writing on the same topic if it seems to have promise. The more you write, the more material you will have for your essay.

Freewriting opens your mind to ideas you might have initially neglected. As you write, new thoughts surface and new examples come to mind. Ellen did the following freewriting in preparation for an essay about foolish mistakes she's made. Notice that with each new example she is more clearly showing the type of person she is. (For another example of freewriting, see page 64.)

Topic: Mishaps in My Life

First Timing: Working in the yard for Mother one Saturday morning. Sunshiny—a good day to work outside. Mom liked flowers and had them everywhere. Gave each of us a choice of which flower bed to weed. I chose the one at the back door; it had yellow flowers and lots of grass. Some of the flowers hadn't bloomed (I found out), so I got busy fast cause we could quit as soon as we finished. When I got through, she came over to inspect. Mouth flies open; asks where her flowers are. I had pulled up everything that didn't have a bloom. The bed was bare, but it looked good to me.

Second Timing: Another smart episode. Mother out of town for the day; I thought I'd surprise her. Bathroom needed painting, so I found some paint in the store room that looked all right. A part of the bathroom was wallpapered, but I didn't think that mattered. Painted the trim white/careless/paint said it was washable. Mom comes back, I proudly show her the bathroom. Mouth flies open again when she see parts of the wallpaper covered with paint. I told her it wouldn't matter because the paint can said it could be washed off. It was then I found out it had to be done immediately.

Third Timing: Worst mess up: was when I was working. Joe Digby/apartment complex/wanted the outside stairs cleaned and painted. Had to take a wire brush, get the rust off first, then paint. I was about halfway through when he drove up to see how I was doing. This time his mouth flew open. I got the directions mixed up and was doing the apartment stairs next door. By this time, I was beginning to wonder about myself.

Activity 4: Freewrite in Timed Periods

Select a topic of your own, or use one that your instructor assigns. Do three five-minute timed writings about the topic, striving for more specific examples each time. If you find you have nothing to say about your topic after the first timed writing, discuss changing your topic with your instructor.

Journal Writing

Journal writing is simply recording your thoughts and ideas in a journal or notebook every day or every few days. Journal writing has no rules, no right or wrong way to write, no way that it has to be. A journal entry can be serious or it can be funny. It gives you the opportunity to get in touch with yourself and to write without having to adhere to guidelines.

The main value of journal writing as a prewriting activity is that the things you write about can serve as a springboard for essay ideas or as a file or reference for good topics. Though the personal experience or narrative essay often can be derived from journal entries, because of its richness in material a journal can be the basis for almost any kind of essay. Notice the various directions in which these two journal entries might lead the writer.

Topic: Lily the Mechanic

July 8

I've been trying to figure out what Lily across the street is doing with her car. She's been out there for the last two days with the hood up and a flashlight in her hand. I wonder if she knows what she's doing or if she's hoping someone will come along and help her.

July 11

Lily's still at it. Now she's got wrenches and other tools, and now sometimes she's underneath the car as well. I wonder if being a mechanic is a good job for a woman: would only other women come to her, or would men have some confidence in her too? It might be interesting to check the yellow pages to see if any woman-run gas stations are listed.

These journal entries might lead the writer to research an essay on opportunities for women mechanics or to write a character sketch on one discovered by looking through the phone book.

Activity 5: Review Topics in Your Journal

Go through your journal and note possible topics for essays. Make a list and keep it with your materials for this course. If you do not have a journal, list some of the topics you have explored in freewriting, and begin to keep a journal in which you explore them, and other topics, further.

Listing

Listing is a method that has several variations and can be used with different kinds of essays. Sometimes the technique involves a single list; sometimes a double one is used.

Using a Single List.   A single list is a simple recording of all of the points you plan to use. After making the list, all you need to do is to go back and group the points in the order you plan to use them. The process essay, since it is concerned with the steps necessary to showing how something is done, is one good place to use a single list . The list helps you focus on what needs to be done in order of time and allows you to see if certain steps are so minor they can be grouped together. An example of prewriting using a single list is shown with the process essay on page 77. The example below also uses this technique.

Topic: Potting a Flower

- Gather things needed: flower pot, potting soil, root stimulator, water, trowel, flower
- Put soil in pot
- Using trowel, make room for flower in the middle of the pot
- Mix root stimulator with water and pour some in the hole
- Place the flower in the hole and pack soil around it
- Pour more root stimulator around the plant until it is wet
- Put flower pot in the sun

This list is already arranged according to the order in which the flower will be planted; however, in your prewriting, you do not have to list in any particular order. Often it is better just to get the points down and then reorganize them later.

Using a Double List.   A double list is used when you want to emphasize two parts of a topic; for example, similarities and differences, pros and cons, problems and solutions. An example using this technique is shown on page 131 with the comparison-contrast essay. The double list on the following page was used in planning a problem-solution essay to determine whether the problem or the solution should be emphasized. The completed list made it clear that the writer had stronger points to make about the problem than about the solutions; therefore, that was what he would emphasize in his essay.

Topic: Obesity in Children

Problem	Solutions
• More overweight children every year (give statistics)	• Parents can promote physical exercise
• Obesity in children produces obese adults	• Kids can be taught how to eat properly and avoid fatty foods
• Society is very hard on overweight kids	• Children can be given professional help—child psychologist or psychiatrist
• Obesity causes lack of self-esteem and depression	
• Obese children have higher cholesterol and other health problems	
• Obese kids often can't wear clothes like what other kids wear	

Activity 6: Make Lists

Do one or both of the following.

1. Work with a partner. Each of you should work alone to create a list of eight or ten steps necessary to make an object. Jumble up the list so that it is not in order. Then switch papers with your partner and put each other's lists in the correct order.

2. Choose a partner and decide on a topic for a pro-con essay. One of you list as many points supporting the topic as possible; the other list points against the topic. From the two lists, determine which side of the issue is stronger and how you would approach it in an essay.

Reporter's Formula

The reporter's formula involves the questions used in the lead paragraph of journalistic writing: WHO, WHAT, WHERE, WHEN, WHY, and HOW. With this type of prewriting, all that is necessary is to look at the subject and ask questions about it to help you gain material for your essay. Questions such as WHAT happened? WHEN and WHERE did it happen? WHO was involved? WHY did it happen? and HOW did it happen? give you insight into the topic that will help to organize your essay and gather material from which to work.

Using the reporter's formula works well with a number of different essay forms but especially with personal experience and narrative essays, since they both tell a story. An example of using this formula in prewriting is given below. Since Jamie vividly remembers the exact time and place of the accident she is writing about, this strategy works well for her paper.

Topic: An Automobile Accident

- WHAT—a tragic automobile accident
- WHEN—November 27 at 2:00 o'clock on a sunny afternoon
- WHERE—On a curvy and hilly two-lane road just out of Sibley, Mississippi
- WHO—two men in a red car/driver of a white pickup truck/two friends and me
- WHY—other car was going too fast
    —the driver was intoxicated
    —couldn't negotiate the hill and curve
- HOW—the red car going at a high rate of speed side-swiped a white pickup truck in front of my car
    —truck spun headlong into my car, causing death of two people in the red car
    —the three people in my car were hospitalized in serious condition

Activity 7: Use the Reporter's Formula

Work with a partner. One person will interview the other about a memorable incident in his or her life. Use the reporter's formula to conduct the interview, and write brief notes about each point. After the interview is completed, the person who conducted it should give an oral account of the incident to the rest of the class. Afterwards, you can switch roles with your partner and repeat the process.

Synthesizing

Synthesizing is putting together or combining information on a given subject. This technique is often used after surveying and analyzing data because it calls for combining the results to reach conclusions about the data studied. For example, suppose you decide to do a survey of music. You interview a number of people to determine the kind of music they like and why. Your survey may look like this:

Topic: Musical Talents and Interests

1. Are you male or female? _____ Age _____
2. What kind of music do you listen to most? _____

3. Which male artist do you prefer? _____

4. Which female artist do you prefer? _____

5. Which band do you like best? _____

6. Where do you listen to music most? _____

7. Which do you prefer? (circle one)—jazz, country, pop, western, reggae, classical, religious, other

8. What kind of music do you like least? _____

9. Do you play a musical instrument? _____

10. If so, what kind of instrument? _____

After all of the data has been gathered, it is time to decide on what you want to emphasize in your essay and why it is important. To do this, you would look at the information you got from various questions and combine it to make new points. For example, this survey may have shown you that people who play guitar are most interested in country and reggae music, and that fifteen-year-old women overwhelmingly prefer male to female artists. This is what is meant by synthesizing, putting information together based on the analysis of your data.

It is possible to use synthesizing with more than one kind of essay; for example, the cause and effect essay could benefit from this technique. However, the evaluation essay on page 163 uses this method quite effectively.

Activity 8: Synthesize Information for an Essay

Work in a group. Select a topic to write about that involves collecting information in some way—either through a questionnaire or survey or by doing library research. Set up several categories that you want data for. Have each group member collect a portion of the data. Then discuss how you would assemble the data in an essay—that is, how you would synthesize the information you obtained.

Activity 9: Culminating Activity

From the list of possible essay topics on the next page, choose four. Do the following for each:

• Think of an audience that would be interested in the topic.

• Determine your possible purpose for writing about it.

• Decide on the tone you might use.

Now focus in on each topic by applying a different prewriting strategy to each. If necessary, adjust your audience, purpose, and tone as you zero in on the specific aspects of the topic that you will be covering. After you have completed the assignment, choose one of the topics and compare your approach with others who worked with the same topic.

↘ **Possible Topics**

- Careers for 2000 and beyond
- Divorce
- Lasting impressions
- Student apathy
- Travel
- Peer pressure
- Women in politics
- Suicide
- Discipline
- Television and violence
- MTV
- Family planning
- Sports
- Memorable moments
- Loyalty
- Jobs and school
- "Couch potatoes"
- Civil disobedience
- Friendship
- Pollution

Keep this assignment so that it may be used with activities in Chapter Two.

Steps in the Writing Process: Drafting

Now that you have looked at ways to prewrite, you should see that prewriting is an invaluable step in helping you formulate your thoughts and gather your material. The next step is the actual process of writing itself; here you will write a first draft of your essay.

As we have said earlier, some things never change in writing. They remain the same because they are important to making writing understood, to giving it clarity of purpose, audience, and tone. The first of these is formulating the thesis, the kernel of the paper. This statement, which occurs early in an essay, is the one idea that holds the paper together and on which everything else is built.

Though you may not have realized it, all of the prewriting techniques you used in the previous chapter were designed to get you to the point where you could write a thesis statement. By the time you finished listing or brainstorming or clustering or any one of the other strategies, besides having some idea of what you would include in your paper, you had the basis for a thesis. You knew what you were going to write about and the approach you would take. Because of its importance, a detailed discussion of what makes a good thesis statement follows.

Creating a Thesis Statement

The thesis statement is the main idea or controlling purpose of your paper. It is usually stated in one sentence and might even be called a one-sentence summary of the paper. It almost always is in the introduction so that the reader has a clear idea of your subject and the stance you will take on it.

Thesis statements will vary depending on the purpose of your paper, as shown below:

- For a paper whose purpose is to persuade, the thesis states the position you will take; therefore, the thesis statement will be arguable.
- For a paper whose aim is to give information, the thesis may simply be a statement announcing the topic.
- For a paper whose purpose is to describe or to narrate, the thesis may express the mood created or the emotion of the moment. Occasionally in such papers, the thesis may be implied without directly being stated.

A thesis should never be an open-ended question. If such a question *were* written as the thesis, the reader would have no idea of what is being supported; so it must be a declarative sentence or a focused question. Furthermore, the thesis should be restricted, which means that it should cover only those points you intend to discuss. At the same time, it should not be so broad that it would be difficult to cover the material. Look at the examples below.

POOR: The Equal Rights Amendment was ratified to give women the ability to hold jobs without discrimination, to end prejudice toward races and gender, and to put a stop to the double standard.

BETTER: A primary reason the Equal Rights Amendment was ratified was to end discrimination in the workplace.

The first thesis is too broad because it includes racial prejudice as well as gender bias and because the last part of it, "to put a stop to the double standard," does not make clear whether it refers to the job market or elsewhere. The second thesis, by contrast, is focused in on one specific aspect of the topic that could easily be addressed in an essay.

In addition to focus, a thesis should have unity—it should have a single purpose, not two conflicting ideas in the same sentence.

POOR: College costs an average of 6 percent more every year, which keeps some students from attending; on the other hand, many still find a way to go.

BETTER: College costs an average of 6 percent more every year; nevertheless, many students still find a way to go.

The first example addresses both students who can and cannot attend college, which negates any unified or consistent approach to the topic. The second example focuses the paper to just one of those populations.

The thesis is like the rudder of a ship; it tells the reader where you are going, and it doesn't lead him or her adrift. Because of this, you should spend some time thinking about how you are going to state the thesis for your paper. A good critic can look at your thesis and know what your paper will say and what kind of essay you are writing. Learn how to develop that sense yourself.

Activity 1: Rewrite Thesis Statements

Correct the thesis statements below by referring to the points made in the previous discussion. Then state briefly what was wrong with the original versions.

1. The World's Fair in New Orleans was a disaster because of the way the press criticized the way it was run, but it was exciting for little children and had many good food booths.
2. Unless people are conscious of pollution, the world will be destroyed by the year 2050.
3. Since politicians are constantly bombarding each other, how do they expect anyone to know who is right and who is wrong?
4. Rap music is a popular form of art because it is creative and original and because it follows the traditions of other spontaneously developed music like jazz.
5. TV commercials are obnoxious to the person who is intent on watching a good show; on the other hand, they provide entertainment in the antics of the performers and they provide a good opportunity to take a snack break.

Activity 2: Draft Thesis Statements

Write thesis statements for the four topics you worked with in the last exercise in Chapter One. Remember to make each thesis statement reflect the purpose for your paper. Use your improved thesis statements in the preceding exercise as models.

Focusing on Audience and Tone

As pointed out in Chapter One, you should have a good idea of your audience before you even begin to approach your topic. By the time you are ready to write, though, you should have homed in on that audience very specifically. Because your audience varies in background, age, knowledge, bias, and general interest, the details you use as well as your writing style can also vary. For example, you would probably write in a clear, simple style with an easy-to-understand vocabulary and examples for young readers. You might use longer sentences and more abstract terms and concepts if your audience were more mature. And you might use very specialized language if you were writing on a technical subject for a specialized audience. Unless you keep your readers in mind, you will have no assurance that they will understand or be interested in what you are saying.

The tone of the paper—the attitude you assume toward your writing—should also be clearly defined by this time. Tone also comes out in the way you write—for example, whether you approach your subject seriously, lightheartedly, or angrily. It is affected by your use of details and through your choice of words or diction. Once you establish the tone, it should be the same throughout the paper.

Nearly all effective papers have some identifiable tone. In those that don't, the writing is not as interesting. It tends to be dull and lifeless.

Activity 3: Write for a Different Audience

The following piece, entitled "Democracy," was written by E. B. White on July 3, 1943. Recast it so that one of the following audiences can understand White's feelings about democracy.

- A group of seventh-grade students
- A group of exchange students from an Eastern European country
- A group of kindergartners

> We received a letter from the Writers' War Board the other day asking for a statement on "The Meaning of Democracy." It presumably is our duty to comply with such a request, and it is certainly our pleasure.
>
> Surely the Board knows what democracy is. It is the line that forms to the right. It is the don't in don't shove. It is the hole in the stuffed shirt through which the sawdust slowly trickles; it is the dent in the high hat. Democracy is the recurrent suspicion that more than half of the people are right more than half of the time. It is the feeling of privacy in the voting booths, the feeling of communion in the libraries, the feeling of vitality everywhere. Democracy is the score at the beginning of the ninth. It is an idea which hasn't been disproved yet, a song the words of which have not gone bad. It's the mustard on the hot dog and the cream in the rationed coffee.
>
> Democracy is a request from a War Board, in the middle of a morning in the middle of a war, wanting to know what democracy is.

Activity 4: Analyze Tone

In the sample below, "High School Graduation," Maya Angelou establishes her attitude about her topic immediately. Read the passage and then answer the questions that follow it.

> The children in Stamps trembled visibly with anticipation. Some adults were excited too, but to be certain the whole young population had come down with graduation epidemic. Large classes were graduating from both the grammar school and the high school. Even those who were years removed from their own day of glorious release were anxious to help with preparations as a kind of dry run. The junior students who were moving into the vacating classes' chairs were tradition-bound to show their talents for leadership and management. They strutted through the school and around the

campus exerting pressure on the lower grades. Their authority was so new that occasionally if they pressed a little too hard it had to be overlooked. After all, next term was coming, and it never hurt a sixth grader to have a play sister in the eighth grade, or a tenth-year student to be able to call a twelfth grader Bubba. So all was endured in a spirit of shared understanding. But the graduating classes themselves were the nobility. Like travelers with exotic destinations on their minds, the graduates were remarkably forgetful. They came to school without their books, or tablets or even pencils. Volunteers fell over themselves to secure replacements for the missing equipment. When accepted, the willing workers might or might not be thanked, and it was of no importance to the pregraduation rites. Even teachers were respectful of the now quiet and aging seniors, and tended to speak to them, if not as equals, as beings only slightly lower than themselves. After tests were returned and grades given, the student body, which acted like an extended family, knew who did well, who excelled, and what piteous ones had failed.

1. What is the tone that the writer establishes?
2. What kind of language does she use to establish the tone?
3. What are some specific words and phrases that strengthen the tone?
4. How does she carry the same tone throughout the piece?

Using an Appropriate Style

Style has to do with the way you write. It is shown through your choice of words, your use of dialogue and of repetition, and through the rhythm of your sentences. Style is recognized in writing much the same way that it is recognized in music and art or architecture or dress. It is just there, and sometimes it is difficult to pinpoint.

More than anything else, however, the style you use should incorporate language that is clear and not cumbersome or repetitious. Your sentences should vary in structure to add interest and greater variety to your writing. The words and expressions you use, the length of your sentences and paragraphs, the overall flow of your writing—all of these things combine to make your own distinct style.

Depending on the situation, your style can, and should, vary from formal to informal. A formal style is characterized by a precise and carefully chosen vocabulary, a fairly complex sentence structure, and an absence of personal references. It is appropriate for formal, serious situations. An informal style includes most of the stories you heard as a child, but also any writing in a lively, conversational tone. The more you write, the more you will develop your own distinct style and learn to adjust it as circumstances dictate. For the purpose of your writing for this book, you will want to make your style suitable for a well-written essay.

Activity 5: Compare and Contrast Styles

As a class, discuss the differences in the styles of the E. B. White and Maya Angelou pieces you read on pages 22 and 23. Be ready to point out what makes each distinctive. You might also look for other writings on the same topics that use a different style.

Getting Words on Paper

Now that you have looked at developing a thesis for your paper, zeroing in on your audience and tone, and using an appropriate style, you may be asking, "But what about the actual writing? How do I know where to start?"

For the purposes of this course, one answer lies in knowing what the assignment is that your instructor has just given you. As you will see from the essay instruction later in this book, you will usually have some idea of how to address your topic before you start. The important thing is not to get hung up when you start drafting your essay by thinking that you must have a perfect draft the first time. Even the best professional writers write and rewrite and then rewrite some more. If you can just get your thoughts down, you can polish your paper later.

As you gain more experience with writing, you will see that it is far more than sitting down and dashing off words. It is thinking and thinking and thinking! It is thinking about your objective or thesis; it is thinking about the information you want to present and how best to present it. It is this "how to present it" aspect that the rest of this chapter will deal with.

Knowing the Essay Form

You are probably familiar with the form that is taught in school for almost all essays: the introduction, the body, and the conclusion. Usually the minimum number of paragraphs is five; however, instructors are always glad to see students expand their work to include more if the writing is good. Ways to develop each part of the essay are included in the following discussion for the benefit of those who are unfamiliar with different forms or who tend to use the same kind of writing with each essay.

The Introduction

The introduction is usually only one paragraph in essay writing, but it can always be extended to include more paragraphs if needed. It sets the tone for the essay, letting the reader know if the paper will be light and humorous or serious or sarcastic. Whichever tone is established in the introduction should then be carried throughout the paper.

The introduction should invite the reader to read the essay; in other words, it should be interesting to the point someone will want to read it. Because of this, you should think carefully about how you will write it and what it will say. If the introduction is dull, the reader will likely not get past it (unless, of course, that reader is the instructor, who *must* read it).

The introduction will also include the thesis, which lets the reader know what the paper will be about. Even though it is possible to put the thesis elsewhere, one of the best places for the thesis is the last sentence of the introduction. In that way, it is next to the body of the paper, which makes it easy for you, and the reader, to move into the body.

The introduction may be developed in at least seven distinct ways. Each of these is included in this discussion, but it should be recognized that often a combination of methods is used. Think of what your paper is about and choose the method that works best for it.

The Inverted Pyramid or Funnel Approach.   The inverted pyramid or funnel approach is probably the easiest method to use. With this approach, the first sentence is broad and general. Words are usually used in this sentence that are repeated in the thesis; in other words, they point toward the thesis. Each sentence in the introduction narrows a little more to the last sentence, which is the thesis. As the description indicates, the introduction looks like a funnel or an inverted pyramid.

Wallace K. Ferguson and Geoffrey Brunn in *A Survey of European Civilization* use the inverted pyramid to come to a workable definition of history in the example below:

> Ideally the subject of history is man and all that man has thought, said, and done since the dawn of civilization. For practical purposes, however, history cannot include every thought, every word, every action or event in which man has been involved. For of all the thoughts, words, and actions of millions of men through countless generations, only a minute fragment can be known today. And even that minute fragment can be known only imperfectly through such written records as survive, and through the mute evidence of those things man has made which have withstood the ravages of time. The history that we can know, the history that we can learn and study, is, therefore, something less comprehensive than history considered as the sum of all past events. It is recorded history. It differs from history as we first defined it in much the same way that our present memory differs from the sum total of innumerable and largely forgotten thoughts, words, and actions of our entire life. It includes only those things the memory of which has survived and is still available today. History, then, might be defined by analogy as the recorded memory of mankind.

As you look again at the paragraph, you can see that each sentence narrows the definition of history until it focuses on the thesis that the writers will work with: *History, then, might be defined by analogy as the recorded memory of mankind.*

The Short Anecdote Approach.   Using a brief anecdote is another way to introduce your paper. An anecdote doesn't have to be humorous; it is just a short account of some incident that happened. Anecdotes make the introduction interesting and cause the reader to want to find out about the entire essay.

The following anecdote, from a selection entitled "La Causa," was used to introduce a description of the writer's work with the United Farmworkers. The anecdote clearly shows how, with the influence of union leader Cesar Chavez, author Jessie de la Cruz first became involved with the group.

> Late one night in 1962, there was a knock at the door and there were three men. One of them was Cesar Chavez. And the next thing I knew, they were sitting around our table talking about a union. I made coffee. Arnold had already told me about a union for the farmworkers. He was attending their meeting in Fresno, but I didn't. I'd either stay home or stay outside in the car. But then Cesar said, "The women have to be involved. They're the ones working out in the fields with their husbands. If you can take the women out to the fields, you can certainly take them to meetings. So I sat up straight and said to myself, *"That's what I want!"*

The Survey Approach.   The survey approach, in effect, surveys the whole essay and lets the reader know what the paper is about and the major points that will be discussed. A thesis is still used with this approach as with other introductions; quite often it appears at the end of the introduction, but it may come earlier.

A student essay entitled "Bulldozer Education" uses this approach. The thesis is the first sentence, with the rest of the introduction expanding on the thesis to explain what the paper will be about.

> School dropouts are an inevitable consequence of two things: of compulsory education and of the thinking of professional educators that most students are pretty much alike. A thoughtful analysis will show first that some students simply can't be educated beyond a certain level and that they only become rebellious when faced with advanced work that they can't do, and, second, that students come in an infinite variety that makes the idea of sending all of them through the same kind of courses highly suspect.

This paragraph was the introduction to a persuasive paper. The writer was trying to influence the reader to accept his beliefs and thus felt he needed to establish in the beginning what he would cover in his paper. The survey approach worked well for him just as it will with many other kinds of essay.

Using Quotations.   Using pertinent quotations in the introduction can also be an effective way to start your paper. While quotations may often be used in other types of introductions such as anecdotes, they can also be used as the kernel around which the introduction is built. The important thing is to have just the right quotation, one that says exactly what you want to say. If you can find such a quotation, you have already helped the reader to visualize what you are writing about.

An example of an essay using this type of introduction is given below. It is taken from James Fenton's "Mistakes People Make About Poetry."

> Writing from Ravenna to Thomas Moore in 1821, Byron said that he could "never get people to understand that poetry is the expression of an excited passion, and that there is no such thing as a life of passion any more than a continuous earthquake or an eternal fever." And he added as an afterthought: "Besides, who would ever *shave* themselves in such a state?" It's worth hearing this from Byron of all people—Byron who could fill his days with riding, lovemaking, and drinking and then sit down late at night in an excited passion and pen an extraordinarily large number of stanzas. But Byron's standards in passion were high. There was no such thing as a *life* of passion, and there was no such thing as a *life* of poetry.

Without the quotations from Byron, Fenton's introduction would have had little impact. The two quotes are an absolute necessity to support his assertion concerning the mistakes people make about poetry.

Using Questions.   Asking questions in the introduction as a lead-in to the subject of your essay is another useful approach. When questions are used, they serve to arouse the interest of the reader; the paper, then, should go on to provide the answers. In this paragraph, from Alexander DeConde's "Washington's Farewell, the French Alliance, and the Election of 1796," the writer's question is in the middle of the introduction, and he answers it in the two succeeding sentences, which he then extrapolates on in his essay.

> When in 1789 George Washington became the nation's first president the French alliance was the cornerstone of American foreign policy. It largely had made possible American independence and had established American foreign policy orientation. At the end of Washington's second term, in fact as he prepared his farewell to public life, the life-giving alliance was practically dead and the United States was virtually at war with France. Why, in eight formative years, did such a drastic reversal in

foreign policy take place? A full answer to this question would be long and complex; yet by looking closely at the election of 1796 and by reviewing the Farewell Address in its political context we may find a partial answer as to how the alliance received its mortal wound. We may also find additional reason for revising the traditional interpretation of the Farewell Address as a wise, timeless, and unbiased warning to the nation.

Setting the Scene.   Setting the scene in the introduction is an appropriate way to begin an essay that has as its purpose to describe something, be it person, place, or thing. It is also a useful approach in essays that tell about a personal experience. As you read the opening to Jacob Bronowski's essay entitled "The Creative Mind," picture what he sees and hears and feels and what he later calls a universal moment, the experience of mankind.

> On a fine November day in 1945, late in the afternoon, I was landed on an airstrip in southern Japan. From there a jeep was to take me over the mountains to join a ship which lay in Nagasaki Harbor. I knew nothing of the country or the distance before us. We drove off; dusk fell; the road rose and fell away, the pine woods came down to the road, straggled on and opened again. I did not know that we had left the open country until unexpectedly I heard the ship's loudspeakers broadcasting dance music. Then suddenly I was aware that we were already at the center of damage in Nagasaki. The shadows behind me were the skeletons of the Mitsubishi factory buildings, pushed backwards and sideways as if by a giant hand. What I had thought to be broken rocks was a concrete power house with its roof punched in. I could now make out the outline of two crumpled gasometers; there was a cold furnace festooned with service pipes; otherwise nothing but cockeyed telegraph poles and loops of wire in a bare waste of ashes. I had blundered into this desolate landscape as instantly as one might wake among the craters of the moon. The moment of recognition when I realized that I was already in Nagasaki is present to me as I write, as vividly as when I lived it. I see the warm night and the meaningless shapes; I can even remember the tune that was coming from the ship. It was a dance tune which had been popular in 1945, and it was called "Is You Or Is You Ain't Ma Baby?"

Defining a Word or Phrase.   Sometimes defining a word or phrase that will be used throughout the paper is a good way to introduce your essay, especially if the term is unclear to the reader. In the example that follows, William Zinsser, from his book *On Writing Well,* begins his essay called "Words" with a general definition of "journalese," warns readers away from using it, and then, in a second paragraph, defines it with specific examples.

> There is a kind of writing that might be called journalese, and it is the death of freshness in anybody's style. It is the common currency of

newspapers and of magazines like *Time*—a mixture of cheap words, made-up words and clichés which have become so pervasive that a writer can hardly help using them automatically. You must fight these phrases off or you will sound like every hack who sits down at a type-writer. In fact, you will never make your mark as a writer unless you develop a respect for words and a curiosity about their shades of meaning that is almost obsessive. The English language is rich in strong and supple words. Take the time to root around and find the ones you want.

What is "journalese"? It is a quilt of instant words patched together out of other parts of speech. Adjectives are used as nouns ("greats," "notables"). Nouns are used as adjectives ("top officials," "health reasons") or extended into adjectives ("insightful"). Nouns are used as verbs ("to host"), or they are chopped off to form verbs ("enthuse," "emote"), or they are padded to form verbs ("beef up," "put teeth into").

Though these seven ways to introduce an essay are not the only ways to begin a paper, they should help you see that the introduction has a definite pattern. This part of the essay, as well as the body and conclusion, must have a plan. The introduction should state what the paper will be about, give the position of the writer, and then lead into the essay.

A well-written introduction also has some relationship to the conclusion. As will be shown in the discussion of the conclusion, both should fit together much like the pieces of a jigsaw puzzle.

Activity 6: Write an Introduction

Choose two of the topics you worked with in the final exercise in Chapter 1. Then write an introduction for each topic, using a different approach for each. Underline your thesis statements; then share your work with a partner and choose which of your topics has the better introduction. Save your better introduction to be used in the next activity.

The Body

The body of the essay, which is nearly always at least three paragraphs in length and is quite frequently longer, is the "meat" of the essay. It contains support for the thesis in the form of examples and/or illustrations, statistics, details, and facts. The more support you provide, the better your paper will be.

Generally, each paragraph in the body begins with a topic sentence that directly relates to the thesis. Because of this structure, it is easy to outline an essay, using the topic sentences as subheads under the thesis statement. Exceptions, of course, exist in writing as with anything. Occasionally, as with the narrative or personal experience essay, a topic sentence may be implied rather than stated. And sometimes the topic sentence is not the first sentence in the paragraph.

As with the introduction, the body of the paper can be developed in several different ways; sometimes the methods are combined. The most frequently used forms, however, are chronological order, cause and effect order, order of importance, spatial order, and comparison/contrast order. A discussion of each of these follows, with suggestions for its use.

Chronological Order.   Chronological order is time order. With this method of organization, events are traced backward or forward. Biographical and historical studies generally use this order, as do technical processes that involve sequential steps. For example, if your paper were about presidential debates, you might begin discussing the latest debates and their impact; then you would work backward to the first presidential debates which were via radio rather than television. The time order would be from the latest to the earliest.

Chronological order is one of the easiest organizational methods to use, because the order is already built in for you. The only trick is keeping the details in that built-in order. The personal experience essays in Chapter Four use chronological order.

Cause and Effect Order.   Cause and effect order analyzes the causes of a given situation and the circumstances that led to it, or it begins with the effects and works back to explain the cause or causes. A paper whose topic is the effects of a major disaster on the lives of people and communities is one that could be developed using this pattern. The following would be a good way to implement such a topic.

THESIS SENTENCE: The effect of the 1996 crash of TWA flight 800 in the Atlantic Ocean soon after take-off, killing all 230 aboard, can scarcely be measured in the lives of those who lost loved ones.

Point One: Families were destroyed and hopes for the future were shattered.
Point Two: Whole communities had their structures dramatically altered.
Point Three: Emotional scars will never go away in those left behind.

A paper such as this deals with the effects—what happened after the crash. A paper could also be written that focused more on the possible causes of the crash than on the effects. For samples of essays using cause and effect order, see Chapter Eleven.

Order of Importance.   Order of importance, sometimes called climatic order, presents examples or points according to how important they are. "Most important" might mean strongest; it might also mean most common. Usually the most important point is given last, though not always: when you are explaining four reasons why students quit school, for instance, you might well want to start with the most common one.

The pro-con essay generally uses order of importance. The thesis is given; then examples are presented and points are made, with the strongest point last. The student model in Chapter Twelve, entitled "To Evaluate or Not to Evaluate," is an illustration.

Spatial Order.   Spatial order can easily be used with descriptive or evaluative essays. It is what its name implies—organizing according to space. An essay that researches dialects in different regions of the United States, for example, could use this pattern. A description of a place or person or event could also benefit from this form. In describing the interior of a house, for example, you could begin with what you see as you enter the front door, then move consecutively from room to room.

Comparison-Contrast.   A comparison-contrast format is developed by show-ing the similarities and/or the differences in the people, places, or ideas pre-sented. It is important to note that a paper of this type should be developed around a single point of comparison and have a single purpose.

Comparison-contrast may be organized in one of three ways: subject by sub-ject, point by point, or a combination of the two. For example, suppose you were writing a paper that compared Eustacia Vye in Thomas Hardy's *The Return of the Native* to Catherine Earnshaw in Emily Bronte's *Wuthering Heights*. The single principle, which you would state in your thesis, might be that Eustacia Vye and Catherine Earnshaw's deaths were symbolic of their lives. You could develop the essay by discussing each character separately (subject by subject), or you could organize it by making the following points about each:

> *Point One:* Eustacia died by drowning, trying to get away from a place she loathed. Catherine died giving birth to a child whose father she didn't love.
>
> *Point Two:* Eustacia never got what she wanted in life—to leave Egdon Heath. Catherine never married the man she loved—Heathcliff.
>
> *Point Three:* Eustacia was considered wild and even a witch because of her nonconformist ways. Catherine was considered wild because of the way she followed Heathcliff.

For samples of essays developed using comparison-contrast organization, see Chapter Ten.

Other ways of developing the body of the essay besides those shown here are also possible. Many essays, for example, use a combination of several methods. The significant point is that you should be conscious of how you are writing your essay instead of just writing without thinking. Each of the essay chapters that fol-low offers additional insight into organization and development.

Giving good support is a *must* in putting together the body of the essay. If you give the reader no tangible details or information, he or she is left with a feel-ing of emptiness, of having wasted time reading your essay. In other words, the thesis cannot stand alone; it needs development.

Activity 7: Develop a Topic

Below is a list of topics. Look back over the different ways to organize an essay and put beside each of the topics your idea of the best way to develop it. After you have finished with the list, choose one of the topics and write a thesis statement for it. Then write three supporting points for that thesis in the order in which you would present them.

1. Why the honor system for taking exams does (does not) work
2. Impressions of the harbor at sunset
3. Women and equal pay
4. Abolishment of interscholastic sports
5. How to say "no" gracefully
6. Little towns and big cities
7. Two presidents: Lincoln and Washington
8. Frustrations of a literature student
9. Triathlete training and competition
10. Climate patterns in the United States

The Conclusion

As mentioned earlier, a good conclusion should fit with the introduction like two pieces of a jigsaw puzzle. In other words, the conclusion should tie together what you have said just as the introduction interested the reader in what was to come. The conclusion finalizes the essay, drawing it to a close.

As with the other parts of the essay, the conclusion may be developed in a number of different ways, and these ways may also be combined. The conclusion does not have to be as long as the introduction, but it does have to have a definite plan. Read through the techniques given below and learn how to vary your conclusions instead of using the same format every time.

Restating the Thesis. Restating the thesis in slightly different terms and then broadening out with general statements is one way of developing the conclusion. This is the opposite of the funnel type of introduction; using the two together gives your paper a sort of hourglass format.

For example, the conclusion that follows was taken from William Zinsser's essay "Words," which began with a definition of journalese and ended by encouraging writers to use the right words: "Take the time to root around and find the ones you want." His conclusion ties in perfectly with this introduction.

> Remember, then, that words are the only tools that you will be given. Learn to use them with originality and care. Value them for their strength and their infinite diversity. And also remember: somebody out there is listening.

Summarizing the Main Points. Summarizing the main points is probably the simplest and most used type of conclusion. It takes little effort to look back over your paper and restate the important points that you have made. Almost any kind of essay can make use of this approach.

The conclusion that follows is from an essay "Our Children Can't Read." After citing a number of reasons why children can't read, the writer gives suggestions to increase reading. The paper concludes by summarizing those suggestions and then making a few concluding statements.

> The solutions aren't drastic. Adopt a "book buddy" program. Set up an adult/child literacy program. Create a library outreach program. Create a high school volunteer-tutor program. These programs cost almost nothing and ask of us only our time. Will they work? The children of this country are its most precious resources. Programs such as these might help us preserve that resource.

Key Words or Phrases.   Emphasizing key words or phrases is another possibility for concluding your paper, especially if terms were used in the introduction. The words or phrases should be those that stand out and which bear repeating in the conclusion. Eileen Herbert Jordan used a variation of this technique in her essay "The Grand Delusion: Smoking Was Cool Until It Left Me Cold." Here is her introduction:

> In the first 45 minutes of *Casablanca* Humphrey Bogart smoked ten cigarettes. I smoked two. It was 1942, I was 16, and so wrapped was I in the enchanted shadowy haze of Rick's Café Américain that I paid no attention—I could have smoked a pack. Everybody in *Casablanca* moved about in a wonderful soft-focus fog, the air about their heads ever cloudy. The piano, muffled in the smoke, had a special kind of intimacy that made one ache just listening to the notes. I was convinced as I watched that love, doomed or otherwise, never would flourish in any other atmosphere quite so well. I was very young and my sense of doom ran high.

In the conclusion of the essay, in which she describes the difficult path she took to stop smoking, she picks up the mood and some of the details from the opening paragraph—but uses them for a different purpose:

> Oh, once in a while now, when smoke blows my way, I have a memory—of a certain night, a certain weekend, a certain song. I close my eyes and sniff, and then go on. In my next coming I'm going to feature fitness as my lifestyle; my body will be superb as I run and jump and jog with my beloved, instead of languishing in smoke-filled rooms. I suppose in *that* life thereafter I will shiver with nostalgia every time I catch the scent of sweat. You simply never know.

The conclusion is reminiscent enough of the introduction that the two are tied together effectively.

Using a Succinct Quotation.   Using just the right quotation can sometimes be an effective way to draw your paper to a close. If you can find a quotation that fits well with one that you have used in the introduction, so much the better. If not, use a quotation that sums up your paper in a concise way. Use a book of quotations, such as Bartlett's, to help you in finding one that fits.

Be careful not to overuse this type of ending, however, because it soon becomes trite to see a quotation at the end of every essay. On the other hand, sometimes a person will say something that fits exactly with what you want to say. Look at this conclusion of a character sketch from *The New York Times* depicting Major Mike Collins, one of the crew on the Gemini 10 space capsule:

> He is fascinated with his business. "To get a good, unobscured look at earth, the stars and everything, to perform useful work out there; to me, that's just fascinating in itself," he said.

An essay by Joseph Wood Krutch entitled "Conservation Is Not Enough," from *The Voice of the Desert,* also uses a concluding quotation effectively:

> In our society we pride ourselves upon having reached a point where we condemn an individual whose whole aim in life is to acquire material wealth for himself. But his vulgarity is not one step removed from that of a society which takes no thought for anything except increasing the material wealth of the community itself. In his usual extravagant way Thoreau once said: "This curious world which we inhabit is more wonderful than it is convenient; more beautiful than it is useful; it is more to be admired than it is to be used." Perhaps that "more" is beyond what most people could or perhaps ought to be convinced of. But without some realization that "this curious world" is at least beautiful as well as useful, "conversation" is doomed. We must live for something besides making a living. If we do not permit the earth to produce beauty and joy, it will in the end not produce food either.

The most important thing the conclusion should do is to present a finality to the paper, leaving the reader with the sense that the paper is complete. That means that new ideas are not discussed in the conclusion; they would cause the reader to wonder why they weren't dealt with earlier in the essay. The four conclusion methods described above are by no means the only ones that can be used; however, they are the ones most often found in student papers. Whether you use these forms alone or in combination, remember that the real purpose of the conclusion is simply to draw the paper to a close.

Activity 8: Write a Conclusion

Write a conclusion for the topic you chose in Activity 7, using one of the techniques discussed in this chapter. When you have finished, see how well your conclusion fits with your thesis statement. If it does not work as well as it should, rewrite it so that it reads smoothly.

Steps in the Writing Process: Revising

By the time you have come this far with your paper, you are probably thinking, "Thank goodness, I'm through!" But that's not really true. You are at the last step of writing, and if you don't complete this step, your paper will be much like a house that has been built without the finishing touches of wallpaper and paint.

But just as a house can wait a few days to have the finishing touches added to it, so can—and should—your paper. Set it aside for a day or two and don't think about it. In that way, when you pick it up again, you will see it with a fresh eye. You may find things that aren't clear or that you want to add to your paper to make it read more smoothly. After you have formed the "wait-a-day" habit, you will see how valuable it is, and you will plan your time to allow for the rest period.

The fact is, though, that revising your paper is a necessity. Once you pick it up again, you see it more objectively—as if you were the reader instead of the writer. Now you have to make everything as clear for that reader as possible.

Working with a Peer Evaluator

Revision means more than just correcting errors, though that is a part of it. It means actually rewriting the first draft to accommodate the changes that you will make from reading it and rereading it. One of the best ways to see your paper objectively as you begin this process is to share it with another student; in other words, to have a peer evaluate your essay. The peer evaluation process is not hit and miss; it is designed, often by the instructor, to accommodate the particular essay you are writing. The questions vary according to the essay form and according to what has been taught with the essay.

A good peer evaluator does not simply look at your paper trying to find misspellings and grammatical errors; he or she should read critically, looking for gaps in structure and other communication problems you might have overlooked because of being so close to your topic. Your peer can see your paper more objectively and, since he or she often is writing the same sort of essay, has the advantage of knowing what the instructor has taught. In addition, since you will be evaluating your peer reader's paper, he or she is more likely to give you suggestions that will enrich your paper so that you will do the same in return. A good peer evaluator is invaluable to a good paper.

Once you have your peer evaluator's comments in hand, you should look over them critically and try to accommodate them as much as possible. You should also be aware on your own of the kinds of errors you are likely to make and be especially conscious of them as you revise. For example, if you know that you are apt to make errors in run-on sentences or tense shifts, be particularly attentive in looking for these. Or perhaps you have a tendency to be too wordy; you "go around the world" to say what you want to say. Then when you revise make sure that, rather than trying to impress the instructor with volume, you have written succinctly and to the point, saying what you wanted to say and then moving on.

As you start revising your paper, forget about the amount of time you put in drafting it; that is irrelevant to its worth. Your task now is to work with what you've written, changing, correcting, and adjusting it to make it as good as possible.

Following a Revision Strategy

The revision process makes the most sense if you break it into three readings for three distinct purposes: (1) checking for content, organization, and clarity; (2) checking for grammar and style; and (3) checking for spelling, punctuation, and capitalization. By the time you reach the third reading, you will be familiar enough with your essay to have caught errors that would have eluded you on a first reading.

Checking for Content, Organization, and Clarity

Checking for content, organization, and clarity is the first step in revision. You begin here because if you had to go back and change content—what you have said—after you corrected how you said it, you may have to do everything over again.

With this reading, you are checking to see if the content truly is what you meant it to be according to your thesis. Reread your thesis; then look at the support you have for it. Check to see that you have enough examples, illustrations, details, and facts to back up your thesis.

If you haven't done so already, try making a rough outline of your paper to see if the topic sentences relate directly to the thesis. If they don't, something is amiss and needs to be changed to make the relationship stronger; maybe some points should be deleted and others added. Check also to see if the order of your points is as it should be or if perhaps you have placed one of your points out of order. Note as well if something—an example, a definition, an explanatory sentence—has been left out that would make your paper clear. If you find places that are ambiguous, change them to read more smoothly so the reader can understand them better.

Another point to note as you read for smoothness is to see if you need to add transitions. Transitions are like bridges; they make going from one point to another easier. Transitions can be words such as *therefore, however, though, but, and, or, undoubtedly,* and *nevertheless* or phrases such as *it is a fact that, it is true, on the other hand, as a result,* and *for example.* Such connectors not only tie sentences and paragraphs together; they also show the reader how various ideas relate to each other.

Paragraphs can also be connected with a different kind of transition called a paragraph hook. This technique involves repeating words from the last sentence of a paragraph in the first sentence of the next paragraph. This kind of transition often sounds less heavy-handed than regular transitional expressions and can be very effective in making your paper flow. An example of a paragraph hook from President John F. Kennedy's Inaugural Address is given below:

> . . . And yet the same *revolutionary beliefs* for which our forebears fought are still at issue around the globe—the belief that the rights of man come not from the generosity of the state but from the hand of God.
> We dare not forget today that we are the heirs of that first *revolution.* . . .

Even though the exact words are not used in this hook, they are close enough to let the reader understand how the paragraphs flow together.

If your paragraphs don't seem to connect clearly enough with the transitional word, phrase, or paragraph hook, try a short transitional paragraph. The transitional paragraph may even be as short as one sentence. It looks back at the preceding paragraph and points toward the next paragraph. President Kennedy used this technique effectively in his historic speech on civil rights, as shown below.

> It is not enough to pin the blame on the other person, to say this is a problem of one section of the country or another, or deplore the facts that we face. A great change is at hand, and our task, our obligation, is to make that revolution, that change, peaceful and constructive for all.
> *Those who do nothing are inviting shame as well as violence. Those who act boldly are recognizing right as well as reality.*
> Next week I shall ask the Congress of the United States to act, to make a commitment it has not fully made in this century to the proposition that race has no place in American life or law.

The transitional paragraph sums up the previous paragraph and creates a bridge to the following one. By making it stand alone, Kennedy is able to emphasize the points he has just made. He has also disconnected it from the paragraph in which he says what he will do the next week, since the ideas do not exactly fit together. The transitional paragraph points backward and forward and thus makes for better reading.

In addition to strengthening transitions, a final important part of this reading should also be to check to see if you have written with your audience in mind. Is it clear for whom the paper is written? Are your style, tone, examples, and language use appropriate for this audience? Are words defined that may be unclear to the reader?

After this first critical reading of your paper, you may need to rewrite parts to make them clearer. You may even find that you need to organize your paper differently. Whatever is needed, now is the time to do it before you read for grammar.

Activity 1: Check for Content, Organization, and Clarity

Use the checklist below, or have a peer evaluator use it, to critique some piece of writing you have recently done. Save the checklist to use with the various assignments you complete in this course.

Checklist for Content, Organization, and Clarity

- Is there a thesis statement that explains the purpose of the essay?
- Does the thesis come toward the beginning of the paper?
- Does the introductory paragraph catch the reader's interest and lead into the body of the essay?
- Does each of the paragraphs in the body support the thesis?
- Are all of the points made relevant to the thesis, or should some be replaced?
- Are the paragraphs in the right order, or should things be moved around?
- Are there enough examples, illustrations, and details to back up the points made?
- Are any parts of the paper ambiguous?
- Are any kinds of transitions needed to make the paper read more smoothly?
- Does the paper reflect a definite audience?
- Are the words, phrases, and examples that are used appropriate to that audience?
- Does the paper have a strong conclusion?

Checking for Grammar, Sentence Structure, and Parallelism

In this second reading, you will be concerned with *how* you wrote your essay. You will check it for grammar and usage errors, sentence structure, and parallelism.

Begin by looking for common grammatical and usage errors: sentence fragments, run-on sentences, incorrect pronoun usage, misplaced modifiers, and tense shifts. A paper must have complete sentences, and it must have continuity in tense. Pronouns should have antecedents and should refer to them properly; modifiers should be near the words they modify. Errors such as these overshadow content, for the message gets lost in the mistakes. A paper not written in complete sentences and moving back and forth between tenses can be very difficult to read. A paper starting in first person and then switching to third person is awkward and confusing. If you have difficulty with any of these language basics, Chapter Sixteen can help you with many of them.

During this second reading, you should also read for style. Check things like variety in sentence structure and appropriateness of language. Make sure that your sentences are neither all very long nor all very short. Make changes if you find that every sentence begins with subject–verb–direct object. See if the style of your paper is consistent, and if your choice of words reflects your style. If you have established a rather formal style, eliminate any informal expressions that have crept in; or make your style consistently informal. Look for wordiness and redundancy—that is, the repetition of the same idea in different words. Check for use of good descriptive adjectives and vivid verbs, as well as for parallel construction in sentences—that is, the balanced repetition of ideas with ideas, words with similar parts of speech, and clauses with clauses. Chapter Sixteen can give you help with many of these style issues as well.

Activity 2: Check for Grammar, Sentence Structure, and Parallelism

Apply the checklist below to your paper after your second reading, or have a peer evaluator do so, to determine any grammatical or stylistic weaknesses. Save the list to use with the various assignments you complete in this course.

Checklist for Grammar, Sentence Structure, and Parallelism

- Is the paper free from sentence fragments and run-on sentences?
- Are pronouns used consistently and correctly?
- Do all pronouns refer properly to their antecedents?
- Are modifiers placed close to the words they modify?
- Was the same tense used unless there was a good reason for changing?
- Is there variety in the length and structure of sentences?
- Have wordiness and redundancy been eliminated?

- Is the style consistently formal or informal?
- Are precise adjectives and vivid verbs used?
- Have nonparallel constructions been avoided?

Checking for Spelling, Punctuation, and Capitalization

This final reading of your paper calls for looking at what sometimes is referred to as the mechanics of your paper—spelling, punctuation, and capitalization. This stage may be what you have always thought of as revision; however, it is really the part of revising known as editing. It is neither more nor less important than the other two parts.

If you are using a word processor, you may think that spelling errors are easy to catch. And they are—to a point. The only problem is that a spell checker on a computer can't catch all errors. One problem is with homonyms, word that are spelled differently but sound alike. For example, the words *their* and *there* are totally different in meaning but they are both spelled correctly; thus the fact that you have used the wrong one will not be caught by a spell checker. Another example is words like *it* and *is,* which are often confused in typing. Again, since they are both correctly spelled words, the spell checker won't indicate an error even if you have used the wrong one. So don't rely on the spell checker exclusively; read the paper over yourself.

If you don't have access to a word processor, you must rely on the dictionary. When that is necessary, one rule of thumb that often works is that if a word looks wrong, it is likely to be wrong. If you are not sure and can't find the word in the dictionary, ask a friend to help you catch your errors.

Another way to help yourself learn to avoid spelling errors is to make a list of words you often misspell and keep it in your notebook with the correct spelling. Put the list in alphabetical order and add to it as you need to. Then refer to the corrected list as you write, since you probably tend to use the same words frequently. By learning to write with the right spelling, you often unconsciously learn to spell the word correctly.

Besides looking for spelling errors, in this reading check your paper for capitalization and punctuation errors as well. As with spelling errors, be aware of the kinds of mistakes you typically make and be particularly vigilant for these. Many punctuation errors, for example, are the result of too many commas or using commas to join complete sentences. Many capitalization errors are the result of carelessness or of using capitals where none are needed. As you get more experience in editing your work, you will find it easier and easier to spot these errors.

Activity 3: Check for Spelling, Punctuation, and Capitalization

Apply the checklist below to your paper after this third reading, or ask a peer evaluator to apply it, to evaluate your spelling, punctuation, and capitalization. Save the list to use with the various assignments you complete in this course.

Checklist for Spelling, Punctuation, and Capitalization

- Are all words spelled correctly?
- Are homonyms or frequently confused words used correctly?
- Do all sentences end with the correct punctuation?
- Are commas used where needed to set off parts of sentences?
- Have unnecessary commas been avoided or eliminated?
- Are semicolons and colons used correctly?
- Are quotation marks placed correctly in relation to other punctuation marks?
- Are only direct quotations, and not indirect quotations, set off with quotation marks?
- Are all proper nouns and adjectives capitalized?
- Has unnecessary capitalization been avoided or eliminated?

When you have finished reviewing and revising your paper, make a clean final draft and hand it in to your instructor. The final draft should reflect changes in each of the three areas of revision.

As pointed out in the beginning of this chapter, even professional writers compose draft after draft before they are comfortable with a final copy. Become a better writer by giving careful thought to each of the revision strategies.

Activity 4: Revise a Draft

Below is an essay that was written by a student. Rewrite it, applying what you have learned in the revision process. Look for errors in content, organization, clarity, grammar, sentence structure, parallelism, spelling, punctuation, and capitalization. After you have finished rewriting the essay, share your version with a partner and discuss the corrections.

FRIEND

The word *friend* conjure up all kinds of meanings. For example in Proverbs 17:17 the Bible records that "A friends loves at all times." Then the dictionary definition of a friend is "a person who knows and likes another." Then the dictionary quoted Shakespeare: A friend should bear his friend's infirmities. While these definitions may be and undoubtedly are, what a friend is supposed to be, I have found more "friends" to be backstabbers, gossipers, and people-users.

I recognize this isn't the way it ought to be; but from my experience I have seen more people who want to use others who are suppose to be friends than those who want to befriend others.

My Dad had a bad experience with a man he thought was a friend. He was being considered for a promotion with his company, his friend was jealous that he was being overlooked. His "friend" went to their employer, and told her that Dad was really not as competent as he seemed; he had actually been doing the work and Dad was getting the credit. He even said Dad had blundered a deal the company was counting on. Nothing could have been further from the truth, but Dad didn't get the promotion. His "friend" did, and he wears this smug expression now when he sees Dad and tries to flaunt his importance. That's not what I call a friend! I used to think a friend was a person who stood by you thick and thin; but now my thinking has been altered.

Just the other day I was in the line of a fast-food restaurant, Mcdonalds's to be exact and I couldn't help overhearing a conversation about a good friend of mine. The conversation went like this

"Did you here what John did to Nancy the other day?"

"No! I can't imagine him doing anything really bad."

"Well, he gave her his class ring and letter jacket; then he had the nerve to go out with a girl named Mary to the beach party. I called Nancy as soon as I saw them together; and I told her he was cheating on her."

"What did Nancy do?"

"She got so mad she called John up and broke-up with him. She told him she didn't believe him and called him a lyar."

All these two girls was doing was gossiping. They didn't bother to find out that Mary was John's cousin; they assumed he was cheating on Nancy and Nancy believed them. Because of their gossiping and not to bother to find out who Mary was, John and Nancy broke up their relationship and stopped going out together. I guess it was better for them not to get married because if they had they might have divorced if Nancy could get so riled up over what somebody said and didn't listen to what John said. Things happen just like that. My mother had a friend whose husband got mad at her when the telephone rang and nobody was on the other end. He thought somebody was on the line and didn't want to talk because he answered the phone. He figured she had a lover. I guess it's hard to tell what people will do behind your back; so he just thought he had it all figured out. Boy, was he wrong my mother's friend would never do anything like that but he wouldn't believe anybody.

But the people who claim to be friends and aren't are those that just use you to their own advantage. I've had several occasions to fine people like that. As soon as they get what they want, they move on to sucker in somebody else. I'll never forget one so-called friend. I thought we were best friends he used to come over to our house all of the time and hang around. We even took him on vacations with us and included him in all of our plans; that is until a new guy came to our school. His dad was president of the bank and the family seemed to be quiet wealthy. This new guy had a sports car, and the girls flocked to him. My "friend" quickly changed loyalties. I felt used I no longer counted. It was like my "friend" didn't even know that I existed. I can tell you one thing, I'll never speak to my "used-to-be friend" again. He and I are threw; I wouldn't give him the time of day if he asked me. I don't even want to hear his name again!!!

Because of my awful experiences, my definition of a friend is not the definition as given in the dictionary or the Bible, it is a person who uses another to their advantage then moves on, it bears more resemblance to the antonyms given in Roget's Thesaurus: "an enemy, a rival, a foe, an adversary, or an opponent." As I always said, if a friend is like that, who needs an enemy?

Kinds of

There are many different types of essays (which are the focus of Chapters Four through Fourteen), but they can be grouped into four general categories: narration, description, exposition, and persuasion.

Narration

Have you ever asked a grandparent or an old family friend to tell you a story about a long time ago? All of us have at some point, because we like to hear what happened in an era unlike our own. When the person responded to your wish, what he or she was doing was narrating an account, telling about events and actions that occurred over a period of time. That is what is meant by narration.

Narration is a basic strategy used in writing and speaking. Its major characteristic is that it depicts a series of related events, usually in chronological order. Occasionally, writers complicate a narrative by using what is known as the flashback technique, inserting a story about something that happened at a prior time. Sometimes writers also use the technique of flashforward to refer to something that will occur later. Whatever techniques are used, the order is important in telling the story.

Essays such as the personal experience essay (the subject of Chapter Four) are narratives because they tell about an experience that happened during a particular time. Other essays also use narrative elements—anecdotes or brief stories—to illustrate points the writer is making. Narrative is made more effective and vivid by the use of descriptive details that help the reader see and hear what is happening and thus vicariously experience the event.

Description

Description is a technique that poets often use because they want to appeal to the senses: sight, smell, taste, touch, and hearing. Poets, however, are not alone in using sensory words; writers of all genres use description to create a verbal picture.

The most effective description creates a dominant impression or mood, depending on the purpose of the writer. For example, a writer describing a place chooses words and images to create a mood and establish an atmosphere.

The dominant characteristic of descriptive writing is that it paints a word picture, an objective one, a subjective one, or a combination of the two. It may give an actual picture of something (objective description), or it may share an impression or feeling (subjective description), or it may do both. Description may be used in all kinds of writing, wherever a verbal picture needs to be created.

The character sketch (the subject of Chapter Five) is one form of descriptive writing. In it, the writer seeks to show what the person is like by observing his or her actions,

Essays

attitudes, mannerisms, looks, speech, and other characteristics. The description makes the person come alive through the pages of the essay.

Exposition

The word <u>exposition</u> refers to a kind of writing that explains something. There are various ways to explain, and an expository essay may use any of them or even a combination of several at once. In exposition, you may tell the steps involved in doing something (the focus of Chapter Six), present a problem and possible solutions (Chapter Seven), define a term or a concept (Chapter Eight), classify information under some general organizing principle (Chapter Nine), show the similarities and/or differences between two things (Chapter Ten), or point out the causes and/or effects of something (Chapter Eleven). What all of these different approaches have in common is that they all explain something.

The primary purpose of expository writing is not to amuse or entertain, though it may do both, but rather to inform or to explain and to give facts. However, it is difficult not to use narration or description or even persuasion in writing in the expository mode. With the exception of explaining the steps in a process, most types of expository writing do not have an absolutely ironclad built-in order; therefore, the writer must work out a plan to present information in the most effective way possible.

Persuasion

When you write a persuasive essay, you are trying to convince the reader to think or act in a certain way. Though you may not be able to prove your point, you offer the most convincing evidence you can to back up your assertion. Usually that evidence is facts, but sometimes it also includes the opinions of experts or other knowledgeable people.

The subject for the persuasive essay must be debatable, at least to the extent that there is a possibility for a difference of opinion on the subject. Otherwise, there would be no need for persuasion. On the other hand, you have been writing persuasive papers to some degree every time you write, because you want the reader to look at your subject in the way that you do. The difference with the persuasive essay is that you recognize the opposition by acknowledging the case on the other side of the issue. However, since you are supporting your own stand, you offer more convincing evidence on that side.

While the persuasive essay per se is totally persuasive, other essays fall in the category of persuasion because their purpose is more persuasive than it is anything else. The evaluation essay judges the good—and bad—about a topic, as does the literary analysis essay, and if the essay is successful you will probably be persuaded to accept the author's opinion. Writing such essays can help you learn how to be judgmental in writing and use proof to back up your assertions.

The Personal Experience Essay

Understanding Personal Experience

Have you ever tried to tell someone about something that happened to you and the other person could hardly wait until you finished to tell about his or her own experience? This kind of thing happens over and over. Your experience triggers the other person's memory of a similar event. Because the stories involve real-life occurrences, they are often surprising, funny, strange, quirky.

Personal experiences are nearly always more interesting than vicarious experiences because we have actually lived them. They are a part of our lives and have helped shape who we are. Often they help us know how to deal with circumstances because they provide a frame of reference: if you have had to move often because a parent was in the military, for instance, the experience helped you learn to cope with new schools. Experiences can also be shared with others who have had similar experiences; together, people can work through problems or just relive the happenings through shared memories. Good times and bad times become real as we say, "This is what happened to me."

Understanding the Personal Experience Essay

The personal experience essay is, as the title implies, a narrative essay in which you will tell about an experience you have had yourself. The experience may also involve another person, and this person may have influenced your life for good or bad. Though the experience may involve a series of related occurrences, such as what happened to make your seventeenth birthday memorable, the sum total of those occurrences should make up one unified experience.

Because what you are writing about really did happen, a personal experience essay is in some ways easy to write: you don't have to go out looking for information. Personal experience essays are found in magazines and as feature stories in newspapers. They capture attention because they are true to life, and the writer's use of sensory language and description makes you feel a part of the story. A well-written account of a mountain climber's harrowing night out alone in a blizzard, for example, can put you right out on the mountainside shivering in the cold.

People write about what has happened to them for a number of reasons:

- to tell something that caused them to have an insight into life that they believe is important enough to share with others;

- to relate an experience they think will be interesting simply because the facts, description, and narration will be new to the reader;

- to relate a personal experience that teaches a lesson or warns the reader, either directly or indirectly;

- to entertain the reader;

- to write about something that is very emotional, disturbing, or upsetting in order to get it off their minds.

These reasons show that writing the personal experience essay can be a therapeutic as well as an enjoyable experience. Often it is not until you actually put your thoughts into words that you can see how much an occurrence or the people involved in it have affected you.

The personal experience essay uses narration in telling about what happened as well as description and sensory details to help the reader visualize the event or to convey a strong sense of place. In addition, the essay may include dialogue if others were involved in the experience, and it often has a strong tone of some emotion such as excitement, fear, or regret. Because of its use of narrative, the personal experience essay must be organized according to a sequence, most often a chronological one.

While the format of a personal experience essay is usually informal, it still must include only the details that have a direct bearing on the experience. For example, if you were describing an experience that happened on a camping trip, you wouldn't discuss the fact that you had to get a canoeing license or that you drove 250 miles to get to the camp unless they were directly relevant to your story. Likewise, you wouldn't tell what happened after you returned home since the focus is on something that happened while you were camping. You would, however, plan to include a personal summary or commentary of the experience either at the beginning or the ending of the paper. This helps tie the essay together and lets the reader understand your purpose for writing.

Student Model

The personal experience essay assignment for one student was to write about an event that was particularly memorable and to do it in such a way that the reader could share the experience. The essay that follows details the unusual events that happened to the writer—all in one day—when she skipped school, taking the family car with her. As you read the essay, decide whether she has brought the situation to life for you.

A Fateful Day

1   I had looked forward to this day for weeks—even months. It was the last week of school, and we all had senioritis. Three other girls besides myself had big plans. I had the family car with Dad's permission, but he had no idea what I planned to do. He thought I was going to school. Little did he nor I know what the day would bring.

2   As soon as we all got to school, we left—to places unknown. First, we drove to a little town about thirty miles away, had breakfast, and got snacks; then we decided to drive to the beach, about thirty miles farther. The day was beautiful, not a cloud in the sky. We envisioned spending three or four hours soaking in the sun and had even stashed our bathing suits in our book sacks just for such "emergencies."

3   Since we were afraid we would meet someone we knew, we took what we thought were back roads to the beach. They were dirt roads, not even paved, but that didn't matter. We were singing at the top of our lungs, "Oh What a Beautiful Day In the Morning," and didn't pay attention to a big puddle of water across the road. It didn't look deep, so we drove right in, but just as we got in the middle of the water, the car stopped. It bogged down—wouldn't go forward or backward. It was stuck!

4   We surveyed the situation and thought we could push ourselves out. Charlene and Bonnie got in the back; Doris got on the right side, and I stayed in the car to try to get it moving, but all our pushing did was sling mud on everybody. What a mess! Now what were we going to do? Here we were in the middle of nowhere playing hooky from school with our clothes in a mess and the car stuck and no one in sight—not even a house. We tried yelling but that didn't help; there wasn't anyone to hear us.

5   So we started thinking of the worst thing that could happen—we could be there for hours since few people traveled on the road at least in that part

6   First, though, we thought about the snacks we had bought. We were starving after this ordeal, so we plunged in the back seat to find the goodies—only to discover that Charlene and Bonnie had been munching on the Oreos and potato chips ever since we had left. So much for that—no transportation now and no food! Things couldn't get much worse.

7   At our lowest ebb, we heard a noise that sounded louder and louder. It was a tractor, just what we needed. The man was headed to his field and heard us yelling and screaming. He got a rope and pulled us out and were we glad. Little did we know, though, that the worst was yet to come— when we told our parents what happened!

—Lauren Maples

Activity 1: Analyze the Model

1. Do you feel that Lauren has brought her situation to life in her essay? Why or why not?

2. How does Lauren get the reader's attention in the introduction?

3. How do her feelings change in paragraphs 2–4? How does she show that her feelings have changed?

4. Do all the details Lauren includes have a direct bearing on the experience? Are there any you think she should have left out or included?

5. How does the writer make you feel about her and her friends' predicament? What sensory details are used to help you "see," "hear," and "feel" the experience?

Guidelines for a Successful Personal Experience Essay

You have just read and critiqued Lauren's paper and seen how a personal experience essay may be put together; now it is time to look at some specific guidelines. Since the personal experience essay is compiled from your own background of knowledge, these guidelines should make it easy for you to write a successful paper.

1. Choose a personal experience that is interesting or unusual or that gives an insight that may be beneficial to others. Lauren's essay shows the trouble students can get into playing hooky, but her other purpose is to entertain the reader with an interesting, though ironic, incident.

2. Identify your audience and use an appropriate tone. The tone Lauren uses is light and borders on the humorous, especially when she and her friends find themselves with nothing left to eat, stuck out in the middle of nowhere. Her audience is other teenagers who have had similar types of experiences.

3. From your prewriting, determine the focus of your essay so that you will only cover the material necessary to describe the experience. Lauren used the Reporter's Formula to determine what to write on. This kept her from including too many details about her "senioritis," which, even though it was the basic reason the incident occurred, didn't have a direct bearing on what happened.

4. Think about your purpose for writing when you select an incident to write about. Lauren's purpose—to write about a memorable event and let the reader share the experience—led her to an amusing incident that almost got her into serious trouble.

5. Make your introduction interesting so that the reader will want to find out what happened; however, don't worry too much about directly stating a thesis in this kind of essay. The thesis may be implied instead or even be stated in the conclusion if the paper is building to that point. Use the introduction to set the tone for the paper and entice the reader to read more. Lauren did this in her introduction by alluding to their being more to the day than she and the girls had planned.

6. In general, use chronological, or time, order in your essay. It is easy to see the time order in Lauren's paper: it moves from the time the girls left school until the time they were pulled out of the mudhole. Some topics, though, may lend themselves to the use of flashback—breaking into the chronological order to allude to a past event that is relevant to the experience. An example might be for a girl to discuss the events leading up to her being selected Homecoming Queen and then flash back to years before when she was in a body cast because of an accident and had fears of never even walking again.

7. In developing your essay, make your paper more interesting through examples, illustrations, and description. In other words, don't just give the facts; make the reader feel that he or she was a part of your experience by showing, not just telling. The student's paper illustrated the girls' carefree attitude through their singing and then their despair in getting stuck. She also described their looking for food and their plans for getting help.

8. Include sensory details to help your paper come alive. Lauren described the beautiful skies, the girls singing and later yelling, the puddle of water and mud, the roar of the tractor, their feelings of being alone.

9. Use transitions where they are needed to help move the action along. Transitions such as *now, as soon as, then, after, next, following, finally,* and *meanwhile* show time order. Lauren's second paragraph began with *as soon as;* and she used *first* and *now* as well as other transitions to make her paper read smoother.

10. Either conclude your essay by commenting on the significance or meaning of the experience, or make these things clear in the introduction. Lauren said

in her conclusion that the worst was yet to come, which meant that when the girls' parents found out they played hooky and all the other things that had happened, they would be in big trouble.

Working with Your Own Topic

Now that you have some basic guidelines for a personal experience essay, the next step is to begin prewriting for your own paper. This, of course, calls for knowing what you will write about.

Choosing a Topic

Here are some specific things to think about as you choose a topic.

- **The experience you choose to write about should have elements that make it interesting or unusual.** It should involve a turning point in your life, a best or worst experience, a learning experience, an experience that involved some conflict or struggle, or simply an interesting, exciting, or informative situation you think others would like to know about. To tell about going to a movie would not be a good topic unless something unique happened that you wanted to share. A snake that slithered down the aisle in the movie theater would be another story, though. It wouldn't matter that the snake wasn't poisonous or that it was someone's pet that had gotten loose. What would matter was the commotion the snake caused and how you responded.

- **Consider your audience as you choose your topic.** Knowing your audience will determine what you will write about as well as the details you will include and the language you will use. A topic that would be of interest to young people or adults is usually altogether different from one that would be suitable for a group of elementary children. For example, most young children could not relate to a near-death experience, but the topic would probably interest young people or adults. The audience, therefore, is one of the first considerations in choosing a topic.

Suppose after thinking about your topic, you decide that since you have moved around quite a bit, you will write about an experience you had starting at a new school. (For other possible topics, see the list at the end of the chapter.) All you need to do is select one such experience that was particularly memorable.

Prewriting Strategy: Review Your Journal

Reviewing your journal is a logical way to begin planning a personal experience essay. Information should be there to help you find an appropriate incident and then recall the experience in detail.

After rummaging through his journal entries, one student decided to focus on a beginning-of-school experience that turned out to be different from what he had expected. He found details in his journal that helped him remember exactly how he felt and then underlined things that he thought ought to be included in his essay.

Topic: Adjusting to a New School

September 9

This morning I really felt out of place since I didn't know anyone. I've been to new schools before, but this one is different; they look at me like I'm some kind of oddball. They're the ones who look strange. Some of them dress in bizarre clothes, and one girl had purple hair. Several guys just wore black; a few of them wore their pants down so low it looked as if they sneezed, their pants would fall off.

September 11

Today we had a class meeting in what passes for the auditorium—this school is unbelievably old and dumpy. No one even listened to the principal—they're so rude! And there are 300 kids in the senior class. I've never been to a school with that many people in one class.

September 12

The cafeteria is as bad as the auditorium. It smells damp and like old food. To make matters worse, they had a food fight today. One girl yelled something about another one, and that started it. It was bedlam. The principal had to come down to stop things. It's a wonder they don't have police officers in the cafeteria after today.

September 14

Today is Club Day—a day for all the clubs to meet so they can get organized for the year. Our homeroom teacher gave us a list of clubs, but I have no idea what I'd like to join. Maybe I'll try the Golden Brush Society or DECA since I like to draw.

September 15

Are things actually beginning to look up? I met Ginger today, the first person who actually talked to me. She offered to show me around the school and helped me meet some people. We had a pep rally and a football scrimmage; she invited me to go with her.

September 16

What a difference a few days make! Some of these weird-looking kids are rather nice when you get to know them. Mrs. Josten called on me in class; she actually knew my name. And I've decided to join DECA, the art society. The art they're producing is more sophisticated than anything I can do—maybe I'll learn something.

The ideas the student came up with from his journal writing were a springboard for points he could make in his essay. Even his narrative framework was more or less in place.

Writing Strategy: Engage the Reader Immediately

A personal experience essay generally tells about an event in chronological order. But that doesn't mean you will have an effective paper if you just begin with the first fact and go on from there. To get your reader's interest, you have to think of an engaging way to introduce the topic, such as making a confession or taking an unusual approach to a commonly accepted truth. This writer decided to bombard the reader with several examples of why the new school seemed so strange, showing his initial despair at ever fitting in.

> Another school—what a drag! That was the way I felt when I had to start all over again in a different school. My feelings must have shown because no one even spoke to me on the first day. All I could see were kooks—guys with low-slung pants, some dressed in black, a girl with purple hair. Not only did they look strange, they acted just as strange. They gathered in cliques and looked at me like I was an outsider. I wasn't the one wearing pants to my knees and a pony tail; I just had normal school clothes on, but you would have thought I was the oddball. To make matters worse, when we had a class meeting, there was so much chitchat that I couldn't hear what the principal was saying. I thought they were downright rude. Besides that, this is a *big* school, with over 300 in the senior class. How was I ever going to get used to this dirty, rundown place and weird people?

This introduction not only got the reader interested; it set the pattern for the rest of the essay. The first few paragraphs in the body elaborated on how the first few days of school went for the writer; then he showed how things gradually began to change when he met Ginger.

Revising Strategy: Use Appropriate Details and Tone

The tone of a personal experience paper, once established in the introduction, should remain consistent throughout the essay. Additionally, the details you use in telling your story should be in keeping with that tone. This writer began his paper with examples showing his bewilderment and anxiety as school began, but he did so in a rather matter-of-fact way. Rereading his first draft, it was easy to see that the following mushy paragraph about meeting Ginger needed to be toned down considerably. Notice the differences in the two versions.

First Draft

I thought I was floating on air when I met Ginger. She was a gorgeous redhead with deep blue eyes. I had never seen anyone who looked more like a goddess. Though she didn't know it, I called her Venus because of her charm; I melted when I saw her. I made up poetry to recite to her and wrote love notes. I began thinking ahead to football games and the winter formal and the prom, and planned to ask her to be my date. I was so in love with her I didn't care what other people looked like, but I did begin to see the girl with the purple hair as just Celia, not "the girl with the purple hair." And the guys who dressed differently were regular guys under that facade. Some of them were the best students in the class. It's funny how one person can change your whole outlook on life. When Ginger began introducing me to everyone, I began to see people for who they are instead of the way they looked. I credit her with helping me change; I wish everyone had someone like Ginger, my dreamboat!

Revision

Meeting Ginger made the difference in my life that year. She introduced me to other students, and it wasn't long before they didn't look so strange. I began to see the girl with the purple hair as just Celia, not "the girl with the purple hair." And the guys who dressed differently were regular guys under that facade; in fact, some of them were the best students in the class. Through Ginger, I began to learn that it's not what's on the outside that counts; it's what's on the inside.

Just as this student revised his essay, you will do the same with yours. Consider the questions below to guide you in revising your paper, or have a peer evaluator use them in pointing out the good and bad points in your draft. For additional points to consider, see Chapter Three.

Revision Questions

- Does the essay focus on a single experience that is an interesting and/or significant one for the writer?
- Does the introduction lead into the essay in an attention-getting way?
- Does the thesis show what the writer's purpose is? If not, where do you find the purpose?
- Has a consistent tone been used throughout the essay? Is it clear who the audience is for the paper?
- Does the essay use some form of chronological order?
- Are sensory details used to make the situation come to life? Does the writer "show" rather than tell?
- Has the writer avoided including details that don't have a direct bearing on the situation?
- Does the conclusion tie the essay together so that the reader sees the point of it?
- Is the paper grammatically correct with complete sentences?
- Has the writer avoided punctuation, spelling, and mechanical errors?

A Published Model

Here is a final model of personal experience writing to look at, this time from a published writer. In it the author, Zora Neale Hurston, recounts her childhood memories of her mother's death and its effect on her. As you read the selection, decide how well Hurston communicates a picture of death and of the emotions she was feeling both during and after it occurred.

A Promise

1   It was not long after Mama came home that she began to be less active. Then she took to bed. I knew she was ailing, but she was always frail, so I did not take it too much to heart. I was nine years old, and even though she had talked to me very earnestly one night, I could not conceive of Mama actually dying. She had talked of it many times.

2   That day, September 18, she had called me and given me certain instructions. I was not to let them take the pillow from under her head until she was dead. The clock was not to be covered, nor the looking-glass. She trusted me to see to it that these things were not done. I promised her as solemnly as nine years could do, that I would see to it.

3   What years of agony that promise gave me! In the first place, I had no idea that it would be soon. But that same day near sundown I was called upon to set my will against my father, the village dames and village custom. I know now that I could not have succeeded.

4   I had left Mama and was playing outside for a little while when I noted a number of women going inside Mama's room and staying. It looked strange. So I went on in. Papa was standing at the foot of the bed looking down on my mother, who was breathing hard. As I crowded in, they lifted up the bed and turned it around so that Mama's eyes would face the east. I thought that she looked at me as the head of the bed was reversed. Her mouth was slightly open, but her breathing took up so much of her strength that she could not talk. But she looked at me, or so I felt, to speak for her. She depended on me for a voice.

5   The Master-Maker in His making had made Old Death. Made him with big, soft feet and square toes. Made him with a face that reflects the face of all things, but neither changes itself, nor is mirrored anywhere. Made the body of Death out of infinite hunger. Made a weapon for his hands to satisfy his needs. This was the morning of the day of the beginning of things.

6   But Old Death had no home and he knew it at once.

7   "And where shall I dwell in my dwelling?" Old Death asked, for he was already old when he was made.

8   "You shall build you a place close to the living, yet far out of the sight of eyes. Wherever there is a building, there you have your platform that comprehends the four roads of the winds. For your hunger, I give you the first and last taste of all things."

9   We had been born, so Death had had his first taste of us. We had built things, so he had his platform in our yard.

10   And now, Death stirred from his platform in his secret place in our yard, and came inside the house.

11   Somebody reached for the clock, while Mrs. Mattie Clarke put her hand to the pillow to take it away.

12   "Don't!" I cried out. "Don't take the pillow from under Mama's head! She said she didn't want it moved!"

13   I made to stop Mrs. Mattie, but Papa pulled me away. Others were trying to silence me. I could see the huge drop of sweat collected in the hollow of Mama's elbow and it hurt me so. They were covering the clock and the mirror.

14   "Don't cover up that clock! Leave that looking-glass like it is! Lemme put Mama's pillow back where it was!"

15   But Papa held me tight and the others frowned me down. Mama was still rasping out the last morsel of her life. I think she was trying to say something, and I think she was trying to speak to me. What was she trying to tell me? What wouldn't I give to know! Perhaps she was telling me that it was better for the pillow to be moved so that she could die easy, as they said. Perhaps she was accusing me of weakness and failure in carrying out her last wish. I do not know. I shall never know.

16   Just then, Death finished his prowling through the house on his padded feet and entered the room. He bowed to Mama in his way, and she made her manners and left us to act out our ceremonies over unimportant things.

17   I was to agonize over that moment for years to come. In the midst of play, in wakeful moments after midnight, on the way home from parties, and even in the classroom during lectures. My thoughts would escape occasionally from their confines and stare me down.

18   Now, I know that I could not have had my way against the world. The world we lived in required those acts. Anything else would have been sacrilege, and no nine-year-old voice was going to thwart them. My father was with the mores. He had restrained me physically from outraging the ceremonies established for the dying. If there is any consciousness after death, I hope that Mama knows that I did my best. She must know how I have suffered for my failure.

19   But life picked me up from the foot of Mama's bed, grief, self-despise-ment and all, and set my feet in strange ways. That moment was the end of a phase in my life. I was old before my time with grief of loss, of failure, and of remorse. No matter what the others did, my mother had put her trust in me. She had felt that I could and would carry out her wishes, and I had not. And then in that sunset time, I failed her. It seemed as she died that the sun went down on purpose to flee away from me.

—Zora Neale Hurston

Activity 2: Analyze the Model

1. How effectively does the author convey her feelings about her mother's death? Explain your opinion.

2. What is the tone of the essay? Does it remain consistent throughout?

3. At what point in the essay does Hurston make clear what her main point will be? Does she communicate that point throughout the story?

4. What was your reaction to the personification of Death? In what ways did it add to or detract from the story being told?

5. How does the personification of Death fit with the other beliefs and customs mentioned in the essay?

6. What phrases or descriptions convey particularly strong images? How do these descriptions contribute to the mood of the essay?

Activity 3: Write a Personal Experience Essay

With a personal experience essay, it is difficult even to suggest possible top-ics; however, in case you hit a blank wall in deciding what to write about, the following ideas may give you a general direction. Remember to keep your audience in mind as you select a topic.

➘ **Possible Topics**

- A frightening incident
- A time I learned I wasn't as clever as I thought I was
- My first day on a job
- My first time away from home
- The first time I ever drove or took a plane ride
- A camping experience
- The time I had a flat tire
- A situation where I felt left out
- A time when gossip or a lie backfired on me
- The happiest experience of my life
- A trip to the zoo

The Character Sketch

Understanding Character

As a child you probably learned from your parents that your character is what you're made of; your reputation is what other people think about you. Those things are probably true. Your character is what you deem most important in life—what you will and will not do. But your character, and the character traits you possess, are also what makes you a unique individual, distinct from other people.

As you think back over your life, the people you remember most are those that stand out because of their characters. They stand out because of something different about them: perhaps it was their disposition, their attitude toward life, the way they always saw the good or bad in people, the risks they were willing to take. Maybe it was the way they laughed, the way they pinched pennies, or some little saying they always used. It could have been the way they sacrificed for others or the way they bullied to get what they wanted. Whatever it was, the memory remains indelibly.

The same is true of those you associate with every day. You meet a new person and immediately evaluate her according to the way she looks, the way she acts, the way she talks, and even by how others react to her. It isn't long before you make a decision about whether you want to get to know her better. It is then that you begin to learn the character traits that make her what she is.

Understanding the Character Sketch

Writing a character sketch is putting on paper something about someone you know or have known. It is painting a descriptive picture of the person with words so that the reader can visualize what the person is like. In doing so, you rely on the descriptive strategies of naming, detailing, and comparing to present the person to the reader. You use dialogue and relevant anecdotes to illustrate the characteristics of the person.

As you pick the appropriate kinds of details to describe the person, you may have several purposes in mind for writing the character sketch:

- to give a better understanding of the subject and his or her importance in your life;

- to entertain your reader with a striking portrait of an unusual person;

- to give a vivid and fair account of the person;

- to focus on certain characteristics that make the person unique;

- to present the person in such a way that you also reveal something about yourself.

When you write a paper about a person, you want the reader to feel at the end, "I know this person; I understand something about the kind of person he or she is." And even though catching a person completely in words is not possible, your impressions shed light on him or her in an interesting way.

At the center of your essay, however, is a vivid portrait of the person. It will very likely include information about his physical features, his behavior, his speech, and his manner of dressing as well as interesting and important incidents that have helped to shape his character. The insights you give into the person's life will not only help the reader visualize the person you are writing about but may also suggest comparisons with other, similar individuals in the reader's experience.

The audience, then, is important to keep in mind in organizing and selecting the details that will help to reveal the person's character. Because you want the reader to walk away with a sharply defined picture of the person, any details that do not add to the central characteristics or dominant traits you are focusing on should be omitted. For example, to describe a fellow worker as the cousin of your Aunt Dee who plays bridge at the country club is irrelevant information. It has nothing to do with your fellow worker. And you would not describe the principal of your school as a person who repairs antique clocks—unless you were focusing on surprising or little-known facts about him or her.

There is no one, preset way to organize a character sketch. Your approach is dependent on what you are emphasizing or what your focus is. For example, you may choose to begin with an anecdote illustrating some noteworthy characteristic of the person, with your thesis making a succinct statement of what you are focusing on. Each supporting paragraph might build more on that characteristic through a description of the person's looks, her actions, and how you remember her. Or you could begin by a physical description of the person, with the body of your paper built on anecdotes or dialogue of remembered conversations. Or you might decide to start by putting the person into the setting in which you best remember him, as sometimes that setting is important in capturing the personality of the individual. In each case, the details you would include would be only those that are relevant to the kind of picture you are trying to create.

The conclusion of the character sketch should bring a finality to the essay, reflecting the qualities or dominant trait you have emphasized. This can be done by giving a quote that sums up the character, by recounting a final anecdote illustrating the dominant trait, or by using a clincher statement that sums up your thoughts.

Student Model

Though some character sketches involve figures from literature, most involve real people that you know well enough to be able to portray fairly. John wrote about his basketball coach who had coached him through high school. He used the prewriting technique of freewriting, though listing or even classical invention would have worked as well.

A Hard Act to Follow

1   Playing basketball was something I did as a little tyke. I learned to dribble and shoot almost as soon as I could walk, so it wasn't unusual that I tried out for basketball in high school. I made the team and found that basketball wasn't a one-man sport; it takes teamwork. At least that was the slogan of Coach Grantham.

2   Coach Grantham was one of those coaches that demand the best. He wouldn't take any slacking off. We learned the right techniques of dribbling and the different kinds of shooting—one-hand push shot, two-hand shot, jump shot, hook shot, tip-in shot, lay-up shot and free throw. I didn't know there were that many shots until I met Coach. We were drilled on fouls and offensive plays and defensive plays and anything else connected with basketball. Coach knew everything, and he tried to teach us everything he knew.

3   Not only did Coach Grantham teach us how to play basketball, but he also taught us how to compete. He said, "Somebody has to win and somebody has to lose; it's not how you win but how you lose that makes a good player." That philosophy helped us maintain our composure when we lost the state title by only two points. Even though we wanted to win badly, somebody had to lose, and if we lost, we were going to do it with character.

4   Coach Grantham was interested in each one of us as a person, too. If we needed a ride home after a game, he took us home; if we were sick and unable to practice, he was considerate; if we had a personal problem, he listened and offered advice. For example, I graduated this year and my girlfriend is still at school. He advised us both to date other people. He said it wasn't realistic as young as we were not to date others, and he was right. We are still friends, but we're not ready to go steady, especially with our being apart.

5   Coach was also interested in our grades. He had a slip sent to each of our teachers at the end of every grading period, and the teachers put down our grades and wrote something about our conduct. If we didn't get what he thought we should, we were "chewed out" and made to sit out a game, even if it were a district game that was important. Sometimes he even helped us gather material for research papers and made sure we did our work on time. He wanted to give us every opportunity for a scholarship in college, but he knew grades were important if we wanted to go.

6   As I look back over the four years with Coach Grantham, I can't think of another person who has influenced me more. I'll always remember him for helping me grow up through the game of basketball. Now that game is the game of life, and his philosophy is even more important. I can hear him with his gravely voice, "All right, John, keep practicing—It's not how you win but. . . ."

—John Fletcher

Activity 1: Analyze the Model

1. What opinion does John put forth of Coach in his introduction? How does he elaborate on that opinion throughout the essay?
2. What do the two slogans which Coach taught his players in paragraphs l and 3 reveal about the man?
3. What method does John use to describe the coach?
4. What are some concrete, specific words the writer uses to show his opinion of Coach?
5. How effective is John's conclusion in tying the paper together?
6. What tone does the writer establish at the beginning of the paper? Is that tone consistent throughout?

Guidelines for a Successful Character Sketch

As you saw in the model, a good character sketch can present a strong, insightful view of an individual. Here are some guidelines to follow when you plan and write your own character sketch.

1. Choose a person who has been significant in your life, one whom you feel you can describe vividly and who would interest your reader. John chose to write about his high school basketball coach, a person who had made a definite contribution to his life.

2. In the thesis, state the slant your paper will take. John's thesis is actually two sentences: "I made the team and found that basketball wasn't a one-man sport; *it takes teamwork. At least that was the slogan of Coach Grantham.*" You know immediately that Coach Grantham was a big influence in John's life.

3. Establish the tone in the beginning and continue with it to the end of the paper. John's paper showed a high respect for Coach from the start and throughout his paper.

4. Develop your paper with enough details to adequately show the character, using anecdotes, description, narration, comparison, and explanation as needed. John described Coach not in appearance (except his voice) but in his actions and his attitude. He used anecdotes to illustrate Coach's philosophy of winning/losing and gave examples of his caring for each player.

5. Use concrete and specific words rather than abstract and general ones. John said Coach listened, was considerate, had a gravely voice.

6. Give incidents from the person's life that illustrate traits about him or her that are typical or significant. The trait of caring is illustrated by the examples in paragraphs 4 and 5; the concern for thoroughness is illustrated in paragraph 2.

7. Include at least three paragraphs to the body of the paper, with each paragraph stressing some aspect of the person's character. Paragraph 2 stresses the fact Coach demanded the best from his players; paragraph 3 shows how Coach taught the players to lose as well as win; paragraph 4 illustrates the coach's personal interest in each player; and paragraph 5 shows his concern about their grades.

8. Conclude the essay with a final statement to support the thesis and summarize the character traits. John's conclusion summarized Coach's influence on him by referring to one of his slogans: "It's not how you win but. . . ."

Working with Your Own Topic

To begin planning your own character sketch, you need to select an individual and a way to approach him or her. If you are like most people, you probably have a fairly wide range of people that have made some sort of impact on you.

Choosing a Topic

The following points should help you to zero in on an appropriate person to write about.

- **Select someone who has impressed you or who has made a difference in your life in some way.** Choose a person you can describe vividly, someone with striking or unusual qualities or one who has had a strong effect on you, either positive or negative. Don't describe an acquaintance that you know very little about, or a person from your past whom you liked but whom you only vaguely remember now. Think carefully, for in describing this person, you will be showing something about yourself and the character traits you admire.

- **Write about someone whose characteristics would interest your audience.** It has been said that almost any individual can be an interesting subject for a character sketch; however, not all audiences are necessarily interested in the same sorts of people. An instructor whose annoying habits of biting her nails, squeaking chalk on the board, hitting the garbage can for attention, and yelling at students might interest some of your fellow students because they could identify with your frustrations. But she may not be interesting to a more general audience unless you could demonstrate that despite her eccentricities you really did learn a great deal from her. Similarly, a sketch about a body builder may seem boring to people who are not fitness enthusiasts, unless you could also include characteristics of the person that made him or her more universally appealing.

After giving consideration to your topic, suppose you decide to write about your grandmother who lived with your family while you were growing up. A number of incidents cause you to remember her, and you think you can portray her in a way that will make other students remember their own grandmothers.

Prewriting Strategy: Timed Writing

Timed writing is one way to bring hazy memories of a person into sharper focus. The following student used a series of timed writings to develop certain facets of his grandmother's personality or to flesh out incidents he remembered.

First Timing: Grandma was a slightly built lady with white hair, glasses, and most often a smile. She liked her room/painted the door and trim an off-white and wallpapered the rest. The wallpaper was old-fashioned looking, just like her. She kept her room spotless/everything was in its place/pictures everywhere of her other children. Some of my cousins called her Nanny, but we called her Grandma.

Second Timing: Every day when we came home from school Grandma had something cooked for us—teacakes, jello pie, brownies, pudding. She could cook the best fried apple and pear tarts of anyone. That reminds me of one time when Mom and Dad had gone to New York on a trip. She cooked spaghetti and meatballs, the worst I had ever eaten! I told her I had to study, so I took my food upstairs and hid it in the attic. I forgot about it, and it wasn't until a year or so later anyone found it. . . .

Third Timing: Grandma loved to work in the yard. She planted four o'clock flowers everywhere—yellow and pink—and told me they only bloomed at four o'clock in the afternoon. I still have some of the seed; one day I'm going to have a yard, and I'll plant my seed and remember Grandma every time I see them bloom. Grandma liked to go to church too. If she were sick, she watched the television and when we came home from church she delighted in telling us how many preachers she had watched. I never saw anyone who liked to listen to preachers as much as she did. I tell you one thing, we had better not say a bad word or she would wash our mouths out. She was kind but she was strict! She believed in being good.

After looking over the three timed writings, the student realized he had more than enough to write a character sketch about his grandmother. He could tell what she looked like, how she acted, and how she wanted him to act.

Writing Strategy: Present Special Aspects of the Person

Use the body of your paper to zero in on the different elements or qualities that make the person unique or special. This student began his paper by describing his grandmother and her room, leading into his thesis *My grandmother was old-fashioned in her looks and her ways, but her kindness and her love of beauty and truth gave her a quality of timelessness.* Then he devoted separate paragraphs to characteristics that exemplified the general traits he mentioned. These are the topic sentences he used in his first draft.

PARAGRAPH ONE: When we came home from school every day, I loved to open the door and smell what Grandma had cooked for our treats.

PARAGRAPH TWO: Grandma could cook treats, but cooking a meal was something else.

PARAGRAPH THREE: Our yard was the most colorful in the block because Grandma made sure we had flowers blooming all of the time.

PARAGRAPH FOUR: Grandma loved to go to church and listen to preachers better than anyone I ever knew.

As you can see, this student used four paragraphs to the body of his paper since he had so much to say about his grandmother. Then his conclusion drew together his picture of her.

Revising Strategy: Make Sure Incidents Emphasize Character Traits

When you have a lot to say about a person, it's easy to lose track of just what you want your readers to see. After reviewing the examples in his paper, this writer realized that at least one of the incidents he chose wasn't as clearly developed as it could be. He chose to revise paragraph 1 of the body so that it showed more clearly his grandmother's kindness to him. Notice the differences in the two drafts.

First Draft

When we came home from school every day, I loved to open the door and smell what Grandma had cooked for our treats. She knew exactly what time the school bus came and had everything out on the table. Her teacakes were the old-fashioned kind that were soft and melted in your mouth, and her jello pie was mixed with cool whip or something to make it fluffy. I made a beeline for the table as soon as I got home and had to be reminded to wash my hands.

Revision

When we came home from school every day, I loved to open the door and smell what Grandma had cooked for our treats. She knew exactly when the school bus came and had plates of goodies hot from the stove waiting on the table. Sometimes she baked old-fashioned teacakes that melted in your mouth; sometimes she made jello pie with cool whip that made it fluffy. One time she had popcorn popped and syrup poured over it for us to make popcorn balls. It's funny, I don't remember her sitting down with us. All I remember is we made a beeline for the table and made pigs of ourselves. We never thought at the time that was Grandma's way of being kind and showing how much she loved us.

As you can see from this student's revision, he used essentially the same material, with one example added. By drawing a conclusion about his examples at the end of the paragraph, though, he made it clearer what point he was trying to make.

The questions that follow will help you analyze the first draft of your character sketch. Use them, as well as your peer evaluator's response to them, to guide you as you revise. For additional points to consider, see Chapter Three.

Revision Questions

- Did the writer choose a character who would be interesting to the audience?
- Does the thesis indicate the character traits the writer will develop?
- Did the writer get the attention of the reader in the introduction?
- What is the tone of the paper? Is it consistent throughout the essay?
- Has the writer used a variety of techniques—description, comparison, narration—to bring the person to life?
- Did the writer use concrete descriptive words rather than abstract terms? What are some better words that could have been used?
- How does the writer use anecdotes to portray the person? Are any of the anecdotes confusing or unnecessary?
- Is the writer's organization effective or should some parts be moved around to make the essay clearer?
- Does the writer have an effective conclusion that emphasizes the character traits of the person?
- Has the writer consistently used good grammar and correct sentence construction?
- Does the writer use correct punctuation, capitalization, and spelling?

A Published Model

Here is one more model to study before you write your own essay. This essay, entitled "A Vision of Daffodils," is a character sketch of a teacher who was a great influence on author Al Martinez's life. As you read through his essay, see if you understand what he means when he says, "Seeing is truly believing—when someone believes in you."

A Vision of Daffodils

1   Calla Monlux was not much more than five feet tall and stocky, in a pleasant sort of way. She seemed the prototype schoolteacher of the 1940s, an old maid in a long dress and sensible shoes, stern but relenting. A tiny, knowing smile glows through my memory of her like an

outline in fog, characterizing everything she did. It said she was wise and gentle and liked you just for who you were.

2   My association with her came in the sixth grade at Lockwood School in Oakland, California, where she taught English. I was a poor kid from a broken home, burdened with a drunken, violent stepfather who found pleasure in beating me for no other reason than that I reminded him of my mother's first husband, my father.

3   Halfway to hell at age ten, I ran away from home frequently, stole whatever I could get my hands on, fought endlessly, and stuttered badly, all of which made me somehow special to Miss Monlux. Teachers knew more about their students then; I'm sure she knew everything about me. The stuttering was obvious. In the first few weeks of class, she inaugurated sessions of oral recitation. I tried it once but couldn't put a thought together without stammering.

4   Miss Monlux wanted me to try again but when I refused, she relented. She had an idea. I could write what I couldn't say and turn it in to her. I have wondered since if she sensed in me a raw talent to create.

5   My first efforts were lame, but she saw something I didn't and encouraged me to continue. Then one evening in the spring of 1941, as the United States prepared for a war that would soon come, I sat on a hillside and watched the lights of my neighborhood blink out during an air-raid alert. I compared it to the stars going dark and wrote with a singularity of purpose I had never before experienced. Miss Monlux read it and smiled that tiny, knowing smile.

6   You have a very special gift," she said, "and it can take you to a very nice future. But it needs nurturing." She sat me down after school and told me to close my eyes. Then she read me parts of a William Wordsworth poem: "I wandered lonely as a cloud/That floats on high o'er vales and hills,/When all at once I saw a crowd,/A host, of golden daffodils;/Beside the lake, beneath the trees,/Fluttering and dancing in the breeze."

7   When she asked if I could see them, I said no. "Visualize," she insisted. "The sun is warm. The breeze touches you." She read the poem for me again and again, each time describing, each time demanding, each time transforming words into imagery.

8   And then I saw them.

9   The daffodils emerged in a corner of my mind all buttery and golden, and the breeze touched my face with the warmth of a baby's kiss. My eyes still closed, I described what I saw and felt, and Miss Monlux, in a tone blending pride and knowledge, said, "You've learned the most

important lesson you'll ever learn about writing. You've learned to visualize. Now put on paper what you see in your heart."

10   I wrote with a passion that has never left, for she had defined for me not only who I was but who I would always be, forever attempting to translate into words what I visualize in my head. In so doing, she altered the course of my life . . . and eliminated a stammer that she never directly addressed. She didn't have to.

11   Her push, and her lessons in the days that followed, allowed me to overcome a dismal childhood and gave me new tools to pursue a life free of emotional pain and physical violence. I think often of Calla Monlux and the moment she set me traveling on a new path. I see her as though it were yesterday, the small, knowing smile still glowing across the years.

12   The vision is clear.

—Al Martinez

Activity 2: Analyze the Model

1.   How effective is the writer in conveying the character of Calla Monlux? Are you able to "visualize" her even as she wanted Martinez to visualize the daffodils?

2.   What aspects of the teacher does the writer present in the first paragraph? How do these set the stage for the rest of the essay?

3.   How do the third and fourth paragraphs flesh out the description in the first paragraph?

4.   Describe the one thing Monlux does that particularly changes the course of the writer's life.

5.   How does Martinez's use of the phrase "A tiny, knowing smile..." in paragraphs 1, 5, and 11 tie the essay together?

6.   To what extent is this character sketch also a portrayal of the writer's character?

Activity 3: Write a Character Sketch

Since the character sketch must be about someone who has affected you in a particular way, the suggestions below only serve to enhance your memory and to help you select someone who has had a significant impact on your life.

↘   **Possible Topics**
*   Someone who surprised or disappointed you
*   A particularly memorable grade school or high school teacher
*   A person who helped you make an important decision and stood by you through it

- A person who has affected your life—for good or bad
- A relative who showed concern when you had a problem
- A religious or youth leader who gave you advice with a struggle
- A sibling who constantly irritates or supports you
- A person who taught you something about yourself
- A person who caused you to look at your own set of values
- A friend who helped you change your outlook on life

The Process Essay

Understanding Process

From the time you learned what your parents were saying to you, you were given directions about what to do. They began as simple instructions—take one bite at a time, chew your food properly, don't put too much in your mouth, swallow your food. Of course, you don't remember these simple directions, but they started you on the road to learning how to do something. As you grew older, you learned how to tie your shoes, how to skate, how to ride a bicycle, and how to interact with classmates when you went to school.

While the directions you were given were a natural part of growing up, they nevertheless were important. As you think back on them, you can remember the results of following them correctly or the consequences otherwise. The directions you follow now are much more complex and often involve intricate steps. In school or at work, they are usually written down and demand careful attention.

Understanding the Process Essay

The expository essay you will learn about in this chapter is called a how-to or a process essay because it gives directions or instructions about how to complete a task, or it tells how something is done. It explains the steps necessary in chronological terms, or it gives information about the subject so that the reader knows the process involved.

The process essay can be one of two types: informational or instructional. Informational essays do not necessarily have steps that must be followed in a precise order, but they still need to explain how to do something by presenting it as a step-by-step process. Students often write about topics that are more informational than instructional; for example, "How to Make Friendships That Will Last," "How to Keep Your Cool When Your Boyfriend Cheats On You," or "How to Show Your Parents You Are Responsible." None of these involves steps that are sequential, but each offers information that shows "how to" do something. The sample essay in this chapter entitled "How to Interview for a Job" by Marianne Jones, a student, is a good example of this type of essay.

Instructional essays, on the other hand, are easy to spot because they give sequential steps in a process and explain what is needed for each of the steps. They show how to accomplish a task and use transitional words to show the order in which things are done. Most students do not find this type of essay difficult to write because it has a built-in order: the order in which steps must be performed. Topics chosen for the instructional essay range from "How to Make a Gingerbread Man" to "How to Fix a Flat" or "How to Drive with a Standard Shift."

Informational and instructional essays are easy to identify because of the clarity of the directions and/or information given. They leave the reader with the knowledge of how to accomplish a task or cope with a problem. Such essays are often found in magazines and newspapers and are recognized by the use of the words "how to" in the titles of the articles. For example, the title of one article in *Prevention Magazine* was "Listen to Your Body" with the subtitle "How to Decode Six Strange Messages." *Reader's Digest* carried an article called "Ten Ways to Win at Work" by Tom Peters, which lists ten ways to help one's career along the road to success. "How to Get the Lead Out of Gasoline" was a step-by-step process article published by Consumer Reports in the Baton Rouge *Advocate Newspaper.* As you can see, the title of each of these articles was a dead giveaway that a process was involved.

Process essays are used to explain many job-related or medical procedures. For example, when you visit the dentist's office, he or she may give you a pamphlet explaining how to take care of your teeth properly. Though you don't think of this as a process essay, in effect, it really is. It follows essentially the same format as the directions you will follow in your essay. It has an introduction explaining what the pamphlet is about, a body that gives the steps needed for caring for your teeth, and a conclusion showing what to expect if the directions are followed.

Student Model

The assignment for the process essay for one student was to write about something in which she was interested, something she had actually done that would be beneficial to other students in the class. Marianne had been quite successful in obtaining a job she had kept for two years, one which she thought would be a part of her future. Several times her employer had commented on the ease he had in the interview. Marianne chose the topic of how to interview for a job because of her good experience.

Marianne arrived at her thesis when she decided to organize her essay into three steps of preparation—mental, emotional, and physical. Even though she did not actually write the introduction until the end, she had her thesis in mind, which made it easy for her to know how to organize the paper.

As you read through her essay, note how she arranges it so that it is an informational essay that helps the reader learn something from her knowledge. Note also the ease with which she moves from one point to the other by using clear transitions.

How to Interview
for a Job

1   In today's world where there are so many applying for the same job, it is important to make the interview count. Since an interview is a face-to-face encounter, it usually indicates there is some degree of interest on the part of the employer. He has probably already seen your resume and is impressed with it. It is up to you, then, to make the employer feel that you are the best person for the job. The steps which follow are suggestions born out of experience. Almost without exception, if the job is truly available, they will guarantee success.

2   Preparation for the interview essentially falls into three categories: mental, emotional, and physical. Each of these three areas is equally important, all necessary to being totally prepared for a successful interview.

3   The first thing to do is to be prepared mentally, which means to know as much as possible about the position, the company, and the qualifications for the job. An employer is impressed if you have "done your homework" prior to the interview. He can easily see that you are knowledgeable and qualified for the position because you know what his needs are and have taken the time to study them. For example, a friend of mine, Darryl, learned about a position that was open in Florida. Though his degree was in industrial engineering and the job specified electrical engineering, he applied. The company hired him because he was knowledgeable enough and eager to learn whatever else was necessary for their position. He has since advanced many times in the company.

4   Along with the knowledge necessary for the job interview, being mentally prepared, as in Darryl's case, means being mentally alert. If you have the option of scheduling the interview, schedule it at the time of day in which you are most wide-awake. If you are a night person and like to sleep late, don't schedule the interview for 8:00 o'clock in the morning. You will likely be less attentive and not give the best impression.

5   The second area of preparation is emotional, which means to be in the right frame of mind and have a good attitude. A smile and a hearty hand-shake let the employer know that you are self-assured, you have an air of

confidence, and are at ease in his presence. This may take practice on your part since you are meeting him for the first time and since the interview is crucial. However, take the time at home to think through exactly what you will say when you meet your prospective employer. If you are still uncomfortable, practice smiling in the mirror and say out loud how you will introduce yourself and what you plan to tell him. Be positive in your attitude and in your speech; never speak negatively. At the same time, use correct English; never use slang. Even though standard English may not be spoken in that particular job, knowing how to speak correctly will make a good impression. Establishing a good rapport with the interviewer by being at ease in your actions and maintaining eye contact will help him in directing his questions to you so that he can determine your suitability for the job.

6   The third way to prepare yourself for the interview is physically. Most students think this comes first, but if you are prepared mentally and emotionally, being prepared physically is probably the easiest thing to do because it comes naturally. It goes without saying that physical preparation means being neat and clean and wearing clothes appropriate to the job being sought. For example, applying for the job of shipping clerk doesn't mean that you need to wear dress clothes for the interview. On the other hand, applying for a position in an office means you will not wear shorts or sundresses. It means wearing the kind of clothes you will be wearing in that position. Having your hair neatly combed, fingernails clean, and the appropriate clothes show that you are prepared for the interview physically.

7   It is easy to see that being prepared for the interview mentally, emotionally, and physically will enhance your prospects for getting the job you are seeking, especially if you have the skills necessary for the job. As with Darryl, the good impression you make on your prospective employer will give you the added boost to secure your position. It will also build your confidence and make you feel at ease as you begin your new job.

—Marianne Jones

Activity 1: Analyze the Model

1. How did Marianne follow the thesis statement in the organization of her paper?

2. How well did her paper flow? To what extent were her transitions appropriate?

3. How would her paper have differed if she had used examples from her own experience rather than another person's experience?

4. Are you convinced that the interviewing experience is as easy as Marianne says it is? Why or why not?

5. What steps, if any, would you have added to Marianne's paper? For example, do you think she should have given some discussion to how a person finds out a job is available, something that might be a factor in preparing for the interview?

Guidelines for a Successful Process Essay

You have just read and critiqued Marianne's paper and have seen how a process paper is put together even before looking at specific guidelines. When a paper reads smoothly, you aren't aware of the writer's adhering to directions; however, it is evident Marianne was aware of them. As you study the following guidelines, you will find they work with any process paper—instructional or informational.

1. State the subject in the introduction, the process to be described or the event that happened. Include in the introduction why you are writing about the subject as well as the thesis. Marianne's paper states the subject of her essay in the first sentence of her paper. She then explains that she has learned from personal experience the best way to apply for a job, and she lists the necessary steps. Her thesis, in paragraph 2, concludes the introduction.

2. Also use the introduction to set the tone for the paper—humorous, light, serious, or conversational. The introduction to the job interview essay sets a tone that is serious but informal. Marianne uses language that others would understand, and her ideas are easy to follow.

3. List the ingredients, tools, equipment, or supplies at the beginning of the paper so the reader will know what is needed early on. In the job interview essay there are no ingredients, tools, equipment, or supplies mentioned, as none are needed. However, the steps for a successful interview are given as a part of the introduction, which is as it should be.

4. Use the number of steps in the process to help you decide on the number of paragraphs you will need in the body. Steps that are very small can be put together so that the paper is not too choppy. On the other hand, no steps can be omitted. The writer of the interview essay organized her paper into three steps. She divided one of the steps into two paragraphs (3 and 4) to show two aspects of mental preparedness. Both ideas were closely related, so she counted them as one step, using four paragraphs for the body.

5. Use chronological order when you are explaining steps that must be done sequentially, as is usually the case in process essays. When there is not a built-in chronological order, use an order that makes sense to you. Note that in the job interview essay, Marianne gives reasons for putting the steps in the order she does.

6. Use a variety of transitions to show a progression of thought. At the beginning of the first paragraph of the body of the essay, the writer says,

"The first thing to do is . . ."; the second paragraph begins with "The second area of . . ."; and the final paragraph of the body begins with "The third way to prepare. . . ." Throughout the paper, a variety of transitions were used: *however, at the same time, on the other hand.*

7. Keep parallel structure in your paper. In the job interview essay, the writer uses the same structure—"first," "second," and "third"—in beginning each of the points. This is as it should be in order to be parallel. The first transition usually sets the type of transitions that will be used to introduce each point; however, common sense dictates that it would be inappropriate to enumerate points if there were as many as six or eight of them. A better approach might be to use words and expressions like *first, next, then, once you have,* and *finally.*

8. Include illustrations, examples, or anecdotes to make your paper clearer and easier to follow. Examples and/or illustrations are given to enhance each of the points in the interview essay. Notice the specific examples used in paragraphs 4, 5, and 6.

9. Give negative as well as positive instructions. If you know something won't work but you tried it anyhow, it is likely the reader will do the same thing. Your experience might help him or her avoid a pitfall. The job interview essay points out two things that shouldn't be done: never speak negatively and never use slang.

10. Use humor if you can do it effectively; on the other hand, don't sound corny in an attempt to be humorous. Humor is not used in the interview essay; on the other hand, if the introduction had used humor, it would have set the tone for the essay and allowed humor to be used throughout.

11. Organize the conclusion so that it relates to the introduction by either restating the thesis, summarizing the steps, or possibly explaining the last step in the process. The interview essay concludes by restating the steps used in the interviewing process: being prepared mentally, emotionally, and physically. Together the introduction and the conclusion form a funnel: the introduction begins in a broad statement and narrows down to the thesis. The conclusion begins with a restated thesis and broadens out to a general statement.

Working with Your Own Topic

Now that you have been given guidelines for writing your process essay, the next step is to begin prewriting on your own. This calls for knowing what you will write about first.

Choosing a Topic

Here are some things to keep in mind as you choose a topic.

- **You must write from personal experience.** You cannot tell a person how to fix a flat tire unless you have done so or unless, of course, you have read the directions that someone else has written. You cannot tell a person how to deal with a bratty sister or brother unless you have one who is a constant challenge to be around. So give some thought to the subject first, making sure that you are familiar enough with it to give someone else information about how to cope with the problem you are telling them about or how to do something according to your instructions.

- **You must know your audience.** Usually, you will write for a general audience, which means that you must be concise yet give enough details so that the reader will not have questions. If, however, you are writing for a specialized audience that uses a particular jargon, you will need to define terms if you also expect an inexperienced reader to understand your subject. For example, to tell a person unfamiliar with the workings of a zoom-lens camera how to use it, you would need to define particular features not found on other cameras.

Suppose you have chosen the topic "How to Be a Landscape Engineer." Since this is clearly just a fancy way to say "How to Mow the Lawn and Tend the Flower Beds," you can also be pretty certain that this is a topic that many of your classmates, who will be your audience in this case, will know firsthand.

Prewriting Strategy: Listing

One of the best ways to prewrite for a process essay is to make a list of all of the steps necessary for doing what you have in mind. The following example shows how you might prewrite by listing for this topic.

Topic: How to Be a Landscape Engineer

3. Cut the grass in one direction. To mulch, cut again in the opposite direction.

7. Rake the grass and bag it if the lawnmower doesn't catch the grass (saves the back)

4. Make sure all of the hedges are trimmed to the right height (a good thing to have a tape measure handy to avoid having them look like mountains and valleys)

5. Weedeat around the flower beds (just don't let the weedeater eat up the flowers—remember)

6. Run the edger along the sidewalk to make the yard look professional
1. Be sure to bring the right tools—a gas or electric lawnmower, weedeater, edger, rake, hoe, blower, and trash bags
8. Blow off the walk (don't blow the grass in the street)
2. Bring a sweat rag (a hot job in the summer time) and plenty of water (don't dehydrate)

As you can see from the list, the order is not necessarily the order in which the paper should be written. That is why the writer went back and put numbers beside the points to show the order he thinks they need to be presented in. The little notes beside the points are reminders of incidents that could be incorporated in the paper to "flesh out the points" with examples and illustrations from personal experience. This would make the paper more interesting to the reader.

Writing Strategy: Combine Small Steps

Once you have your steps in order, your goal will be to write an essay that flows smoothly and interestingly from point to point. For this paper, the writer began by creating a thesis statement that reflected the humorous and yet frustrated tone he wanted to carry through the paper: *Two years later and two hundred miles away, the steps in yardwork still haunt my dreams: mow, rake, weedeat, edge, blow, trim (or was it trim, edge, weedeat, mow, rake, edge?).*

After an introduction focusing your topic and approach, you would divide your essay into paragraphs stressing how you fine-tuned the job of landscape engineer. It would be pretty dull to have eight paragraphs with eight different steps just to mow a yard, so you need to come to some conclusion about what can be grouped together. To make his ideas flow smoothly, here is the approach this writer took as he developed the body of his paper:

FIRST PARAGRAPH: tools and personal items (points 1 and 2)
SECOND PARAGRAPH: cutting and mulching (point 3)
THIRD PARAGRAPH: weedeating, edging, trimming hedges (points 4–6)
FOURTH PARAGRAPH: cleanup (points 7–8)

Since this paper is to be tongue-in-cheek, it could include humorous asides to emphasize how clumsy the writer was or what happened with the first job. But through it all, the main objective would be to tell someone how to get the job done. This would be an interesting paper to write and fun for your peers to read.

Revising Strategy: Eliminate Unnecessary Details

Once you have completed your first draft, check to be sure that you haven't used so much detail in explaining any step that the way to actually do the step is not clear. Notice how the revised third paragraph of the body of this paper tightened up the explanation and made the process much easier to understand without losing the writer's humorous tone.

First Draft

The next step in being a landscape engineer makes the title fit. It involves the fine art of "manicuring" the lawn so that it looks professional—using the weedeater, edger, and trimmer. To begin with, make sure the weedeater has string; then cut around all of the shrubs with the weedeater. Just don't use the weedeater in the flower beds. It's not what its name implies—weedeater; it cuts flowers, too. You'll have to use your hands to do that job. To make the edge of the flower beds look really good, turn the weedeater so that it is perpendicular or at right angles to the ground and cut a little trench around the flower beds. Next, get the edger and trim around the sidewalks. It makes the grass seem higher and gives the yard a finished look. The final part of manicuring the lawn is shaping and trimming the hedges. The first time I used the trimmer, I really had fun. The house had hedges in front of the windows on either side of the front door. I started on one side and did well without measuring, so I started on the other side. You should have seen what happened! The hedges looked more like a mountain slope when I finished than two rows of even hedges. Besides having a difficult time weaseling out of doing such a bad job, I learned a valuable lesson—carry a yard ruler and measure as you trim.

Revision

Once you have finished cutting, the next step involves the fine art of "manicuring" the lawn so that it looks professional—using the weedeater, edger, and trimmer. To begin with, cut around all of the shrubs with the weedeater—making sure, of course, that you don't let it eat any nearby flowers as well. To make the edge of the flower beds look really good, turn the weedeater so that it is perpendicular or at right angles to the ground and cut a little trench around the flower beds. Next, get the edger and trim around the sidewalks. This makes the grass seem higher and gives the yard a finished look. The final part of manicuring the lawn is shaping and trimming the hedges. Use your yardstick and measure as you trim so that you don't end up with totally uneven hedges, as I did on my first—and last—job for one customer.

The questions that follow will help you analyze a process essay. Read through them carefully and apply them to your writing, and have a peer evaluator do the same. Chapter Three contains additional lists of revision questions.

Revision Questions

- Does the introduction state the purpose for the paper and give an explanation of what it will be about?

- Is the tone of the essay understood from the introduction and carried throughout the paper?

- If the essay is informational, are clear steps given to show that it describes a process?

- If the essay is instructional, are the steps in correct chronological order?

- Does the essay show firsthand experience or knowledge of the topic?

- Do the transitions show a progression in the organization of the essay?

- Does the title reflect the whole paper?

- Are imperative or action verbs used to help the reader visualize the process?

- Is the audience clear?

- Are all sentences succinct, clearly worded, and punctuated correctly?

- Are all words used and spelled correctly?

A Published Model

Here is a final model—this one by a professional writer. In an essay entitled "The Ultimate Outdoor Workout," Catherine Fredman gives directions for burning calories, fighting stress, and shaping the body—all by exercising out-of-doors. As you read her essay, note the specific steps she gives to take before hiking, what to wear, how to pack up, and what to do on the trail.

The Ultimate Outdoor Workout

1   Toss off your flip-flops and lace up your hiking boots. Summer's muggy, sweaty weather is giving way to those perfect crisp days of autumn—prime time to hit the hiking trails!

2   More and more Americans are falling in love with this rewarding sport. According to the 1994–1995 National Survey on Recreation and the Environment, hiking and backpacking are the two fastest growing outdoor activities, posting respective growth rates of 93 percent and 73 percent over the past 13 years. What everyone's discovering: Hiking is a great workout—for body, mind and spirit.

3   Hiking is like a powered-up walking workout. It involves adapting your
stride and speed to changing terrain: hopping boulders, scrambling up
hills, braking down steep slopes, cruising along the flats. You use all your
muscles in this dance with nature—your legs and arms to propel you, your
back to support a pack and shift your weight, your stomach to stay aligned.
And a deep breath of clean, sweet-smelling air is so much more enticing
than a lungful of weight room funk.

4   To help you get off on the right foot, we've gathered together all the
info you'll need—on boots, packs, snacks and more. So read on, then get
out and hit the trails!

5   Before you head off into the woods, trek to your local bookstore or outdoor supply store for a book on day hikes in your area. Most have detailed
descriptions of each trail, including the distance, the altitude gained and
the approximate time it takes to complete the hike. You also might ask the
salespeople at an outdoor equipment store to recommend some local
favorites since they're likely to be hikers themselves.

6   National, state and county parks have the best-marked trails, as well as
friendly rangers and informative trail maps. National Forest and Bureau of
Land Management areas often have dirt logging roads, but detailed maps
of these roads may not be available. You can always call the district ranger
station for tips; the telephone number is in guidebooks, as well as in the
blue government pages of your local phone book.

7   To plan your day hike, figure that your average speed in a hilly, forested
area is about 2.5 miles per hour, assuming you're reasonably fit. Add
another hour to your total hike time for every 1,000 feet of elevation
gained. Factor in the time it will take to get to the trail head, and the hours
of full daylight that you will have left for exploring a new area. It's also a
good idea to add an extra hour or two of "cushion" time whenever you
hike somewhere new in case it takes longer than expected.

8   Experienced hikers often say that the rights boots are like good friends:
They support you when the going gets rough, and they never rub you the
wrong way.

9   When you buy boots, keep in mind this useful equation: Every extra
pound on your feet is roughly equivalent to five extra pounds on your
back. For day hiking you don't need expensive, stiff, beefy backpacking
boots designed for carrying heavy loads. Leather-and-fabric trail-hiking
boots ($60 to $90) are lighter and more flexible, with a stiff enough mid-
sole to help you keep your balance when scrambling over rocks. Or you
might choose the even lighter approach shoes ($65 to $90), the hot new
trend in outdoor footwear. These look like built-up cross-trainers, and are
designed for the quick-moving, multi sport athlete who trots down trails,
bikes up mountains and tackles rock faces. Above-the ankle models are
your best bet to keep irritating pebbles from getting inside.

10   Try on lots of different boots to find the pair that really fits your feet. And don't automatically go by shoe size; your size in a boot is often a half or even a full size larger than it is in streetwear. Look for something that's comfortable from the start—the salesperson's claim that they'll feel better once they're broken in just isn't true.

11   After boots, socks are your most important purchase; nothing ruins a hike faster than sore or blistered feet. And when it comes to blister protection, socks are your secret weapon. Stay away from cotton—it sponges up the moisture in your boot, keeping your feet damp and making them less resistant to blisters. Opt for wool instead, as it absorbs up to a third of its weight in moisture without feeling wet. If wool is too itchy, try a softer wool/nylon sock. Or wear a thick liner sock made of a moisture-wicking synthetic, such as acrylic or polypropylene, under a wool outer sock.

12   Above the ankles, dress in layers that you can easily add or subtract, depending on wind and temperature. By-pass cotton and other natural fibers for CoolMax, polypropylene, Capilene and other moisture-wicking synthetics that will keep you cool and dry. Although shorts are a lot breezier, long pants protect your legs from brush and brambles, and they make it a lot easier to spot disease-bearing ticks.

13   Even if you use a comfy, battered book bag at first, sooner or later you'll want to purchase a pack designed for day hiking. It should be water-repellent or waterproof, have two outside pockets for water bottles, key clips and oversize zippers with easy-to-grasp pulls. For maximum comfort, look for a sternum strap, which fits above your breasts and takes some of the stress off your shoulders, and a waist belt (preferably padded), which shifts the weight load to your hips and prevents the pack from bouncing from side to side. Packs with these features cost between $30 and $65.

14   Try out several packs before you buy one to ensure a comfortable fit. Toss in whatever gear is handy in the store and take a walk around the floor. Check for proper fit: Does the pack fit snugly against your back without extending up past your shoulders or down past your natural belt line? Are the shoulder straps contoured to avoid chafing? Does anything poke or protrude? Are the straps the right length—neither too long nor too short?

15   Your pack should be ample enough to carry the following day-hike essentials:

- Map and guidebook
- Rain gear and a pair of dry socks
- Lunch and water
- A first-aid kit, plus sunscreen, insect repellent and either moleskin, Second Skin or some other blister remedy
- Toilet paper

- Plastic bags for trash removal
- A flashlight with fresh batteries—the woods get dark earlier than you think
- A cigarette lighter—it's more reliable for starting fires than matches
- A whistle—three evenly spaced blasts is the universal SOS signal
- Extra stuff like camera, a field guide on birds or flowers and perhaps a pair of binoculars

16   Outhouses or public toilets are rarely there when you need them, so be prepared with a stash of toilet paper and plastic sandwich bags. In order to prevent pollution, the National Outdoor Leadership School recommends digging a six-inch-deep cat hole with your boot heel or a handy stick at least 200 feet from any water source. After you've communed with nature, place the used toilet paper in the plastic bag, tuck it in your pack (animals will dig it up if you bury it), and kick the dirt back over the hole.

17   Like a car that runs better with premium gas, you'll have more energy with the hiker's equivalent of high-octane fuel: carbohydrates, which are easier to digest than proteins and fats. Plan to take along foods you like that won't get mushed or soggy or require much preparation. Bagels are more durable than bread, for example, and oranges hold up better than apples. Crackers and low-fat cheeses are a good option. Pack dried hummus that can be quickly rehydrated, bean salad, or vegetable-packed tabbouleh. And be sure to pack a few sweets—like low-fat oatmeal raisin cookies— for a late-afternoon boost.

18   GORP—"Good Ol' Raisins and Peanuts"—is the archetypal trail mix, but you can improve upon it with add-ins such as dried apricots, cranber- ries and cherries, cereal, and sunflower or pumpkin seeds. Prefab every- thing: Cut up all your ingredients at home and put them in plastic bags, so you don't have to slice and dice on the trail.

19   Bring plenty of water—at least two quarts per person—because you can't count on finding potable water on the trail. It's easy to get dehydrated, especially if it's a cool day with a light wind and you're hiking at a slight altitude with your mouth open. Avoid the fatigue and wooziness of dehydration by drinking *before* you feel thirsty—and drinking a lot.

—*Catherine Fredman*

Activity 2: Analyze the Model

1. Does the writer explain in the introduction why she is writing about the sport of hiking?
2. What process is actually explained in the essay?
3. What kind of order did the writer use in developing her essay? Did you think the order was effective? Why or why not?

4. Does the writer give reasons and explanations for what is needed on the hike? Is she clear?

5. Who was the audience for this essay? Do you think the list of things to carry in the pack is useful for that audience?

6. Do you think the essay would have been better with a conclusion? If so, how could the writer have ended her paper?

Activity 3: Write a Process Essay

The topics below are only suggestions, since a good process essay *must* be based on personal experience or knowledge. The most important point is to make sure that you know your subject well enough to tell someone else how something is done.

As you think about the topic you will write about, think also of the audience—who will be most interested in reading your paper. The audience will determine to what extent you need to go into detail and how many steps are needed.

↘ Possible Topics

- How to bungee jump
- How to water ski or snow ski
- How to juggle work and school
- How to find a way to go to college with little money
- How to choose a mate in marriage
- How to become an expert gardener
- How to work with an obnoxious person
- How to have a relationship with someone your parents disapprove of
- How to drive safely on ice
- How to make a pottery vase
- How to run for a class or school office
- How to lose friends

The Problem-Solution Essay

Understanding Problem-Solution

As a student, you recognize that problems are a given in your life every day. Sometimes they are major problems, such as not having enough money for car insurance, and sometimes they are as minor as choosing where you will go out to eat. But minor or major, they demand a solution of some kind. At times, simply discussing the problem with another person helps you to find ways to solve it. Quite often, too, when another person views the problem from an objective point of view, he or she can help you see it from a different light. At other times, presenting the problem to a group of people can provide many ideas to help solve it.

For example, Bill was concerned that too many children in his neighborhood had nothing to do in the summer. He felt it was a situation that invited trouble because of the lack of recreational facilities and the influence of drugs and gangs in the area. He began a campaign to rectify the problem. He started by calling on business leaders in the community; then he enlisted the help of volunteers from a college fraternity and appealed to the media to publicize a fund-raising event. Church groups became involved as well. Through the efforts of everyone in the community, an outside recreational area was constructed and a gymnasium built. It became a project that was on-going, a project that was beneficial to everyone and one that he remembers with pride. He had identified a real problem and worked systematically with others to find a solution.

Understanding the Problem-Solution Essay

The problem-solution essay is what its name implies—an essay that has as its focus the solution to a problem. Writing such an essay can help you think about problems you have and the solutions that are possible. In some essays, the problem, because of its enormity, gets more emphasis, while the solution may be hardly touched upon because there is no good one or because the writer is not sure of the solution. In other essays, the solution is emphasized more. The writer may feel that the reader already knows the problem; therefore, he or she stresses one or more possible solutions. And sometimes, both the problem and solution are given equal treatment. The topic you choose will help to determine whether you want to place more emphasis on the problem or the solution or whether you will cover both equally. Here are some examples.

- **Problem Stressed.** An essay on quitting smoking, especially if written from firsthand knowledge, could well focus more on the problems—getting motivated to stop, the difficulty of breaking the habit, situations in which it seems natural to smoke—than on the solution, which boils down to just doing it. The problem is more pronounced, and you have more to say about it; therefore, you should stress the problem.

- **Solution Stressed.** Your grandfather has just retired from his job but still has plenty of energy. He has no hobbies and is miserable because he has time on his hands. Although this is a problem, the solutions are quite evident. He could volunteer at hospitals, schools, and community organizations. He could take up a hobby or join an exercise club. The list is endless; therefore, in your essay solutions would get most of the emphasis.

- **Problem and Solutions Equally Stressed.** You see several problems keeping you from going to the college of your choice, but you also see several solutions. For example, your family does not have the money to send you; your grade-point average is not high enough to get a scholarship; the school is not close enough for you to live at home. But you also know that some solutions are possible: work scholarships, state and federal grants, funds from private organizations. Developing each of these points in some detail would result in a paper that dealt with both problems and solutions.

Student Model

The assignment for Joey's essay was to write on a problem he had that other students could identify with. He could emphasize the problem, the solution, or a combination of the two. Joey chose to emphasize the problem, but he offers some solutions at the very end of his paper. You should be able to identify with his problem; perhaps you could add to his solutions.

The Generation Gap

1   The generation gap at our house involves three generations—my grandmother, my parents, and me. It sometimes is so wide that I find it difficult to communicate with anyone and really get them to understand how I feel. The biggest problem which involves all of us is my getting to go where I want to go, when I want to go, and with whom. This creates a problem because my parents and my grandmother don't agree with my choice of friends, and they don't understand that I am the one who is responsible for my actions and no one else. They still want to take charge. I realize there are decades between my grandmother, my parents, and me, but there ought to be some way to bridge the generation gap.

2   For example, even though I love my grandmother dearly, she doesn't understand that times have changed. She comes from the old school which had an 11:00 o'clock curfew. She reminds me that girls had to be in by 10:00 o'clock, and they had to get their parents' approval to date every boyfriend. Without a doubt, Grandma sets her clock when I go out to make sure I am in by then. To stay out past that hour involves more haranguing than I am willing to go through with, even with the support of my parents. She argues that I am up to no good after 11:00 o'clock and that I will only get into trouble after that time. No amount of persuasion seems to get her to see that we are living at the end of the twentieth century, not the beginning, and that times are different now.

3   Besides the time problem with Grandma, I have difficulty with my parents, who quiz me about where I am going and whom I am going with. I honestly don't always know exactly all the places where I will be going. We may start out at my girlfriend's house and end up at a party, and then after I take her home, my friends and I may go somewhere else. If my parents were to try to track me down, they would have difficulty. It would take a special agent to find me at times. I don't mean I am doing anything bad; I just like to have fun with the guys, and we may cruise around to see what we can see. But try to tell that to my parents and see what they will say! The generation gap comes into play because in their time, my father's night would have ended when he took my mother home, and my mother would have quizzed him unmercifully if she thought he was going somewhere else. He would have had to answer to Mom even before his parents if he had gone anywhere else, so it was just as well that he went home early.

4   The problem with my friends, though, is a problem all to itself. I know that I should choose my friends carefully, but somehow we just gravitate together. I suppose the biggest reason I like them is we like the same things, which makes them fun to be with. We have a pretty good rapport; they don't judge me, and I don't judge them. They aren't of my parents'

social group, which is a big deal with my father, but that doesn't matter to me. I couldn't care less if their parents don't have membership in the country club or if they aren't on the dean's honor roll. I know when I need something, they will help me. For example, last week I crashed my car, and my father was so angry he wouldn't let me use the family car while my car was being repaired even though I was paying for it. My friends took me where I needed to go and provided me with transportation. That's what I call true friends!

5   The generation gap is getting to me. There must be some way to bridge it, but at present it seems almost too wide for me to handle. After spending a great deal of time thinking about it, though, I've decided the only solution that will work for me is to do my best to work within the gap by keeping my cool and try to show that I am responsible by doing what I am asked. I might even get up the nerve to tell my father where I am going and what I will be doing most of the time, and once in a while, I might even come home at 11:00 o'clock just to satisfy Grandma. Maybe in this way, my parents and my grandmother won't get angry and jump on my case. Just wait; when I get to be a parent, I will remember what it was like to be young, and I'll help my children to bridge the generation gap. They won't have as difficult time as I've had.

—*Joey Bartel*

Activity 1: Analyze the Model

1. Did Joey make a good choice in emphasizing the problem more than the solution? Why or why not? Could he have emphasized the solution equally?

2. Which point do you think best illustrates best the writer's dilemma?

3. What is the tone of the essay? How does the writer establish the tone?

4. What is the most effective part of the essay? The least effective? Explain why you think so.

5. Whom do you think is most unreasonable in the generation gap—Joey, his parents, or his grandmother?

Guidelines for a Successful Problem-Solution Essay

The guidelines for a problem-solution essay are similar to those that you use for solving problems every day, except that you are putting your thoughts in writing. The techniques are also similar, as you will see in the following points.

1. Select a topic that you have personal experience with or at least a definite opinion about. Joey's paper discusses a personal problem, the generation gap between himself, his parents, and his grandmother. But a nonpersonal topic like ways to overcome voter indifference in your community could also be effective if you have clear ideas and good information about it.

2. Decide on whether you will emphasize the problem or the solution or both. While Joey emphasizes the problem in the student model, a topic like overcoming voter indifference might emphasize solutions, or give equal emphasis to both problem and solution.

3. In the introduction, state the problem, even if you are going to emphasize the solution. The introduction also gives the circumstance and/or the situation as well as states the thesis. In addition, it sets the tone for the paper, which is carried throughout the essay. As paragraph 1 of his essay demonstrates, Joey establishes an informal tone in his introduction that helps him get the reader on his side almost immediately.

4. Include at least three paragraphs in the body of the paper, emphasizing either different aspects of the problem or possible solutions to it. Since Joey's paper emphasizes the problem, each of the three paragraphs in the body of his essay involves a different example of that problem: his grandmother's insistence on his being home at a particular time; his parents' wanting to know where he is going; and his parents' view of his friends.

5. Use examples and illustrations to clarify each point you make. Joey develops his ideas by explaining his grandmother's reasons for her eleven o'clock curfew, the things he does when he is out with his friends, and his and his parents' differing views on what makes a good friend.

6. If the issue is complex, break it down so that it will be clearer to the reader. For example, voter indifference is a many-faceted problem. In order to address it, you might have to explore why there is a feeling of apathy toward the voting process, whether voters feel their votes make a difference, and whether voters feel they can trust elected officials. You would look at the attitudes people have toward government and political parties and whether they feel it actually does any good to vote their convictions. Along with this idea, you might also explore the possibility of some who do not consider it a citizen's duty to vote and therefore don't even register. Some of these areas might have to be presented as background before or during your discussion of aspects of the problem.

7. Generally, organize the paragraphs in the body in the order of importance. Sometimes that order will not be entirely clearcut; you might wonder, for example, if Joey's problem with his parents' wanting to know where he is can be more important than their being concerned over his choice of friends. Usually, the most important problem or the best solution is stated last because you want to conclude your paper on a strong note.

8. Use the conclusion to summarize the solution(s), even if most of the paper emphasizes the problem. By doing so, you show there is a possibility for solving the problem. Note in paragraph 5 that Joey has some tentative ideas for dealing with his parents and grandmother even though he is not sure whether they will work.

Working with Your Own Topic

To begin planning your own problem-solution paper, you need to decide on a topic that will work for you. As with most essays, there is a wide range of possibilities.

Choosing a Topic

Here are some things to keep in mind as you choose a topic.

*   **You must have both a clearly defined problem and one or more solutions in mind.** You may have a lot of ideas on why violence among young children is a problem, but unless you are prepared to offer at least a tentative solution or two, you should not use the topic for this assignment. Similarly, you should not try to emphasize several solutions to the problem of classmates who "borrow" your homework if you have only one good solution but several weak ones to present.

*   **You must know enough about your topic to convince your audience that you are knowledgeable.** Suppose, for example, you are concerned about the number and size of potholes on your street, and you wanted to send the city council solutions for handling their repair. To convince the council that you know what you are writing about, you would need to research the problem and offer viable solutions. On the other hand, if you were writing the same paper for a general audience, research would not be as necessary. You would probably write to express some frustration and the general public would not be as interested in real solutions as much as they would the problem.

Suppose you have decided to write on the subject of compulsive gambling, since you have a friend who has become addicted to video poker. You must now determine how you will develop your paper.

Prewriting Strategy: Determine Your Emphasis

Before you do anything else, you need to decide whether you will be emphasizing the problem, the solution, or both. Start by making a double list, using as many examples as possible to describe aspects of the problem and possible solutions. The length of the lists will show you what to emphasize in your paper. Here is the double list one student developed:

Topic: Compulsive Gambling

Problems	Solutions
• devastating to the person and/or the family because the person loses money he or she can't afford to lose	• try to understand why the person gambles excessively
• may lead to loss of family and job	• try to get the person to understand the enormity of the problem and to accept responsibility for his or her actions
• may cause a person to commit crimes to pay for the habit	• help the person get counseling
• may cause a person to commit suicide rather than face the reality of his or her losses	
• robs the community of otherwise decent law-abiding citizens	
• preys upon people who can least afford to lose money—have a "get something for nothing" syndrome	

Besides helping you determine whether to emphasize the problem or the solution/s, a comparative list such as this will also help you determine if your solutions are viable or whether they will fall flat. This writer realized that the majority of her points dealt with the problem, so she decided to give that the most emphasis in her paper. She then reviewed her list and noted her strongest points.

The following plan shows the aspects of the problem the writer's essay covered and the order in which she dealt with them. If you compare this plan with her earlier lists, you can see that she combined some points since they seemed to fit together.

• Preys upon those who can least afford to gamble
• Leads to loss of family and job because money is used for gambling
• Causes people to commit crimes to pay for their habit—robs community of law-abiding decent citizens
• May cause a person to commit suicide

Writing Strategy: Write a Good Introduction and Conclusion

Once you have decided on the order for a problem-solution paper, the body should be fairly easy to write. But to make this paper as effective as possible, you need a strong introduction and conclusion.

The Introduction.   To make your audience want to read your paper in the first place, you have to make them care about your topic. One way is to use your introduction to involve them personally. The introduction this writer wrote uses an anecdote, which often lends itself well to a problem-solution paper, and ends with a thesis that is a general statement of the problem:

> You never know what a person is going through from outward appearances. Such was the case with my friend Cindy. She seemed happy on the outside, but I soon found out she had a problem she couldn't handle. After school one day she stopped by my house and asked to come in. Her face was red from crying, and she was clearly very upset. As soon as she sat down, she said, "I've messed up, and I don't know what to do." She had a problem with video poker—to the extent she was several thousand dollars in debt with no way to repay the money. She had written so many bad checks the bank had closed her account. *Playing video poker was a problem for Cindy she could no longer handle, a problem many others become addicted to before they realize it.*

The Conclusion.   When writing a conclusion, remember that papers focusing on problems such as this one often don't lend themselves to strong or clear solutions. This writer decided to conclude by offering the few solutions that seemed plausible. Her final statement shows that Cindy will have to bear the ultimate responsibility for ridding herself of her problem.

> After talking at length, Cindy and I tried to find some way for her to solve her problem, beginning with how to repay the money. She began to see that gambling is an addiction like any other addiction, one that she needed help to overcome. She agreed to call Gamblers Anonymous and also to seek counseling from a psychologist who specializes in problems with addiction. She said she only gambled when she wanted to hide her feelings because she was depressed. She looked upon the video poker machine as her "friend" who wouldn't chide her for her failures. It was clear that Cindy's problems were deep-seated and that there was little I could do except show her that she had to get help.

Revising Strategy: Keep the Tone Consistent

Problem-solution essays, especially those about situations that involve you personally, may cause you to react emotionally. Be sure, however, that you don't get carried away with your feelings and sound too strident or angry. Notice how the writer revised this paragraph from the body of her paper to soften the tone.

First Draft

When Cindy shared her problem with me, I was so upset I could hardly contain my feelings. I had known her for years and had no idea she was involved with video poker. My first instinct was to lash out at the gambling industry and those who promote it. I knew they were out for the almighty dollar and didn't care whose lives were ruined. Their advertisements only show the glamorous side of gambling not the pitiful sight I was seeing—a person whose life has practically been ruined by playing video poker until she has nothing left.

Revision

When Cindy shared her problem with me, my first instinct was to blame the gambling industry. After all, their ads promote the glamorous side instead of the side I was seeing. I realized, though, that even though their advertisements are enticing, no one *makes* a person gamble. It is the individual's choice.

The questions below will help you analyze your problem-solution essay. Read through them and apply them to your writing; then have a peer evaluator do the same. For additional points to consider, see Chapter Three.

Revision Questions

* Does the essay deal with both a problem and a solution?

* Does the essay have a clear tone so the reader can understand the problem and the writer's feelings about it?

* Are the points organized so that the strongest or most important point is last?

* If the problem is being emphasized, is each aspect of it adequately described through examples or details?

* If the problem is a complicated one, is it broken down so the reader understands all it involves?

* Is the tone of the paper not overly strident?

* If solutions are being emphasized, are the ones presented viable enough for the reader to believe in?

* If needed, is terminology that can help the reader understand the problem correctly used and explained?

* Are sentence patterns varied and descriptive adjectives used to help the reader see various points?

* Are there spelling and punctuation errors to be corrected?

A Published Model

Before you begin your own essay, here is a final model to study. This essay was originally written by James E. Sheridan in the form of a letter, though we have left off the greeting and closing. The title, a take-off on Jack London's *The Call of the Wild,* clearly shows the writer's frustration as he grapples with the problem of getting rid of beaver dams on his northern Wisconsin property. As you read his essay, note his tone, the way he views his problem, and the many solutions he has tried.

The Gall of the Wild

1   You can't imagine the havoc that the beaver creates on the land. My creek today is an utterly different creek from what it was only a few years ago. In some areas, where beavers have carved out clumps of grass and earth for their dams, it is twice as wide as it once was. The land on either side is marked by canals and well-worn paths created by beavers on their way to harvest trees—*my* trees—and everywhere there are little pointed stumps left by beavers where they felled and carried trees away. When you see what three or four beavers can do to a landscape in a few days, and then you think of the millions of beaver in this country for centuries before Europeans came, you come to realize that the beaver is substantially responsible for the shaping of America.

2   If you have ever seen areas where all the trees have been transformed into dead gray sticks, you have probably been looking at areas where beavers have flooded the trees. The configuration of my land is such that even a low beaver dam will spread water over many acres; in only a few days that water can kill all the tamaracks, black spruce, pine, and various other trees there. So when the beavers build a dam I have to tear it up, and I can't wait too long before doing so. But to tear up a beaver dam is surprisingly difficult to do.

3   The construction of a beaver dam is devilishly clever; you have to dismantle a dam to fully appreciate the genius of its construction. The beavers weave sticks and branches and logs together and deposit clumps of mud and vegetation against the structure so that the flow of the stream presses the muck in place and keeps it there. It is not unusual to find waterlogged logs six to eight feet long and four to six inches in diameter. More common branches are small tree trunks about three inches thick and sometimes eight or more feet in length.

4   To dismantle a dam, I have to stand on it or next to it, then start pulling out branches and tossing them on the creek bank. The branches do not

come out easily; all are entangled with the one being pulled as well as with attached globs of water-soaked foliage and mud. For a branch to come out, I must strain and tug and pull with all the power my back and shoulders can generate. When I do, and am well into a mighty effort, the branch suddenly gives way, and I am thrown violently off balance and go hurtling backwards into the creek. On other occasions, as I am grimacing with effort and opening my mouth to pant and grunt, the end of the branch, laden with muck and foliage and water, springs out of the dam to slap me across the mouth and drive the muck down my throat.

5   I used to wear breast-high waders for the work, but it was slightly awkward to move in the waders on the irregular top of the dam and the uncertain mud at the bottom. Moreover, each time I rocketed backwards into the creed, the waders filled with a couple of hundred pounds of water and threatened to carry me bouncing along the bottom of the creek like a bloated walrus. So now I go out in old trousers and shirt and tennis shoes. It is messier and less comfortable but easier to work and also safer.

6   All the time I am engaged in dismantling the dam, black flies, no-see-ums, and assorted other carnivorous insects, realizing that it is difficult for me to brush them off with hands that are coated with muck, have their way with me. (No-see-ums, as you probably know, are very tiny insects, virtually invisible—hence the name—who bite like Siberian tigers.)

7   It is not enough simply to put a hole in the dam large enough to allow the backed up water to get through. The beavers will repair such a hole in short order and go on to build the dam higher. So I try to clean out the dam down to the very bottom of the creek. I persist in thinking that the beavers will return to the site, see that all their work has been destroyed, and become discouraged and move elsewhere. But all the evidence shows that is not going to happen.

8   No matter how thoroughly I remove the dam, the beavers quickly rebuild, usually that very night. So I must tear it down the following day. The whole thing becomes a matter of perseverance, of determination; who will outlast the other?

9   But I am a human being, an intelligent, reasoning creature, and he is little more than a mouse with a glandular problem. It should be no difficult matter, I reason, to outsmart the dumb animal. One of the first things I tried, some years ago, was to string a rope about six or eight inches over the water at the dam site and hang cans and pieces of metal from it. Well, the beavers paid no attention to it, ultimately building right over it. I am not really surprised; it was a poor idea, hardly worthy of a reasoning human being.

10   Then I acquired a large jug of deer repellent, a fluid that looks like molasses and smells ineffably bad. I spread it around the dam site, but it had no perceptible effect. Next, I obtained a dried castor gland, the

beaver's sexual gland that contains an oily substance and has a strong smell. I soaked it in water and poured the fluid on several spots around the dam. In theory, the beavers would smell it, think the territory had been claimed by another beaver, and leave. (You see how subtle and intelligent that plan was; I am a human being, not a dumb animal.) The rebuilt dam the following morning suggested that the smell simply turned them on and made them work harder.

11   Next, I purchased 50 feet of plastic drain pipe: flexible pipe about 10 inches in diameter with dime-sized holes all along its length. I ran the pipe through the dam, at right angles to it, so that one end of the pipe was 25 feet upstream and the other was 25 feet downstream, each end secured to a sturdy post anchored in the creek bed.

12   I reasoned that since the water would continue to flow through the pipe and thus through the dam, the beavers could go on building indefinitely but the water level would never rise high enough to threaten my trees. Even if the beavers stuffed the end of the inlet pipe with grass or mud, water could still flow through the dime-sized holes along the pipe's length. If ever there was a subtle human intelligence at work, that was the time. I went home that day chuckling with satisfaction at this triumph of human reason over dumb animal instinct. But the next morning I found that the beavers had incorporated the entire pipe, together with the posts that held it in place, into the dam; they had used my pipe as building material!

13   I had to become more subtle and clever still. Beavers, like all sensible animals, fear human beings; they normally flee as soon as a human approaches. All I had to do was to introduce a human presence at the dam site, and the beaver would be afraid to work there. So I bought a cheap plastic radio, battery powered, and after having torn up the dam, hung the radio—tuned to an all-night station—from a tree near the dam site. Next to it, I hung a flashing light. (You see the difference between a human being and a dumb animal?)

14   The next morning, I found I could not get my canoe close to the radio and light until I cleaned away the dam that had been created during the night. It was unusually large for a single night's work; I suspect the music refreshed the beavers and increased their productivity, just as it does for assembly time workers.

15   Of course, I could shoot the beavers (an increasingly attractive notion), but I can't help feeling that there is something profoundly selfish and a bit stupid about coming to a region because I like the natural surroundings and the wildlife, and then killing any wildlife that inconveniences me. Some conservationists in Colorado (the problem of beavers is now nationwide) arranged to trap beavers, pick out the females, and fit them with a birth control device, so the population will inexorably decline. I like that idea,

but since I can't distinguish between male and female beavers, I am afraid that if I were to take that approach I might only create a lot of constipated male beavers.

16   It would also be possible to catch them in live traps and then deal with them. (What marvelous possibilities for revenge leap to mind! I could put flaming aspen slivers into the beaver's gums. Or nail his tail to the hubcap of my truck and then drive rapidly over a rough road. Or defrost him in the microwave.) In fact, I tried live traps some years ago but did not catch a single beaver. In any event, if I catch one, I have to take him miles away to release him. And, while en route, I will probably pass somebody from that place bringing his beavers to my area.

17   Oh well, I am confident that I will win out in the end. After all, I am a human being, and the beaver is a dumb animal. Ultimately, there can be no contest.

—*James E. Sheridan*

Activity 2: Analyze the Model

1. What is the tone for the letter? Where is it established? Does the writer carry it through to the end?

2. How does the writer get the attention of the reader in the introduction and make clear the enormity of the problem?

3. It takes the writer seven or eight paragraphs to define the problem. How would you explain it in a few words?

4. Can you visualize the construction of a beaver dam by the way the writer describes it?

5. What does it take, according to the writer, to dismantle the dam?

6. The writer thinks he can solve his problem by finding a way to keep the beavers from building. What are some of the solutions he tries?

7. In your opinion, does the fact that none of the solutions work weaken this essay? Why or why not?

8. Do you think the writer really believes what he says in the final paragraph? If not, what is his purpose in writing it?

Activity 3: Write a Problem-Solution Essay

The topics below are merely suggestions, since you must have some personal knowledge of the subject or a strong opinion concerning it. Keep in mind an appropriate audience who would most want to read your paper, or use the audiences suggested with some of these assignments for variety.

↘   **Possible Topics**

- As a candidate for the school council, prepare a position paper discussing possible solutions to a school problem.
- Write a letter addressing a problem at a place where you have worked and offer solutions to that problem.
- Write a teen column for the newspaper about a typical problem such as being self-conscious or overweight that you feel you have solutions for.
- Explain the problems involved with sharing a room with a sibling of the same sex and offer several solutions.
- Address either the problems older people have when they are unable to care for themselves or possible solutions to their dilemma.
- For students with this problem, research solutions for going away to school when a person has little or no money; write a paper on what you've found.
- Address the problems involved in being handicapped (if possible, deal with a handicap you are aware of personally).
- Share your solutions for prioritizing your time to allow for study, extracurricular activities, and a social life.
- Focus on either the problems or the possible solutions in selecting a career.
- Address a relatively minor problem in your everyday life that you can write about in a humorous, tongue-in-cheek, or exaggerated tone.

The Definition Essay

Understanding Definition

When you were a child, how many times did you ask an adult what a word meant? It may have been the first time you heard the word or the first time you heard it in that context. You may have even made up words that meant something special to you. One student remembers that when she was little she coined the word *stocked* to mean her socks were wrinkled in her shoes. It wasn't until her mother understood the meaning of *stocked* that the student could get her help in straightening the socks. Another student used to use *viz* to mean *scissors*. He, too, had to make his meanings understood to get what he wanted.

Learning the meanings of words also made up a part of your early education. One of the first things you did as a student in elementary school was to learn how to spell words and define them. That was absolutely necessary to form a reservoir of definitions from which you could draw as you progressed in school. That reservoir now holds you in good stead because you have continued to fill it with new words and definitions.

In the twenty-first century, with continued developments in areas like space travel, the Internet, and computer research, more words will be coined and more definitions will be added. For the person who wants to keep abreast of the times, learning new words and their definitions will be a necessity.

Understanding the Definition Essay

The definition essay draws not only on the dictionary definition of a word but also on an extended definition. A dictionary usually defines a word in three parts: (1) the term being defined, (2) the class to which it belongs, and (3) the characteristics that distinguish it from other classes; thus, a truck (term) is a four-wheeled vehicle (class) used for transportation (characteristic). The definition essay begins with some sort of formal definition like this; however, it extends or develops the formal definition to include varying aspects of the subject.

A definition essay may build on the meanings of a concrete term like *truck* or *canoe* or *golf* or *vase*. It may also involve an abstract term such as *happiness* or *democracy* or *patriotism* or *love* or *generosity*. With a concrete term, your extensions of the definition would probably involve facts that you would either have to know or be able to find through research. For abstract terms, whose meanings vary according to the person who is defining the term, you may have to draw more on your own experiences or things you have personally seen or heard to make a definition come to life. Whatever approach you choose must be clear to the reader so that he or she understands what you are trying to define.

There are several ways that you may choose to extend a definition, whether it is of an abstract term or one that is tangible. If you were writing about a Newfoundland dog, for instance, you might (1) compare it with something similar (a Newfoundland dog is like a black bear in that both are big and have black fur); (2) discuss how it is used (for pulling sleds and as a pet); (3) show its origins and development (originated in Newfoundland in the 1600s and still used as a working animal today); and/or (4) show what it is not (the Newfoundland dog is not ferocious like a Rotweiller).

This extended definition could then be fleshed out using a combination of methods—explanation, description, analysis, specific examples, and any personal knowledge of the Newfie. You could, for instance, describe some situations showing its strength or endurance as a worker. Perhaps you owned one and could add anecdotes about its behavior and loyalty, since some personal knowledge about a topic generally makes a paper more interesting to read. By the end of your paper your reader would have a clear, many-faceted definition of what this particular dog is.

Writing a paper defining an abstract term usually calls for personal reactions. For example, in defining *happiness* you might begin with the dictionary definition but then devote much of your paper to incidents in which you or other people experienced the feeling.

Student Model

The theme of definition demands thought, but it is not extraordinarily difficult to write. Ellen's assignment was to write about a topic that she could identify with and that she thought would also have meaning to her peers. She chose the subject "The Dropout," which she developed from using the prewriting technique of classical invention. As you read through her paper, note how she combines the methods for defining given above.

The Dropout

1   A dropout is usually defined as one who quits school before he gradu-ates. While that is the technical definition, the extended definition goes fur-ther. It includes a person who limits his opportunities for success in life. It also often includes a person who risks not only his own life but those of others by resorting to illegal means to make a living because of his limited capabilities. A dropout, then, is a loser not only to himself but also to soci-ety because of the limitations and restrictions he automatically incurs.

2   Most often those who drop out do so without thinking of the repercus-sions. They may get behind in their studies and aren't willing to do what it takes to catch up. They usually end up working at fast-food restaurants or service stations or other low-paying jobs for the rest of their lives. Some also make the mistake of getting a job while going to school, and when they see a paycheck coming in, they think the job is more important and drop out of school. They accept short-term goals and forget about the future until it creeps up on them, and then it is too late.

3   Quite often, without the educational background needed, the dropout must work two jobs in order to raise a family and provide the necessities. Such was the case with my friend Tim's brothers and sister. He is the only one in his family to finish high school; all of his siblings dropped out before the twelfth grade. He was determined he would not be like them because he saw what a difficult time they had making a living with-out an education.

4   It is easy to see the dropout is in some ways similar to the homeless—he loses his education; the homeless loses his home. If the dropout finds it too difficult to make ends meet, he sometimes becomes one of the home-less. He simply drifts from one job to the other because of the lack of needed skills; after a while, he either becomes a ward of the state or takes to the road seeking what he can find to eke out an existence.

5   One of the worst things about dropouts, though, is that too many of them get involved in selling drugs and making fast money when they real-ize what little they can do without an education. When that happens, they're also risking their lives as well as endangering others. Two of my classmates had members of their families killed because of drug deals gone sour; they were dropouts trying to make a fast dollar.

6   Dropping out of school is not the answer because no one wins. Society is cheated by not having productive people and the individual is cheated of what he could have been. Instead of developing latent talents and using them to accomplish higher goals, the dropout usually settles for what he can get. Too often because of his short-sightedness, he passes on a loser mentality to his offspring, and the cycle continues.

—*Ellen Winthrop*

Activity 1: Analyze the Model

1. How does the writer's extended definition of a dropout in the introduction help to explain the term?

2. What are some of the characteristics of dropouts Ellen mentions in the essay? Together, do you think they end up providing a well-rounded, fair definition?

3. To what does the writer compare a dropout? Do you think the comparison is justified?

4. The writer based her essay on people she saw around her rather than on actual research. To what extent, if any, would the paper have been improved if she had done research?

5. How does the conclusion of this essay relate to the introduction?

Guidelines for a Successful Definition Essay

You use the guidelines for a definition essay every day in explaining terms that others do not understand; therefore, it should not be difficult to apply them to your writing.

1. Select a term to define and then focus on particular conditions or circumstances that you will use to extend the definition. For example, Ellen chose to focus on how both the individual and society lose when a person becomes a school dropout.

2. Decide whether you will approach the topic from a personal or more objective point of view. Generally, abstract terms require personal examples—either from your life or from the lives of people you know—to bring them to life; more tangible terms might be treated in a less personal way.

3. Use your opening paragraph to formally define the term and explain your particular approach to it. Be succinct so that your definition is both clear and accurate. Though the formal definition need not be taken directly from the dictionary, it should include the term, its class, and its distinguishing characteristics. Ellen defined a dropout in the first sentence, but then she elaborated on it throughout the introduction, showing a number of distinguishing characteristics.

4. State your approach to the topic in your thesis statement. Ellen's thesis statement, "A dropout, then, is a loser not only to himself but also to society because of the limitations and restrictions he automatically incurs," established the direction her essay would take.

5. Establish the tone in the beginning of your paper and carry it through to the end. Ellen's tone was serious; she seemed distressed because of the

enormous problem dropouts cause for themselves as well as others. But definition essays can also be humorous, sentimental, or even angry.

6. Choose a method of development for the body of the paper that corresponds to the way you have defined the term. Ellen did this by discussing each of the distinguishing characteristics she had mentioned in her introduction: dropouts' limited opportunities for success, their tendency to endanger others by making a living through illegal means, and their generally being losers to self and society. Some definition essays are also developed by discussing what the topic is *not:* A paper about self-made millionaires, for example, might contrast them with timid, reckless, and disorganized people—all qualities successful people tend not to have.

7. Choose an order for your examples that makes sense with the subject matter. Topics such as Ellen's lend themselves to order of importance, in which the strongest example is saved for last. If the term you were defining involved some sort of history, however—flying machines, for example—you would probably want to use chronological order.

8. Develop your paper through specific examples, illustrations, explanations, or descriptions that bring the term to life. Ellen's example in paragraph 3 of Tim's family helps to illustrate the difficulty a dropout with a low-paying job has in supporting a family. Her example in paragraph 5 shows the danger a dropout has who tries to earn a living through illegal means.

9. Conclude your essay by a restatement of the definition, a quote others have used to define the term, or by summarizing the information you have presented. Ellen restated her thesis but then added that dropouts often pass on their short-sightedness to their offspring.

Working with Your Own Topic

If you follow the definition essay guidelines, you should have no difficulty in writing a good paper. But first you must select a topic to work with.

Choosing a Topic

In determining what your topic will be, think first whether you want to define an abstract term or one that is tangible. As you make that determination, keep in mind the following tips.

• **You should select a term that has enough characteristics or qualities to lead to an interesting essay.** Abstract terms are sometimes easier to write about for this reason, because they tend to have different meanings, and thus call up different examples, for each writer. If you choose a concrete term, you must make sure that you have enough to say about it to develop a full-length essay. Many concrete terms—*chapel, beachcomber, Oriental rug, motorcycle* are a few that come to mind—can be made into interesting essays if you are willing to do research into such areas as the item's history, different types that exist, and particularly noteworthy examples. If you cannot find such information, or are bored with the topic before you even begin, look for something else to write about.

- **Make sure you can develop your topic in a way that will interest your intended audience.** Knowing your audience will determine the extent of your definition, its formality and tone, and particularly the focus of your examples. If, for instance, your audience was a cadet training group, an essay about loyalty that dealt primarily with examples of loyal pets might seem quite irrelevant. And an essay on loyalty for an audience of troubled teenagers with little feeling for friends or family might require still different examples.

Suppose, after much consideration, you have decided to write on a tangible subject that you know a fair amount about. The subject you have chosen is a sonnet. Your dilemma is how to develop and organize your essay.

Prewriting Strategy: Classical Invention

Classical invention is a good strategy for organizing your thoughts for a definition essay. Instead of trying to answer every question in each part, you might choose to take each of the five parts to classical invention and use them as a guide to develop your paper. One student writing about the sonnet organized her thoughts in this way:

Topic: Sonnet

- Definition: a fourteen-line lyric verse, having a five-foot iambic line and a set rhyme pattern, often abba abba cd cd cd or abab cdcd efef gg
- Comparison: like blank verse with five-foot iambic line, but different because sonnet is rhymed
- Relationship: can cause feelings such as joy, love, happiness, anger, and sorrow
- Circumstance: developed in the 1200s in Italy; often written to express love or the beauty of nature, but really can be on any topic
- Testimony: writers like Shakespeare, Elizabeth Barrett Browning, and John Donne masters of the form

After looking over her ideas, the student decided she wanted to give her definition paper more of a personal touch. She realized that one of her main purposes in defining sonnets was to show how enjoyable they were to read because they express the writers' personal thoughts and feelings. She decided to develop some of the ideas in her last three points by focusing on noteworthy sonnets of the three writers she had mentioned.

Writing Strategy: Make the Organization Reflect Your Purpose

The student began her paper by presenting the formal definition of a sonnet. Once she had explained its origins and what a sonnet is and is not, she wrote a thesis statement directing her paper toward how sonnets can express their writer's innermost thoughts, referring specifically to Donne, Shakespeare, and Browning. Her first-draft topic sentences for each of the body paragraphs were as follows:

PARAGRAPH ONE: John Donne's series of Holy Sonnets present the writer's profound thoughts on religious faith and immortality.

PARAGRAPH TWO: While Shakespeare was a master of blank verse in his plays, his sequence of 154 sonnets is almost a narrative of events and resulting feelings involving himself, a dark lady, and another young man or "rival poet."

PARAGRAPH THREE: Elizabeth Barrett Browning's "Sonnets from the Portuguese" describe the great love she had for Robert Browning and the emptiness she felt when they weren't together.

Revising Strategy: Stick to the Topic

Because a definition essay has no built-in format, be careful not to stray from the topic—which is aspects of the word being defined. Notice how the writer corrected this kind of error in the revising stage when she got carried away discussing Shakespeare's plays as well as his sonnets. Changing her topic sentence was one big help in keeping the paragraph more in focus.

First Draft

While Shakespeare was a master of blank verse in his plays, his sequence of 154 sonnets is almost a narrative of events and emotions involving himself, a dark lady, and another young man or "rival poet." The story, however, is loosely constructed, and it is not as important as Shakespeare's overall treatment in the sonnets of the themes of life, love, beauty, and friendship. The highly compressed format of the sonnet is a perfect vehicle for bringing these emotions to life through figurative language. In "Sonnet 116," for example, Shakespeare compares love to a guiding star "constant to the edge of doom." This connection between love and doom recurs in many of Shakespeare's plays as well, most notably *Romeo and Juliet,* whose beautiful verse lines present a highly emotional picture of the "star-crossed lovers." Shakespeare clearly is a master of blank verse as well as the rhymed sonnet pattern.

Revision

Shakespeare's sequence of 154 sonnets is a narrative of events and emotions involving himself, a dark lady, and another young man or "rival poet." The story, however, is loosely constructed, and it is not as important as Shakespeare's overall treatment in the sonnets of the themes of life, love, beauty, and friendship. The highly compressed format of the sonnet is a perfect vehicle for bringing these emotions to life through figurative language. In "Sonnet 116," Shakespeare compares love to a guiding star "constant to the edge of doom." He also personifies love in the same sonnet, saying, "Love's not Time's fool" and "Love alters not with his brief hours and weeks." The beautiful construction of these sonnets helps convey Shakespeare's unique understanding of human nature.

The questions that follow will help you analyze the first draft of your definition essay. Use them, and your peer evaluator's response to them, to guide your revision. For additional points to consider, see Chapter Three.

Revision Questions

- Is the topic limited so that it is defined adequately yet clearly?

- Is the topic defined using the format of term, class, and distinguishing characteristics?

- Is the same tone used throughout the paper?

- Has the audience's knowledge and interest in the topic been considered so that unfamiliar terms have been defined and information already known to the audience been omitted?

- Has each aspect of the definition been discussed with enough information and examples?

- Has research been done when needed to ensure the accuracy of information?

- Are all of the points made relevant to defining the term?

- Are the word choice and sentence structure varied to keep the audience's interest?

- Is the paper free from grammatical and spelling errors?

A Published Model

Before you begin your own essay, here is one final example. "Let Us Prey," by Catherine Collins and Douglas Frantz, is a compiled model that presents many aspects of the term *cult*. As you read the piece, note how they first define what a cult is and then the kind of details they use to flesh out that definition.

Let Us Prey

1   *Cult.* It is the word itself combined with the age-old issue of religious freedom—that most fundamental and hallowed of American rights—that causes so much controversy when one tries to convey its meaning. Although the media and the anti-cult groups use the word pejoratively, the organizations in question argue that centuries ago, Christianity was considered a cult.

2   *Webster's New World Dictionary* gives as a first definition for cult "a system of religious worship or ritual." According to Margaret Singer, Ph.D., a Berkeley, California, psychologist, the actuality is a bit more complicated. "The word describes a power structure," she says. What really sets a cult apart is that "one person has proclaimed himself to have some special knowledge." Actually there are hundreds of cults, she explains, many of which revolve around entirely secular pursuits: psychology, martial arts, even flying saucers.

3   Peter D. Ross, an attorney and member of the Unification Church in New York, contends that the current connotation is "inflammatory"—and there are academics and even mainstream religious leaders who agree there is, at times, some overreaction. "Some anti-cult groups are not simply against cults, but against religion of any sort," says Larry D. Shinn, Ph.D., a Bucknell University professor of religion. "You must make the distinction with cults you make with drugs. I take aspirin, but I don't take heroin."

4   The emergency of so-called cults is not a new phenomenon, says Elizabeth C. Norbeck, Ph.D., dean of the faculty and vice president for academic affairs at Andover Newton Theological School in Massachusetts. As she wrote in the September 1992 issue of *USA Today* magazine, "Historically, new and unfamiliar religious movements (including Christianity) . . . always have generated fear and antagonism disproportionate to their real threat."

5   Who, then, decides if an organization is a cult? Or indeed if it's dangerous? That depends, says Kenneth Lanning, a supervisory special agent

with the FBI, on who's setting the rules. "As a law-enforcement officer I'm interested only when it's involved in criminal activity."

6   Marcia Rudin of the American Family Foundation's International Cult Education Program says these groups interfere with members' ability to think freely and critically. A "cult," she says, uses deception and unethical manipulative techniques of persuasion and control "to advance the goals of the group to the detriment of the individual members, their families and the community."

7   No matter where recruitment takes place, or how long involvement lasts, once a person becomes involved with a cult-like group, leaving can be extremely hard—sometimes impossible. It can be even more difficult for older individuals because time is critical to the recovery process. And time is what many older people don't have a lot of.

8   "When someone leaves a cult, his problems are just beginning," says Rudin of the American Family Foundation. "It can leave a very big hole in a person's life. You've cut yourself off from other people. And to recover you must rebuild those bridges. You have to rebuild your self-esteem and deal with the rage and the shame. And sometimes you have to take care of the practical things: jobs, credit, bank accounts, a place to live, health care, etc."

9   Caroline Marshall (name changed) knows all that. "My life was undergoing radical change. The Pittsburgh (Pennsylvania) company I worked for was in Chapter 11 and I was losing my job. A personal relationship was breaking up and my children were all away and busy with their own lives." Marshall drifted toward Ramtha, a New Age cult based on the teachings of J. Z. Knight, a Washington state housewife who claims to be the entity through which a 35,000-year-old warrior spirit speaks. "Before I knew it, I was caught up. It's far easier than people think," she says.

10   Thus as the age of 58, Marshall left the East and moved to Washington to pursue her studies of Ramtha. It was a decision that cost her two years and approximately $30,000 in savings.

11   As Marshall's involvement increased, she became more and more concerned. The warnings of impending natural and economic disasters were extremely intense and included talk about a race of underground space aliens conspiring with the United States government and feeding on human beings.

12   Finally, Marshall's sons helped her make a break.

13   Anna Hoover (name changed) didn't leave her cult as willingly. For seven years she was a member of the Church Universal and Triumphant. "One day my husband asked me to come home to pick up a package," she says. When she got to the house her entire family, plus three deprogrammers, were waiting. "I was angry. I felt betrayed. It took several days of

talking before I could simmer down and start to listen. Even though I was grateful to my family, it took a long time to get over that anger."

14 Hoover calls her cult experience "a rape—a spiritual and psychological rape. It almost destroyed me."

15 Martin points out another often-forgotten segment of the older population who, although not directly involved with cults, are nonetheless their victims: those who are forced to live a life of total estrangement from their children, and sometimes their grandchildren, who are cult members.

16 Another burning issue for former cult members is regaining some kind of spiritual orientation in their lives, according to Michael Langone, Ph.D., editor of *Recovery From Cults* (Norton, 1993). He did a study in which 87 percent of the respondents said they had some religious affiliation before joining a cult, while 54 percent said they had none at all after leaving the cult.

17 "People become gun-shy," Langone says. "If you're young you have time to work through this—but for an older person, to be alienated from religion is, I believe, a sad thing."

18 It's virtually impossible to anticipate the physical and emotional trauma cult association can unleash. It can also lead to irreparable economic devastation, particularly for older people. And that's just the beginning of the long, dark process.

19 The seduction starts out caring and comfortable. Eventually, it becomes cruel and castrating. By the time a victim realizes what has happened—if he or she ever does—it's often too late. Worse, the destruction can never be fully undone.

20 The debate goes on.

—Catherine Collins and Douglas Frantz

Activity 2: Analyze the Model

1. What is the writers' purpose in this essay? At what point did their purpose become clear to you?

2. Besides the dictionary definition of cult, how else did the writers elaborate on its meaning in paragraph 2?

3. How do other people define "cult" according to the writers?

4. What extensions of the definition of cult do the writers present in the essay? Do the examples they use support the definition of cult that they have established?

5. Besides the emotional and economic loss to those involved in cults, what else do they lose, according to paragraphs 16 and 17? Why is that so important?

Activity 3: Write a Definition Essay

As pointed out earlier, your topic should be one that you are familiar with or want to research. The suggestions below also include a possible direction to go in extending the definition of each topic. Remember, as always, to keep your audience in mind as you choose what to write about.

↘ **Possible Topics**

- New millionaires (names, characteristics of people who have become millionaires in the last five years)
- Responsibility (facing the consequences of one's actions)
- Socialism (what it is and how it works in different countries)
- Best friends (what they are and are not)
- The tango (how it's done and its meaning to various dancers)
- Happiness (according to Peanuts)
- Snobs (how to recognize them in society)
- Ghosts (how they are presented in various pieces of literature)
- Courage (shown by common people in everyday life)
- Criminal lawyers (characteristics that differentiate them from other types of lawyers)

The Classification Essay

Understanding Classification

It would be difficult to imagine a society that had no means of classifying or sorting out things according to a particular method. Pandemonium would result. Every area of life would be affected—not just the classification of species of animals and plants, but even of mundane things such as shopping.

Suppose, for example, you wanted to buy a book. You go into the bookstore and ask for a novel that is required reading, *Wuthering Heights* by Emily Bronte. The clerk says, "Look around; all of the books are out on the shelves. Just browse through what's there until you find it." You survey the scene; there is no order at all. Books on mathematics, science, photography, composition, language, and electronics are mixed in with American novels, English novels, and novels by world authors. It helps little that you know who wrote the book and that her name is written on the spine. There is such a conglomeration of books on the shelves that it would take hours and hours to find *Wuthering Heights.*

That scene would be multiplied if you went into the grocery store to buy items for even one meal. Imagine the time necessary to gather all of the supplies needed if the meats were mixed in with the produce and the cereals were placed with the canned goods and eggs and milk. Clearly, it would be next to impossible to live in a world that had no way of grouping things in some order.

When the earliest humans first began to gather sticks for a fire, they probably sorted them out into small ones to start the fire and larger ones to keep it going. They too were classifying, though they probably weren't aware of what they were doing.

Not only is classification a method for sorting *things* into categories, it is also used in dividing or sorting out the intangible, such as periods of one's life. A young woman, for example, might divide the periods of her life according to the types of schools she had attended: preschool, elementary, middle school, high school, and college. An older man may think of the categories of childhood, adolescence, young adult, and middle age. Other categories for classification could also be used: schools attended, cities lived in, people who were a great influence.

Understanding the Classification Essay

The classification essay uses the same general approach. It sets up a general category to be discussed; then it presents a number of items, people, or ideas that fit into that category. The category functions not only as the general topic of the essay, but also the single organizing principle that holds the essay together.

For example, suppose you are going to write a fact-based essay dealing with some aspect of the community in which you live. The topic and organizing principle of your paper might be the resources available to provide for the welfare of the people. The areas you discuss in developing this paper could be the educational facilities, the recreational facilities, and the religious facilities. A category such as vacant buildings in the downtown area would not be appropriate, since it has nothing to do with the general organizing principle of resources available.

Classification essays can also be based on opinion. You might, for example, classify and discuss the courses you have studied by their level of interest: dull and boring, somewhat interesting, and exciting. Or you might categorize them according to level of difficulty.

A classification essay can also be based on a subject in literature. For example, the supernatural in Shakespeare's plays *Hamlet, Macbeth,* and *Julius Caesar* might be classified according to how the main characters are affected by ghosts. In *Hamlet* the ghost of Hamlet's father causes Hamlet to take revenge on his Uncle Claudius. In *Macbeth* the ghost of Banquo at the coronation banquet causes Macbeth to appear unstable to his guests and begins his decline as king; and in *Julius Caesar* the ghost of Caesar causes Brutus to realize the likelihood of his own death when the ghost says he will see Brutus at Philippi. While there are other evidences of the supernatural in the plays—floating daggers, speechless apparitions, witches—they do not occur in every play and so would not be included in this essay.

Student Model

The classification essay is not difficult to write after you give some thought to the subject, as shown with the student paper that follows.

Jerry's assignment for the classification essay was to write about something that happened to him that he could divide into categories or classes. It could be jobs or people he had met or teachers or fellow students or vacations or any number of things. He was asked to brainstorm about his topic, which he did, and he came up with the subject of former employers. After thinking about those employers for a while, he decided that he would categorize them according to the kind of influence they had in making him decide to be his own boss when he grew up.

As you read through Jerry's paper, note how he makes his introduction interesting and how he constructs his thesis (italicized for your benefit). Note also how he categorizes the three employers who affected him most and later identifies them with names he thinks shows their personalities.

My Employers and Me

1   When I was little, I used to dream of one day having a job and earning my own money. I thought of what I would do with the money, how much I would allow for spending and how much I would save for my future. I imagined the person I worked for would be lavish with praise about my work; he would be generous in allowing me time off when I had something I really needed to do; and he would point to me as an example for other workers to follow. I would, in turn, do my very best to earn his respect.

2   It wasn't until I became a teenager and was old enough to work that I tempered my dreams a little. I chuckle now that I am older to see how much they changed, but change they did, all because my employers weren't what I expected them to be. I'm sure I gave them one hundred percent effort; I can't understand why they weren't what I thought they would be. *Instead, I can easily divide them into three categories: the miserly, the overexpectant, and the grumpy. It's no wonder that I plan to be my own boss; I'm tired of having bosses of my own.*

3   I'll begin with my first employer. I began working for Mr. Addlebrain when I turned sixteen. He ran a hardware store and must still have the first penny he ever made. He watched me like a hawk. When a customer came in for a nut or a bolt, I sometimes didn't charge for it. After all, the nuts and bolts weren't marked, and I had to look up everything in a catalog from different companies. It was just too much trouble; what could giving away something that small have amounted to anyhow? Finally, after working for Mr. Addlebrain for six months, I decided that before he let me go, I would resign. Actually, I didn't resign; I just

didn't show up for work one morning. I figured he would never raise my salary as much as he complained about the cost of nuts and bolts, so I just quit.

4   After my experience with penny-pinching Mr. Addlebrain, I applied for work at Mr. Weatherspoon's gas station. He didn't even ask for references, so it was easy to get a job with him. He gave me a list of things to do right away. I glanced over the list, but I thought I knew how to pump gas and check tires, so I didn't really give it too much thought. It was summertime and as hot as blue blazes, so I tried to stay inside the sales room as much as I could under the fan. At least it was cool in the sales room.

5   I soon realized, though, I hadn't completely read the list. Mr. Weatherspoon yelled as loudly as he could when he saw me. "Why are you doing goofing off? Look at that list I gave you." In big letters he had written, STAY BUSY! DO NOT SIT IN THE SALES ROOM! So much for that. I looked at the list again: "Empty the garbage cans; fill the water bottles, untangle the hoses; sweep up the sales room; pull weeds from the driveway." That was just a start. The next part of the list said, "Customers deserve the best. Wash their windows; check the tires; check the spare tire in the trunk; clean the battery cables; check the battery; fill the windshield washer bottle." All of these were to be done besides putting gas in the car.

6   I didn't last long at Mr. Weatherspoon's station, either. He just expected too much. I could never sit down with all of the things I was expected to do; I was afraid I would forget something. I had to keep the list in my pocket and constantly look at it. At least, I learned a lesson at his station; some day be your own boss so you can expect others to work for you.

7   The employer, though, that made me *know* I was going to college to learn how to be my own boss was Mr. Freggenhopper. His name says it all! Mr. Freggenhopper was about the grumpiest person who ever lived. He owned the franchise for a fast-food chain, and he worked at the one where I was employed. Mr. Freggenhopper complained when we had customers, and he complained when we didn't have customers. He griped about my not working fast enough and about my talking with the customers. After all, I brought him business. My friends came in every afternoon to see me, and they usually bought a coke and fries. Sometimes they even splurged with a double cheeseburger or a quarter-pounder. I couldn't help talking with them about their dates and asking them who they were taking to the prom. But Mr. Freggenhopper didn't see things my way. After three months, he had had enough. He called me into his office one afternoon, and he said I should run for a political

office some day with as much gift of gab as I had. He said he had never seen anyone talk as much in his life and that now I could just carry on my conversations elsewhere. I was fired—again!

8   I couldn't understand what was happening. First, Mr. Addlebrain was so penny-pinching, he let me go over a little thing like not charging for nuts and bolts; then Mr. Weatherspoon expected so much no one could ever live up to his expectations; and finally, Mr. Freggenhopper didn't see how much I was bringing him customers by my friends coming over every day and talking with me. All of this happened in less than a year. It's no wonder that today I'm in college learning how to be my own boss.

—Jerry Bernard

Activity 1: Analyze the Model

1. Does the writer's introduction include a statement of how he is categorizing his topic, and does he stick with his categories throughout the essay?

2. What is the tone of the writer's paper? Do you think his use of this tone is effective or would you suggest another tone?

3. Are each of the points parallel in the way the writer describes them?

4. Do you think the writer could have described any of the situations in more detail? If so, explain.

5. After reading the essay, what impression do you get of the author and of his work habits?

Guidelines for a Successful Classification Essay

Now that you have read an example of a classification essay, you should be able to see that certain guidelines must be adhered to in order to write one effectively. These are given below for you to apply to your own essay as you begin to write.

1. Limit your topic and the divisions included so that a single organizing principle is involved. Jerry uses the general topic of employers and then narrows it to include only employers who caused him to decide to be his own boss. He does not overlap by using employers whom he got along with. Make an outline of your paper if that will help to determine whether all your categories fit.

2. Include at least three classifications. (If you use only two, you may end up with a comparison-contrast essay.) As already pointed out, Jerry's classes are employers who were miserly, overexpectant, and grumpy.

3. Use your introduction to establish your tone and to present the categories you will be discussing. The introduction is usually no longer than two paragraphs. Notice how Jerry begins by discussing his dream of growing up and making his own money in his first paragraph. Then in the second paragraph he narrows his subject down by explaining why his dreams fell through—because of three types of employers. His thesis in this case is two sentences: "Instead, I can easily divide them into three categories: the miserly, the overexpectant, and the grumpy. It's no wonder that I plan to be my own boss; I'm tired of having bosses of my own."

4. Use examples and/or illustrations to support each of the classes of your essay. Jerry divides his paper into a description of each of the employers and then illustrates what was wrong with each one. The miserly employer didn't like his giving away nuts and bolts; the overexpectant employer felt he should always be doing something; and the grumpy employer complained because he talked with his friends too much.

5. Consider using one of the following order patterns to present your ideas:

    *   **Chronological order:** Note that Jerry describes each of the employers he had in the order he worked for them.
    *   **Order of importance or commonness:** "People who affected my life" might be organized in order of importance; "Plants in the Riverside Botanical Gardens" might be organized according to which types are most common. At times, the most important or frequently occurring category is given last; at other times, it is given first. The writer makes it clear in the introduction which order he or she is using.
    *   **Spatial order:** A paper dealing with regional dialects in a state or country could use this order—going, for example, from east to west or from north to south.
    *   **Numerical order—size, volume, weight:** Though not too often used, papers on such topics as the advantages of different size automobiles could be organized numerically.

6. Use transitions throughout your paper to make it read smoothly. Jerry's paper is written in a light, conversational tone, so it was easy for him to move from one class to the other with transitional words. For example, he introduces the first classification with, "I'll begin with my first employer" and moves to the next class by saying, "After my experience with penny-pinching Mr. Addlebrain, I applied for work at Mr. Weatherspoon's gas station." Words and expressions like *next, another, the most important, finally,* and *last but not least* can also help in moving from one point to another in a classification essay.

7. Define terms if your audience is unfamiliar with them. In Jerry's paper, no definitions were necessary; however, if you were writing about the political views of the Supreme Court justices you would probably need to define the terms *liberal, conservative,* and *moderate.*

8. Describe each category fully as well as list the members of each group if that is necessary. For example, to classify members of the Supreme Court into liberals, conservatives, and moderates would probably demand giving their names and explaining why they fit into one category or the other. You would already have defined the terms as best as possible.

9. For your conclusion, use a restatement, or simply stop with the last point. Jerry decided to conclude his paper by summarizing his three employers and then end with "It's no wonder that today I'm in college learning how to be my own boss." His last statement is a direct reference to his thesis and effectively draws his paper to a close.

Working with Your Own Topic

The classification essay is not difficult to write if you follow the guidelines given. The next step is to begin prewriting on your own, which calls for having an idea of what you want to write about.

Choosing a Topic

As you begin thinking of your topic, a few things need to be considered.

*   **You must have several strong examples that support your general organizing principle.** Classification essays can be based on fact, or opinion, or a combination of both, but they will never be successful unless you have enough specific examples that fit your topic. Essays based on fact, such as the kinds of weather in a given area or the regions of the country that twentieth-century presidents came from, must often be researched to make sure you have the facts right. And accurate research becomes even more important if you want to draw any conclusions or offer any opinions about those facts. Essays based on opinion tend to be more interesting and fun to write. Readers are often eager to find out if they agree with your assumptions on topics like the strange habits of family members or things teenagers spend money on; thus, they are more likely to read the entire paper. But such essays are successful only if you have several well-defined examples of the subject and clear views on them that you want to communicate.

*   **You must have information that is appropriate for your intended audience.** If you were writing to the newspaper to suggest the categories into which the sports section might be rearranged, you would write differently from the way you would if your audience were your classmates. Your classmates may be more interested in topics that affect their everyday lives—kinds of relationships, favorite eating places, types of TV commercials, or job-related topics like unusual customers in the check-out

line. By having the audience in mind, you will be more aware of appropriate examples to use in classifying the topic.

Let's assume that after considerable brainstorming, you have come up with the topic of "Indoor Pets." Since you've had several pets over the years, you feel confident that you will have enough specifics to write about. Now you need to determine how to best organize your ideas for a classification essay.

Prewriting Strategy: Find a Single Organizing Principle

A good way to begin is to list as many specific examples as you can that would fit with the topic. As you do this, also write notes about the examples so you can see similarities between them and thus determine a single organizing principle under which you can classify them. The example below shows how one student worked with the "Indoor Pets" topic.

Topic: Indoor Pets

- birds (our parakeet—Chirpy): live in cages—sing—eat bird seed—make a mess—good company—cover cage at night
- tortoises (friend has one): live in aquarium—sleep a lot—fun to watch—don't make any sounds—eat lettuce and celery—move slowly
- gerbils (saw in pet store): make a real mess—go round and round on Ferris wheel toy—never really get anywhere—shred paper—eat gerbil food—fun to watch
- little dogs (our little poodle, Papilion): bark unnecessarily sometimes—have to be carried outside to go to the bathroom—fun to play with—have to be groomed—fed regularly—do tricks
- cats (our Calico cat, Funny Face): scratch furniture sometimes—must have litter box—meow when they want something—good company
- white mice (yuk!): must have cage—fed and cared for—can be let out if watched carefully—fun for children to watch
- fish (goldfish or other): need aquarium—fed fish food—aquarium must be cleaned periodically—fun to watch

After looking over the list for an organizing principle to use in classifying the pets, the student came up with the categories below:

- *Live in cages*—birds, gerbils, white mice
- *Make sounds*—cats, dogs, birds
- *Fun to watch and good company*—cats, dogs, birds
- *Must be cared for every day*—cats, dogs, birds

- *Need little care*—tortoises, mice, gerbils
- *Eat very little*—gerbils, tortoises, mice, fish
- *Sometimes a nuisance*—cats, dogs, birds, gerbils

This second list made it clear that not all pets fit into all categories. However, one organizing principle she noted was that cats, dogs, and birds provide the best company because they make some sound to communicate with their owners. It was easy to see that gerbils, fish, mice, and tortoises don't share this principle.

The writer decided, then, to make the paper more personal. You noticed beside the bird, dog, and cat she had written names of animals who had been a part of her life. She decided that the general category she would write about was pets that had made her happy as a child.

Writing Strategy: Use the Introduction to Focus the Body

To focus the rest of her paper, the student then wrote an introduction that conveyed her feelings about the topic and her stance in writing about it. Notice how she even mentions pets that don't fit her organizing principle to strengthen her case about those that do.

Introduction

Some people like pets that run around in tiny cages all day like gerbils and white mice. Others like exotic animals that they see in the zoo, like emus and ostriches. To me, though, the best animals are those that can be kept inside as pets, especially those that provide company and don't require much care. *As I look back on my childhood, the three that particularly had those qualities were my dog Papilion, my cat Funny Face, and my parakeet Chirpy.*

The thesis statement should also give the order in which you will treat your examples. Here the writer has decided to speak of her pets in the order in which she owned them: her dog, her cat, and her bird. She will develop her paper by writing a paragraph or two about each of them, focusing on the easygoing companionship that they provided.

Revising Strategy: Eliminate Digressions

A classification paper is definitely enlivened by the specific examples you include. But to make those examples as effective as possible, be sure to tightly focus your discussion of them. Check each point that you make against your thesis statement. Even one or two sentences that wander off the point should be eliminated, as this writer did in her revision.

First Draft

Papilion was an easy-to-be-with dog from the day I got him. Mom surprised me with him on my tenth birthday, and he looked like a big ball of black fur. I had begged for a little dog and had no idea I would really get one. I knew Mom liked cats, but I wasn't sure how she felt about dogs. Soon he was amusing everyone in the family with his tricks. He learned to stand on his hind feet and clap his paws together and beg for something to eat. But he was particularly attached to me. He knew when my school bus came and would scratch his way out of the back door and run to meet me. One day, though, he followed me down to a friend's house and when her mother backed her car out, she ran over him. Papilion was killed and I cried and I cried.

Revision

Papilion was an easy-to-be-with dog from the day I got him. Mom surprised me with him on my tenth birthday, and he looked like a big ball of black fur. Soon he was amusing everyone in the family with his tricks. He learned to stand on his hind feet and clap his paws together and beg for something to eat. But he was particularly attached to me. He knew when my school bus came and would scratch his way out of the back door and run to meet me. One day, though, he followed me down to a friend's house and when her mother backed her car out, she ran over him. Papilion was killed and I cried and I cried.

The questions that follow will help you, and/or your peer evaluator, analyze your essay. Read through them carefully and apply them to your writing. Additional revision questions are in Chapter Three.

Revision Questions

- Does the topic involve a single organizing principle?

- Is that principle established in the introduction?

- Are at least three classes or categories of the topic dealt with?

- Are the basics of those classes explained or defined if the audience is likely to be unfamiliar with them?

- Does the paper follow a reasonable order of organization?

- Are appropriate transitions used to show connections between ideas?

- Does the tone of the essay remain consistent throughout?

- Are examples and illustrations used effectively in talking about each class?
- Are sentences structurally sound and punctuated correctly?
- Are there spelling errors or capitalization errors to be corrected?

A Published Model

Now read one more classification essay to get yourself ready to write. The sample that follows, "The Marks of an Educated Man," was written a long time ago and may sound formal or sexist by today's standards, but it clearly is a classification essay. The author, Nicholas Murray Butler, classifies an educated man according to five characteristics. As you read through his essay, you may be surprised that he does not include in his characteristics a high level of education or a wide range of reading, and that he speaks only of men rather than men and women. Look for the traits he does discuss and then note the way he concludes his essay to draw together those traits.

The Marks of an Educated Man

1   A question often asked is: "What are the marks of an educated man?" It is plain that one may gain no inconsiderable body of learning in some special field of knowledge without at the same time acquiring those habits and traits which are the marks of an educated gentleman. A reasonable amount of learning must of course accompany an education, but, after all, that amount need not be so very great in any one field. An education will make its mark and find its evidences in certain traits, characteristics, and capacities which have to be acquired by patient endeavor, by following good example, and by receiving wise discipline and sound instruction. These traits or characteristics may be variously described and classified, but among them there are five that should always stand out clearly enough to be seen by all men.

2   The first of these is correctness and precision in the use of the mother tongue. The quite shocking slovenliness and vulgarity of much of the spoken English, as well as not a little of the written English, which one hears and sees proves beyond peradventure that years of attendance upon schools and colleges that are thought to be respectable have produced no impression. When one hears English well spoken, with pure diction,

correct pronunciation, and an almost unconscious choice of the right words, he recognizes it at once. How much easier he finds it to imitate English of the other sort!

3   A second and indispensable trait of the educated man is refined and gentle manners, which are themselves the expression of fixed habits of thought and action. "Manners makyth the man," wrote William of Wykeman over his gates at Winchester and at Oxford. He pointed to a great truth. When manners are superficial, artificial, and forced, no matter what their form, they are bad manners. When, however, they are the natural expression of fixed habits of thought and action, and when they reveal a refined and cultivated nature, they are good manners. There are certain things that gentleman do not do, and they do not do them simply because they are bad manners. The gentleman instinctively knows the difference between those things which he may and should do and those things which he may not and should not do.

4   A third trait of the educated man is the power and habit of reflection. Human beings for the most part live wholly on the surface of life. They do not look beneath that surface or far beyond the present moment and that part of the future which is quickly to follow it. They do not read those works of prose and poetry which have become classic because they reveal power and habit of reflection and induce that power and habit in others. When one reflects long enough to ask the question *how?*, he is on the way to knowing something about science. When he reflects long enough to ask the question *why?*, he may, if he persists, even become a philosopher.

5   A fourth trait of the educated man is the power of growth. He continues to grow and develop from birth to his dying day. His interests expand, his contacts multiply, his knowledge increases, and his reflection becomes deeper and wider. It would appear to be true that not many human beings, even those who have had a school and college education, continue to grow after they are twenty-four or twenty-five years of age. By that time it is usual to settle down to life on a level of more or less contented intellectual interest and activity. The whole present-day movement for adult education is a systematic and definite attempt to keep human beings growing long after they have left school and college, and, therefore, to help educate them.

6   A fifth trait of the educated man is his possession of efficiency, or the power to do. The mere visionary dreamer, however charming or however wise, lacks something which an education requires. The power to do may be exercised in any one of a thousand ways, but when it clearly

shows itself, that is evidence that the period of discipline of study and of companionship with parents and teachers have not been in vain.

7   Given these five characteristics, one has the outline of an educated man. That outline may be filled in by scholarship, by literary power, by mechanical skills, by professional zeal and capacity, by business competence, or by social and political leadership. So long as the framework or outline is there, the content may be pretty much what you will, assuming, of course, that the fundamental elements of the great tradition which is civilization, and its outstanding records and achievement in human personality, in letters, in science, in the fine arts, and in human institutions, are all present.

—Nicholas Murray Butler

Activity 2: Analyze the Model

1. Do you agree with the qualities Butler says make an educated man? Why or why not?

2. What examples might a current day writer use instead of those Butler uses?

3. What do you deduce about Butler's training and background from this essay?

4. Do you think that contemporary writers would follow such a specific format in a classification essay as Butler does? If not, in what ways might they vary it?

5. What are five ways you as a student would classify an educated person?

6. Why do you think Butler chose not to include one's education, reading habits, or travels?

7. In the conclusion, how does he make up for not including those attributes?

Activity 3: Write a Classification Essay

As with other essays, the topic you choose should be one with which you are familiar; however, the suggestions below may help you in your selection. Some slants to the topics are given to help you direct your thinking into the categories needed for a classification essay. Remember, though, that the categories and examples must be appropriate for your audience.

↘ **Possible Topics**

- Teachers—those you have learned most from, negatively and/or positively
- Habits—annoying habits of (moviegoers, parents, athletes, etc.)
- Friends who aren't really friends
- Oldest, youngest, and middle children in a family
- Television programs—examples of the best or worst
- Books—best sellers to avoid, to take along on a summer vacation, etc.
- Gifts for the person who has everything
- Goals—your short term or long range ones
- Kinds of phobias (height, closeness, crowds, etc.)
- Drivers who can be a menace on the road

The Comparison-Contrast Essay

Understanding Comparison-Contrast

It's almost impossible to carry on an extended conversation without using the two words *like* and *as*. The reason, of course, is that they help us experience things through our senses. We say, "The sun is *as* hot *as* fire" or "My feet feel *like* ice cubes." Both carry with them a picture or a feeling we can imagine. We see the fire or we feel the ice.

We use similar expressions when we try to explain the unfamiliar or to establish a superficial similarity. For example, we say, "He is as slow as a snail" or "The comet was like a fireball." These are ways we help others "see" what we are talking about. At times, we speak of contrasting ideas in a similar manner, but we show the differences instead of the similarities. In speaking of twins, we might say, "They are as different as night and day." With an expression like this, we get a sense not only of their outward appearance but also of their actions.

Many of the expressions that help to make comparisons or contrasts are similes—phrases or sentences saying something is *like* or *as* another object. Metaphors and analogies are also used. Metaphors make comparisons by saying something *is* whatever one is describing: not "The road looked like a sheet of glass" but "The road *was* a sheet of glass." Analogies are similar; they make comparisons by explaining an unfamiliar thing in terms of something more familiar. For example, we describe the human heart as being analogous to a pump, or we compare a computer to the human brain. In both cases, a picture is conjured up in our minds by comparing something we know well to something we know less well.

Using similes, metaphors, and analogies, then, is one way to emphasize the similarities and differences between two things. But many comparisons and contrasts are also made on a literal level. When you see a movie whose plot reminds you of another film you saw recently, you may mentally compare the two by ticking off their similarities. Or in deciding which of two winter jackets to buy, you may contrast their colors, their styles, and the different materials they are made of in an effort to see which one better suits you. In situations like these you may scarcely be aware of the thinking processes you are going through, but each time you compare or contrast two things you are gaining a better understanding of the qualities of each.

Understanding the Comparison-Contrast Essay

The comparison-contrast essay shows similarities and/or differences between two persons, places, things, or ideas. Along the way, it makes use of the same techniques of comparing and contrasting that we use in our daily thoughts and conversations, including creating metaphors and analogies. At times, an essay may show only similarities or only differences; however, more often than not both comparison and contrast are used.

The purpose a writer has in developing a paper is the determining factor in what approach will be used. For example, if a student wants to show how difficult it was for her to decide between two universities, she will probably focus on the similarities between them. Both may be privately owned; have similar facilities, numbers of students, and faculty; and offer similar academic courses and athletic programs. On the other hand, if she wants to show what made her select one rather than the other, she would probably both compare and contrast them. She would then show both how they are alike and how they are different, in this case probably emphasizing the differences. Her purpose directs her approach.

Usually, comparison-contrast essays are organized in one of three ways: (1) discussing each subject separately, (2) discussing each subject point by point, or (3) using a combination of the two. Using the subject of the two universities, look at the way they might be organized with the three methods given below.

- **Discuss Each Subject Separately.** Using this approach, you would mention everything about University A first—its facilities, number of students and faculty, academic courses and athletic programs—taking two or three paragraphs to make your points. Then you would do the same thing with University B, writing another two or three paragraphs before drawing together the points in the conclusion.

- **Discuss Each Subject Point by Point.** With this method, you could divide the body of your paper into four paragraphs, discussing both University A and B in each paragraph. Paragraph 1 would discuss the facilities; paragraph 2 would discuss the faculty and student body; paragraph 3 would discuss the academic courses; and paragraph 4 would discuss the athletic programs. The conclusion would tie together the similarities and/or differences found.

- **Use a Combination of the Two Methods.** With this approach, you would still probably divide the body of the paper into four paragraphs. Paragraph 1 would discuss University A in terms of its facilities, faculty, and student body, whereas paragraph 2 would discuss facilities, faculty, and student body of University B. Then paragraph 3 would discuss academic courses and athletic programs at University A, with paragraph 4 covering the same aspects of University B. As with the other methods, the conclusion would draw the points together, showing similarities and differences.

Though some topics work well with any of these methods of organization, the purpose for your paper or its focus may well help you determine which method to use. For example, if your paper's focus is to show the differences between two cars, you might decide that the most interesting approach would be to discuss each car's features separately, as in method 1.

Student Model

The comparison-contrast essay is a natural form of writing since it involves explanation as well as some argument or persuasion. In addition, it can hardly be written without using such descriptive elements as similes, metaphors, and analogies. One student, Bob Williamson, chose as his topic for this essay two friends who were twins. The focus of his essay was their separateness even though they were minutes apart at birth. As you read, notice the various points of comparison and contrast that he uses.

Separate Yet Together

1   The first time I saw Chris and Carey, I didn't think they were brothers even though they had the same last name. It was the day school started, and we were all a little scared. Few in the class knew each other, so it wasn't until about a week later that I learned they were siblings. When I found out they were twins, I just stared at them; they were not at all alike in the way they looked, in the way they talked, or in the way they acted, though later they didn't seem quite so different.

2   To begin with, Chris was small, even to the point of looking frail. He had a cowlick in the back of his head that made his hair stand straight up. His hair was light brown, and his eyes were greenish gray. On the other hand, Carey was two or three inches taller than Chris and well built. He had dark brown hair and dark brown eyes. His hair was never

out of place even as a little boy. They didn't seem to come from the same mold, and it wasn't until I met their mother and father that I realized Chris looked like his father, and Carey looked like his mother.

3   Not only were their looks different, but the way they talked was different. Chris had a problem with a cleft palate when he was born, which made him talk with a nasal twang. Sometimes he sounded like a frog; other times, he sounded like a horn. He had surgery later and was able to talk normally, but at the time, his voice was different. Carey didn't have that problem, so he seemed to take advantage of Chris's inability to speak plainly. He never stopped talking, which sometimes got him into trouble. Behind his back, we called him "Motor Mouth," because his motor never stopped.

4   The way Chris and Carey acted, though, was as different as their looks. Chris was shy and withdrawn and as quiet as a mouse; he seemed afraid to speak and cried often. Maybe it was because he was afraid we'd make fun of him because of the way he talked. At any rate, he stayed close to the teacher at school and close to his mother at home. As he grew older, though, he grew out of his timidity and got into as much as mischief as the rest of us. I guess he made up for the first few years. Carey, however, was always loud and outgoing; he was the ringleader of every prank we pulled. He made friends easily and could "talk his way out of a paper bag." There was never a dull moment when he was around.

5   Sometimes, though, both Chris and Carey got into trouble. I remember one day the twins talked me into hitching a ride with them on a freight train that came close to their house. We waited until it got to the railroad crossing and slowed down. Then Carey got on first and pulled Chris up. The top of the car looked a long way off from where I was standing, so I was leery of getting on. But after they "double-dog" dared me, I let them pull me up, too. At first, we felt free as birds and thought it was great fun; that is until the train picked up speed and headed across town. Then we all got worried, even Carey.

6   Besides getting into trouble together, both boys enjoyed the same sport, soccer. Every Saturday morning and Sunday afternoon, they played; every time there was a tournament, they were in it. I'll never forget what their uniforms looked like one weekend during a tournament. I was invited to go with them and their parents to Florida for a tournament, and it rained the whole weekend. In spite of the rain, they played. Their uniforms were so muddy, they looked as if they had been playing in a pigsty instead of a soccer field. Instead of white and black, they were all black—a muddy black! But they were ready to play the next time even if it rained.

7   Years have passed since I first met Chris and Carey, and they have continued to be different. Chris is studying to be an environmental engineer and works in that field while going to the university. Carey is studying to be an architect and works long hours in a job with an architect firm. Their parents have accepted their separateness and have allowed them to live in different apartments with roommates of their own. They continue to see each other often but lead separate lives. And I continue to see each of them, because, after all, both are my friends.

—Bob Williamson

Activity 1: Analyze the Model

1. In his introduction and thesis, how does Bob set the stage for his paper?

2. Which of the three methods did he use to develop his essay? Why was this choice effective (or not effective)?

3. How does the writer set up his paper so that you begin to see similarities as well as differences?

4. What are some figures of speech the writer uses—similes, metaphors, analogies? What did his use of these techniques add to his paper?

5. How did the writer's last paragraph draw together the essay?

Guidelines for a Successful Comparison-Contrast Essay

Once you have a topic to work with, a comparison-contrast essay is not terribly difficult to write. Following the guidelines below will help you produce a good essay.

1. Choose items that are related in some way so they can be compared or contrasted. When Bob chose the topic of his friends who are twins, he automatically had the same general class: two boys. On the other hand, he could not have chosen to compare one boy with a horse. The two would have had nothing in common to provide a logical basis for comparison.

2. Compare according to a single organizing idea. Bob's organizing idea was that the boys were twins and yet they were more different than alike. Once you've established that principle, go on to build a thesis related to it. Note Bob's thesis, at the end of his first paragraph, expanded on the differences— the way the boys looked, the way they talked, and the way they acted—but also pointed out that later the twins didn't seem so different.

3.   Choose a method of development that works well with your organizing idea, keeping in mind the three methods used for comparing and contrasting. Bob's purpose was to show how different the twins were, and the method he chose was the second one—comparing and contrasting the two boys as he made each of his points.

4.   Use specific and relevant examples for support. Two of Bob's examples showing the twins' similarities and differences involve the way they look and talk.

5.   Use both real and figurative comparisons—that is, similes, metaphors, analogies—to show how the two subjects are similar or different. Bob says Chris sounded like a frog and called Carey a Motor Mouth.

6.   Give equal treatment to both elements that you are discussing. Bob describes each of his friends according to the way they looked, the way they talked, the way they acted—even to getting into trouble together—and their goals in life.

7.   Use transitions to help the reader understand the similarities and differences in your subject. Transitions such as *as, like, likewise, resemble, similar to,* and *just as* show similarities while *although, but, even though, however, in spite of the fact that, on the other hand,* and *otherwise* show differences. Bob's paper showed more differences, and his paper reflects that in the transitions he used—*even though, on the other hand, but, however.*

8.   Draw the paper to a close in the conclusion by restating your thesis, by summarizing the main points, or by ending with the last major similarity or difference. Bob ended his paper by showing the last major differences between the two boys—what they are studying to do and by explaining how their parents accept their differences.

Working with Your Own Topic

Now that you have read Bob's paper and have seen the guidelines he followed, you can begin planning a paper of your own. First, of course, you must know what you will be writing about.

Choosing a Topic

A successful comparison essay always has three major qualities: a valid basis for comparison, a limited focus, and information that will catch the reader's attention. Here are some specific points you should consider as you select a topic.

•   **You must have items that can reasonably be compared and/or contrasted.** In other words, the subjects you write about must have some basic similarities, even if you decide to focus on their differences. For instance, it would be possible to contrast two modes of travel—say, airplanes and trains—because even though they are quite different, they also have some commonalties. On the other hand, to compare a novel you've read with the movie version of a different novel probably would not work, as you would have no logical basis for comparison. At least a general familiarity with your topic is vital; however, there is no reason why you cannot research a topic for additional similarities and differences.

- **You must have equal amounts to say about each item.** Even if you've selected two items from the same general class, you can't write about them successfully if you only have good information about one of them. For example, you couldn't compare and contrast kinds of houses in Boston and Tucson if you have three or four points to make about those in one city and only one or two about those in the other. Either be prepared to get information to fill in the gaps, or select another topic.

Since you are to write a comparison-contrast essay, let's assume that you have given some thought to what you will write about. You have narrowed it to two places where you have lived—in the country and in the city—and you know you have things to say about each. Now you must decide how to develop your essay.

Prewriting Strategy: Double Listing

To get to the single principle around which you will develop your essay, use a double list, as this writer did, to jot down all of the ways the two places can be compared.

Topic: Country life vs. city life

Living in the country	Living in the city
• Fresh air	• Smog
• Scent of grass and hay	• Smell of cars and motors
• Free to roam in woods and nature	• Hassle of getting from one place to another
• Little crime	• A lot of crime
• People know each other	• Don't know even neighbors
• Live in separate house	• Live in apartment
• Go places without worry	• Fear of being harmed
• Few gangs, drugs	• Gangs, drugs everywhere
• Live close to family	• Live far away from family

When the writer finished her list, she realized she had a definite point of view to communicate. She decided the single principle she would work from would be the sense of freedom she felt in the country contrasted with the lack of freedom in the city.

Writing Strategy: Choose an Effective Organization

Once you know the general organizing principle you will use with your topic, you can decide which method of development will best make your point. This writer began by quoting from the cowboy song "Home on the Range," very definitely showing which home she preferred. She decided she could drive home her point most effectively in the body with a point-by-point comparison, continually emphasizing the difference between country freedoms and city constraints. Combining and then fleshing out some ideas on her prewriting list, she came up with the following organization:

PARAGRAPH ONE: going from place to place
City: hassle of traveling; traffic jams; infrequently running buses
Country: freely visiting friends and neighbors, biking and walking on safe, empty roads

PARAGRAPH TWO: the outdoors
City: smog, pollution, smell of cars and buses, diesel engines and smoke
Country: fresh air, sunshine, scent of new-mown hay, fresh-cut grass

PARAGRAPH THREE: crime; gangs and drugs
City: drug sales in park even in good neighborhoods; break-ins; gang tagging
Country: no problems yet—at least not where I live

Revising Strategy: Make the Order Consistent

Once you have decided on the best order for organizing your details—in this case, first the city and then the country for each point to be discussed—it is a good idea to stick to it throughout the paper. Notice how this writer talked first about the country in her second paragraph and how she corrected this problem in her revision.

First Draft

The air in the country is unbelievably fresh and clear. The only scent is that of new-mown hay and fresh-cut grass and sunshine. That may sound funny, but Mother used to say I smelled like sunshine after playing outside. Country air is so refreshing, it makes me want to "drink it in." In contrast, I never really understood what smog and pollution were until I moved into the city. Not only is the odor from the diesel trucks overwhelming, but at times the sky is even hazy with smog and smoke from refineries. Pollution is also unhealthy. I can't remember when I ever had an earache until I flew from the country back to the city. I was in so much pain, I went to a specialist who told me it was the pollution in the city after being out in the country fresh air.

Revision

I never really understood what smog and pollution were until I moved into the city. Not only is the odor from the diesel trucks over-whelming, but at times the sky is even hazy with smog and smoke from refineries. Pollution is also unhealthy. I can't remember when I ever had an earache until I flew from the country back to the city. I was in so much pain, I went to a specialist who told me it was the pollution in the city after being out in the country fresh air. The only scent in the country is that of new-mown hay and fresh-cut grass and sunshine. That may sound funny, but Mother used to say I smelled like sunshine after playing outside. Country air is so refreshing, it makes me want to "drink it in."

The questions that follow will help you analyze a comparison-contrast essay. Apply them to your first draft, and have a partner do the same. Additional lists of points to consider at this time can be found in Chapter Three.

Revision Questions

- Is the topic one that can be compared or contrasted according to a single principle?

- Is the purpose for the paper made clear in the opening paragraph?

- Are roughly the same number of points made about each item being discussed?

- Are specific and relevant examples used for support?

- Are similes, metaphors, and analogies used to help the reader see similarities and differences?

- Once the order is established, is it used consistently throughout?

- Are transitions used effectively but not overused?

- Does the paper have a sense of audience?

- Are all sentences grammatically correct?

- Are there punctuation errors and spelling errors that need correcting?

A Published Model

Here is one last piece to examine. In this introductory material from Charles Dickens's classic *A Tale of Two Cities,* Dickens compares and contrasts the two kingdoms of France and England and their rulers in not such a pretty light. As you read through this excerpt, note the similarities and differences between the two.

The Period

1   It was the best of times, it was the worst of times, it was the age of wisdom, it was the age of foolishness, it was the epoch of belief, it was the epoch of incredulity, it was the season of Light, it was the season of Darkness, it was the spring of hope, it was the winter of despair, we had everything before us, we had nothing before us, we were all going direct to Heaven, we were all going direct the other way.

2   There were a king with a large jaw and a queen with a plain face, on the throne of England; there were a king with a large jaw and a queen with a fair face, on the throne of France. It was the year of Our Lord one thousand seven hundred and seventy-five.

3   France was rolling with the exceeding smoothness down-hill, making paper money and spending it. Under the guidance of her Christian pastors, she entertained herself, besides, with such humane achievements as sentencing a youth to have his hands cut off, his tongue torn out with pincers, and his body burned alive, because he had not kneeled down in the rain to do honour to a religious procession which passed within his view, at a distance of some fifty or sixty yards. It is likely enough that, rooted in the woods of France and Norway, there were growing trees, when that sufferer was put to death, already marked by the Woodman, Fate, to come down and be sawn into boards, to make a certain movable framework with a sack and a knife in it, terrible in history. It is likely enough that in the rough outhouses of some tillers of the heavy lands adjacent to Paris, there were sheltered from the weather that very day, rude carts, bespattered with rustic mire, snuffed about by pigs, and roosted in by poultry, which the Farmer, Death, had already set apart to be his tumbrils of the Revolution.

4   In England, there was scarcely an amount of order and protection to justify much national boasting. Daring burglaries by armed men, and highway robberies, took place in the capital itself every night; families were publicly cautioned not to go out of town without removing their furniture to upholsterers' warehouses for security; the highwayman in the dark was a city tradesman in the light; the mail was waylaid by seven robbers, and the

guard shot three dead, and then got shot dead himself by the other four, "in consequence of the failure of his ammunition" after which the mail was robbed in peace; prisoners in London gaols fought battles with their turnkeys, and the majesty of the law fired blunderbusses in among them, loaded with rounds of shots and ball; thieves snipped off diamond crosses from the necks of noble lords at Court drawing-rooms; musketeers went into St. Giles's to search for contraband goods, and the mob fired on the musketeers, and the musketeers fired on the mob, and nobody thought any of these occurrences much out of the common way. In the midst of them, the hangman, ever busy and ever worse than useless, was in constant requisition; now, stringing up long rows of miscellaneous criminals; now, hanging a house-breaker on Saturday who had been taken on Tuesday; now, burning people in the hand at Newgate by the dozen, and now burning pamphlets at the door of Westminster Hall; today, taking the life of an atrocious murderer, and tomorrow of a wretched pilferer who had robbed a farmer's boy of sixpence.

5   All these things, and a thousand like them, came to pass in and close upon the dear old year one thousand seven hundred and seventy-five. Environed by them, while the Woodman and the Farmer worked unheeded, those two of the large jaws, and those two of the plain and the fair faces, trod with stir enough, and carried their divine rights with a high hand. Thus did the year one thousand seven hundred and seventy-five conduct their Greatnesses, and myriads of small creatures—the creatures of this chronicle among the rest—along the roads that lay before them.

—*Charles Dickens*

Activity 2: Analyze the Model

1. How does the writer get across in the introduction what a difficult time the year 1775 was in both England and France?

2. What specific elements does Dickens compare and contrast in the piece?

3. What is the basic purpose of paragraphs 3 and 4—to show similarities or differences? Explain your answer.

4. What is the general feeling you get about life in the two countries? How do the rulers appear to react to conditions?

5. What tone does the writer use in the essay? Does that tone suggest anything about the future? If so, what?

Activity 3: Write a Comparison-Contrast Essay

Since you have already been thinking about what you want to compare and contrast, the topics given below should only add to your list of possibilities. You may also use these ideas as springboards for other topics. Keep in mind as you choose a topic the guidelines for a good comparison-contrast essay.

↘ **Possible Topics**
- Two friends or relatives who could be compared
- Two movies you have seen with similar characters/situations
- Knowledge and understanding
- Hotels versus bed and breakfasts
- A foreign car and an American car
- Two presidents of the United States
- New York and Los Angeles
- Technical writing versus newspaper reporting
- English rugby and American football
- Two pets you have had

The Cause and Effect Essay

Understanding Cause and Effect

If you know any children who are around the age of two, you know that their favorite question is *why?* As soon as you answer the question, they will ask it again and again, in a never-ending cycle. It matters not that they don't fully comprehend your answer; what matters is that they are gathering a little more information and storing it in their memory banks. The constant *why* questioning is their way of finding answers.

Understanding cause and effect begins with the why—why do certain things happen? Why does the wind blow? Why doesn't it stop blowing when it encounters a big object like a building? Why does it travel at high rates of speed at times and slower at other times? You see the effects and feel the effects of the wind, but it is not until you study about wind velocity and currents that you learn the causes.

It is almost impossible to think about an effect without looking for a cause. For example, you woke up this morning with a sore shoulder (effect), and you wondered why (cause). The answer probably lies in what you did yesterday. Maybe the cause was that you shoveled snow or lifted weights or did some other strenuous exercise. But now let's say you take some aspirin or ibuprofen for the pain. You expect some effects, the most likely one being that your soreness is relieved; but you might have others such as tiredness or stomach upset as well. These are simple cause and effect relationships. More complex ones exist and are not as easy to comprehend. For example, sometimes when you analyze a situation, the effects become causes of other effects or vice versa.

The search for causes, or why something happened, is fundamental to people of all cultures. Greek myths tried to explain why thunder roared, why the sun was hot, and even how the world began. While you may not be concerned with things of this magnitude, when you fail an exam, you begin to think of the reasons, the why. Perhaps you stayed up too late the night before or you didn't get the right notes or your mind wasn't focused. All of these are the causes; your failure on the test is the effect precipitated by the causes.

What you were doing as you thought about why you didn't do well was to analyze the causes. You explored the conditions (causes) that brought about the resulting failure (effect). Analysis, then, is a part of understanding cause and effect relationships that occur every day.

Understanding the Cause and Effect Essay

The cause and effect essay focuses on a situation or condition and then asks either *Why?* (causes) or *What's the result?* (effects) based on evidence that is accurate and reliable. The topic chosen and what the writer knows about it determine what will be discussed: causes, effects, or a combination of the two.

If you choose to write about the outbreak of the Ebola virus, for example, you might focus on the effects worldwide. You would probably begin by describing the cause—the virus—in your introduction and then discussing its effects in the body of your paper. With a topic like the deterioration of your neighborhood, you might focus on the causes. A paper taking this approach might start by describing how bad the neighborhood has become—the effect—and then go on to discuss the causes for the deterioration. A paper on the rise in poverty among children in America might focus on both causes and effects, beginning with the causes and moving on to the effects.

Since your aim in writing a cause and effect essay is to offer a good explanation of some relationship, it is necessary to think through or investigate the topic rather thoroughly. For example, if your paper is on the causes of insomnia, you might relate it to things like too much caffeine, too much excitement before bedtime, medicines that provoke wakefulness, and several other possible causes. Before you began writing, you would need to determine which are the most likely causes, which are probable, and which are unrelated to insomnia; and then focus only on the clearest ones in your paper. A paper concerned with effects would be developed following the same procedure, as would one dealing with both causes and effects.

A cause and effect essay can deal with *possible* causes or effects, as long as you make clear that your ideas are only plausible rather than definitive. For example, a question such as "Why do some people succumb to suicide pacts?" may not have absolute answers because nothing scientific has been proven to be the actual cause. Still, it is possible to speculate about causes based on the best available evidence.

What you should not do, however, is succumb to faulty logic. The fact that one event happened before another is not proof that the first caused the second. To believe, for example, that a black cat running across the road in front of you on the way to school caused you to fail a test is to create a cause and effect relationship where none actually exists. This is what is called false cause and effect. There must be a valid connection between the cause and the effect in order to make an association.

Not only is cause and effect analysis a good way to write about happenings that occur every day; it is also effective in writing about literature. In writing a cause and effect paper about a particular work, you would determine why a character acts as he does, what events brought about a crisis in the story, and what effects happened as a result of the causes.

The final effectiveness of a cause and effect essay, whether literary or otherwise, rests with your ingenuity and your willingness to explore all facets of the topic.

Student Model

In the paper that follows, Sarah chose to write her cause and effect essay on student apathy, a topic that gave her great concern. As you read through her paper, note that she describes the effect—student apathy—in the introduction and then traces the causes to three different reasons.

Student Apathy

1   In looking back over my high school years, one of the things which concerned me most was that some students didn't care. It didn't matter to them what their GPA was. They only studied enough to pass, and they never aspired to make the honor roll. If I had to describe their attitude toward school in terms of colors, it would be gray because gray isn't either black or white. It's blah! It expresses their outlook, their actions, and their noncommittal attitude toward everything. Student apathy was the worst problem we had.

2   Once I asked one of the girls in my chemistry class why she didn't study. She never took her book home and tried to bum notes from me to study just before exams. Her reply was that no one at home cared what she did. Her parents were divorced, and she lived with her grandmother. Living conditions were not the best at home, so she had no incentive. The only reason she stayed in school was that she knew she wouldn't be able to get a job without a high school diploma. As a result, she just got by with enough work to pass and that was all.

3   That attitude was multiplied over and over, and it spilled over into the clubs and extracurricular activities. We barely had enough club members to hold meetings and those who did come didn't want to hold an office. I approached the principal about why this was a problem. His answer was that most students must ride the school bus and don't have a way to get home after extracurricular activities. He even scheduled clubs to meet during school time, but that helped very little. Most students still weren't interested. I guess they had formed the habit of not participating, and it was hard to get interested in something they had never done.

4   But the straw that broke the camel's back was their lack of interest in applying for scholarships and grants to go to college. Surely, I thought, they would be interested in getting help to go to a university, but that was futile, too.

When the guidance counselor came in to give us information about what was available, I only saw two or three students who were interested enough to even write down where to send their transcripts. Since I worked in the guidance office, I asked Mrs. Davis what she thought caused so much apathy. Her reply was that some students had never been motivated to seek higher goals in life; they only looked at short-term goals. They thought being doctors, lawyers, politicians, ministers, or teachers was too far beyond their reach. They were content to seek minimum wage jobs and exist on that salary.

5   When thinking of how apathetic my fellow students were, I am saddened. I realize a person must be motivated from within and that he cannot help who his parents are and may be able to do very little about his situation, but I think our society will reap the results of this kind of attitude. My goal is to do what I can to improve my world, and one way I can do it is to become involved in educating little children. I want them to believe they can do anything they choose to do, and be anything they want to be. I want the future to be adazzle with bright colors of red, blue, yellow, green, and orange.

—*Sarah Brown*

Activity 1: Analyze the Model

1. How does the writer describe student apathy in the introduction?
2. What is the writer's thesis statement? Do you think it could have been better focused? If so, how?
3. Are the causes explained in chronological order or in order of importance? Why do you think the writer chose this order?
4. The topic this writer deals with has possible rather than absolutely definitive causes. How did she make sure these causes were plausible?
5. For each cause of student apathy that she discusses, the author begins by giving an example. How effective is this technique?
6. How well does the conclusion tie the writer's paper together?

Guidelines for a Successful Cause and Effect Essay

As you think about writing your cause and effect essay, there are several techniques you can use to make your writing smooth and effective.

1. Limit your choice of a subject to something you can explain within the framework of a five-to-ten paragraph essay. Sarah's topic of student apathy was narrowed to include situations within her school.

2. Consider your audience as you write so that your choice of words and examples will appeal to them. Sarah wrote for an audience that was interested in improving the attitudes of students and their participation in school activities. Parent groups or school personnel could benefit from her insight into the causes of student apathy.

3. Compile a chain of causes and effects to determine their relationship and to see whether the causes, the effects, or both need to be emphasized. The student paper

began with the effect (school apathy) and worked back to three causes (no incentive to study, a habit of not participating, and concern only with short-term goals).

4. Make your thesis statement reflect the focus of your paper. Sarah's thesis, "Student apathy was the worst problem we had," leads her into a discussion of the causes of apathy.

5. Be sure that the evidence is reliable and accurate. Remember that just because one event happened before another doesn't mean one was the cause of the other. Especially if you are dealing with possible causes, get information from people in a position to know. Note that in paragraphs 3 and 4 Sarah spoke with both the principal and a guidance counselor at her school to determine why students were so apathetic.

6. Organize your paper either in chronological order—that is, the order in which the causes or effects occurred—or in order of importance. Sarah's paper used the second of these orders. The last point begins with "The straw that broke the camel's back . . . ," indicating her belief that unwillingness to pursue ways to further their education was the strongest evidence of student unconcern.

7. Use transitional words to make your paper flow better as you discuss the chain of causes and effects. Transitions that work with cause-effect include *since, because, as a result of, consequently, therefore, possibly* and the repetition of words like *cause, reason, effect,* and *is due to.* Sarah used a number of these in her essay.

8. Use examples and illustrations to make the causes and effects clear to the reader. Sarah began each paragraph in the body of her essay with a different manifestation of student apathy, then went on to discuss a possible cause of it. Each example painted a different picture of how students didn't care.

9. Sum up the chain of cause and effect in the conclusion by making direct reference to the introduction or by restating the chain of cause and effects. The student paper's conclusion (paragraph 5) referred to the effect (student apathy) and then showed what she planned to do about the situation. She also referred to wanting the future to be adazzle with bright colors, a direct reference to the gray she saw in her student body in high school.

10. Keep the tone consistent throughout your essay. Sarah showed concern from the beginning to the ending of her essay. She said she was saddened by what she saw.

Working with Your Own Topic

Sarah's paper showed the necessary elements for a cause and effect essay. She explored the chain of cause and effect and determined that she would emphasize the causes that resulted in a certain effect. You will follow the same sort of thought processes as you plan and write your own paper.

Choosing a Topic

As you begin to think of what you will write about, the first place to look, of course, is within your own personal experience, knowledge, and interests. In addition, keep these points in mind.

- **Be sure there is an identifiable cause and effect relationship within your topic.** In order to determine if such a relationship exists, you may have to gather information by interviewing people or doing other research. The question "Why?" or "What's the result?" is where you will start. Why did the president send troops to Bosnia? What are the results of making students wear uniforms in elementary schools? If you cannot come up with definitive or at least very plausible answers supported by evidence, your topic is not appropriate.

- **Be sure you have enough causes or effects to discuss.** If you want to write about causes, you generally need at least three to write an effective paper; the same goes for effects. If, however, you are writing about both causes and effects, you might have fewer of each.

Now that you are beginning to focus on your topic and the chain of cause and effect, let's assume that you have decided to write about increased traffic in your city. Your preliminary plan is to give equal treatment to both effects and causes.

Prewriting Strategy: Clustering

Clustering as a prewriting technique works well with the cause and effect essay. The reason, of course, is that with clustering you not only uncover ideas; you also show the relationship of one idea to another. Clustering for a paper that will focus on both cause and effects might look like what this student did. Notice that after he wrote down all his points, he clustered all his causes to the left and all his effects to the right, to keep them straight.

Topic: Increased Traffic

A cluster like this can show you how much detail you have about the various causes and effects. This writer, for example, realized that even though he had thought of more effects, they could be summarized rather quickly. The causes, however, were more complex and would take longer to explain. He decided to devote the majority of his paper to discussing causes and to conclude with a briefer explanation of the effects.

Writing Strategy: Use a Bridge between Cause and Effect

A topic like traffic involves an issue that most people in an area can easily identify with. This writer began with a thesis statement that not only focused the direction of his paper, but also expressed his personal frustration with the situation: *Sitting in my fourth traffic jam in a recent week, I had plenty of time to ponder not only the reasons for why traffic has gotten so heavy, but what has happened to people's lives—and tempers—as a result of it.* This statement led naturally into his discussion of the causes he had isolated in prewriting.

When writing about both causes and effects, a bridge paragraph can be an effective way to make a transition from one to the other. Here is the bridge paragraph this writer used when he had finished his discussion of causes:

> So there really are a variety of reasons for all the traffic jams, depending on when and where they occur. A few are based on bureaucratic stupidity, but others are just the natural occurrences of any modern city. The effects, however, are uniformly awful, and hardly any of them seem preventable.

Notice how this bridge paragraph sums up the causes before turning to the effects. From here it would be easy to go into a discussion of smog, no parking places, and the like.

Revising Strategy: Check for Faulty Logic

Be sure with a cause and effect paper that you don't suggest one thing caused another just because it happened first. Notice how this writer revised to eliminate such an error:

First Draft

. . . And frayed nerves on the way home from school or work can lead to frayed nerves at home. For example, after enduring one particularly bad traffic tie-up last week, everyone in our family was jumpy and irritable. It wasn't surprising that the phone didn't ring once all night.

Revision

. . . And frayed nerves on the way home from school or work can lead to frayed nerves at home. For example, after enduring one particularly bad traffic tie-up last week, everyone in our family was jumpy and irritable. It was lucky no one called after dinner—whoever answered the phone probably would have started a fight with the caller.

The questions that follow will help in the analysis of a cause and effect essay. Have a peer evaluator apply them to your first draft; then do the same yourself. For additional points to consider, see Chapter Three.

Revision Questions

- Does the topic involve a definite cause and effect relationship?
- Does the thesis statement reflect the focus of the essay?
- Does the writing style make clear for whom the essay is written?
- Is the tone of the paper consistent from beginning to end?
- Does the paper demonstrate that all causes and effects are at least plausible? Has false reasoning been avoided?
- Does the order of the essay—chronological or order of importance—seem appropriate to the topic?
- Are there enough transitions to make the paper flow smoothly?
- Does the conclusion relate to the introduction?
- Are sentences and details arranged to make the explanation of the cause and effect chain coherent?
- Is the paper free from sentence structure, capitalization, and punctuation errors?

A Published Model

This final model, "Reservoirs Speed Up Earth's Spin," explains the various effects one scientist attributes to people's storing water in artificial reservoirs. As you read the essay, look for the various effects the writer connects with this cause.

Reservoirs Speed Up Earth's Spin

1   In the realm of science fiction, humans steer large asteroids into Venus, smacking our sister planet in order to spin it faster so that it can support life. In the realm of fact, humans have managed to unwittingly alter the rotation rate of Earth itself, according to a NASA geophysicist.

2   Storing water in artificial reservoirs has shifted enough mass around on the surface of Earth to speed up its rotation and cause the planet to wobble, says Benjamin Fong Chao of the Goddard Space Flight Center in

Greenbelt, Maryland. In particular, Chao has studied the effect of 88 huge reservoirs, most of them located in the Northern Hemisphere, that now hold about 10 trillion tons of water.

3   Shifting this water from the oceans to the continents has moved mass from near the equator to higher latitudes, closer to the axis on which Earth spins. That has caused Earth to rotate faster in much the same way that a spinning skater speeds up when he pulls his arms closer in.

4   Chao says that the faster spin has shortened the day by about eight millionths of a second over the past 40 years, since the first mega-reservoirs were constructed. The speeding up counteracts the natural slowing down of Earth's rotation. Friction caused by the tides acts as a brake, slowing the rotation by about one thousandth of a second per century. Other natural factors, caused by changes in the atmosphere and oceans, also influence Earth's rotational speed.

5   In addition to speeding up Earth's rotation, the water reservoirs have also caused the planet to wobble because they are spread unevenly around the globe. The wobbling has changed the location of the axis on which Earth rotates. Thus, the North Pole has moved about 24 inches toward western Canada since the early 1950s. This is a significant fraction of the 39 feet (12 meters) of polar drift observed over the past hundred years, Chao says. The North Pole also shifts location due to such natural factors as changes in atmospheric and oceanic mass and from other causes, which are not completely understood.

6   Understanding such changes, small as they may seem, is vital to NASA's efforts to track satellites and distant spacecraft. "If you want to know where interplanetary spacecraft are, you have to know where you are," says Chao. "If we don't correct for these variations and you try to track a spacecraft which is 100 million miles from you, the error can be very large."

7   Chao suggests that reservoir construction also has slowed the continuous rise in sea level around the world. By storing water on the continents in the form of reservoirs and farm ponds, people have effectively removed water from the oceans. Without the presence of these reservoirs, Chao says, sea level would be about 1.2 inches higher than it is today.

8   Even major reservoirs don't account for most of the water stored by humans. Chao's 88 reservoirs account for perhaps 40 percent of the total amount of water stored to date. Smaller reservoirs could also have an as-yet-unknown impact on Earth's spin.

—Doug McInnis

Activity 2: Analyze the Model

1. What contrast does the writer set up in the introduction?
2. Where does the thesis statement for the essay occur? What is it?
3. What are some of the effects that Dr. Chao attributes to huge reservoirs?

4. Is this essay written for a specific or a general audience? What makes you think as you do?

5. How does the writer make clear that the effects he mentions also have other causes? Do you think the information he presents strengthens or weakens his essay?

Activity 3: Write a Cause and Effect Essay

As stated earlier, topics for the cause and effect essay can come from your own personal experience, from interviewing others, or from research. With all of these possibilities, it should be a relatively easy task to find a topic from which you can work. The suggestions below should give you some direction, however, if you think you are facing a blank wall.

↘ **Possible Topics**

- A recent social trend—its cause/effects
- Secondhand smoke—effects
- Poor grades—causes and effects
- Teen suicides—reasons why and effects
- Drug/alcohol abuse—effects on society
- Tutoring and/or mentoring programs—effects
- Unfair hiring practices—causes
- Dishonesty in schools, the work place—causes and effects
- Staying up too late—effects
- Youth volunteers—effect on nursing home residents, hospital patients, children in camps (or any place volunteers help with)

The Pro-Con Essay

Understanding Pro-Con

Very seldom does a day go by that you aren't confronted with an issue that has
two sides to it, one that requires that you take a stand or make a decision for or
against something. This doesn't necessarily mean that you must get into an argument, but you are still faced with two sides of a question. You must decide
whether you are for it (pro) or against it (con). For example, you have just
accepted a job, but another position becomes available that you had applied for
and want badly. You are in a quandary about what to do, so you must weigh the
pros—points in favor of taking the new job—against the cons—points against
doing so. On the one hand, the new job would probably make you happy and be
more fulfilling than the one you just accepted. On the other hand, you feel a
moral obligation to keep the first job and fear getting a reputation as irresponsi-
ble if you quit it so quickly. This is a tough decision, but situations like this arise
fairly often, making it necessary to look at both sides of an issue.

Often newspapers run two sides of a political question on the editorial
page—one presenting pro points, the other presenting con points. This helps the
public to understand the two points of view and thus determine which one they
most agree with. Understanding both sides of a question is very important during elections for public office or when school boards or city councils have issues
that they want a community to decide on.

In your classes, your instructor may ask an open-ended question on a controversial topic such as assisted suicide in order to get you to think, hoping that
some class members will see the pro side and support it while others will take the
opposing position. The discussion may get lively, but that is all right; each group
sees things from different perspectives.

It would be dull indeed if everyone thought alike. Having an opinion about something helps you to sort out all of the facets of the question and then determine on which side of the issue you will stand—pro or con.

Understanding the Pro-Con Essay

The pro-con essay is often called a persuasive or argumentative or even an assertion-with-proof essay, but whatever name you use, the bottom line is that you are presenting two sides of an argument. As you do so, however, you are also attempting, through the strength of your logic, to make the reader accept your reasons for supporting one side rather than the other.

Clearly, then, the subject you choose must be argumentative; that is, it must have two sides—a pro side and a con side. Often just using the word *argument* makes people uneasy, but as we will use it, argument means "a debate or discussion," not "an angry disagreement." In writing your pro-con essay, you will try to argue that your opinion is right by backing it up with reasons and evidence. While emotions may be involved in persuasive speaking or conversation, the pro-con essay appeals more to the reasoning or understanding of the reader.

The subject matter of a pro-con essay need not be earthshaking, but it does have to involve some debatable issue. There has to be the possibility of a difference of opinion or there is no argument. Many kinds of essays involve taking a position on a subject and supporting it with various kinds of evidence; however, with a pro-con essay you will offer definite reasons in an attempt to convince your reader.

The pro-con essay, like other essays you have written, has a thesis, but it also has an antithesis—that is, a statement that supports the opposite point of view. To illustrate: suppose you are writing a paper about the value of the high school diploma. Your thesis might be "Because of the continued lowering of graduation standards, the high school diploma has very little value today." The antithesis, which may or may not be directly stated in the essay, could be "The high school diploma still serves a need in securing jobs because many employers demand a diploma." Both the thesis and the antithesis have points to support them, and you need to acknowledge both. The thesis, however, must have more support than the antithesis. If you find in developing your paper that it does not, you may decide to flip-flop your argument.

Most pro-con essays follow a very simple format. In the introduction, you would use the inverted pyramid style, beginning with general statements and ending with the thesis. Once you have stated your position, you would begin the body of the paper by addressing all the objections to the position and refuting them. Then you would present a number of points supporting your position, building up to a final appeal which may be the paper's conclusion.

Other approaches are possible. If you are taking a stand on a position that has a lot of arguments against it, you might want to refute them one by one. You would do this by presenting each point, then using your evidence to show why the point is weak or untrue. Or you might want to use most of the essay to support your own position, especially if it is a strong one, and only briefly acknowledge the arguments against it toward the end of the essay.

Some arguments can best be handled by beginning with a chronology of events leading up to your position. For example, suppose you have severe asthma and are trying to convince your doctor and the medical profession of the impact of environment on your condition. In the introduction, you would explain the events that have caused you to believe as you do. In the first paragraph of the body, you would acknowledge that you have no scientific proof, but you have reasons to think that your asthma is affected by the environment in a particular city or state. Your essay would continue with more convincing evidence, leading to a final conclusive appeal at the end.

While other methods of organization are possible, they all involve essentially the same steps: state your position, refute the opposition, and provide reasons and support for your position in order to convince the reader to agree with you.

Student Model

The pro-con essay should involve a topic you feel strongly enough about to argue in a convincing way. Sharon's topic was that students should be allowed to evaluate their teachers. As you read her essay, see whether you are convinced by her argument.

To Evaluate or Not to Evaluate?

1   For the past thirteen years, counting kindergarten, I have been subjected to teachers of all sizes and ages. Some have been men; some women; some have been black; some white; some have been Oriental; some Spanish. Some have been intelligent; some have been just plain dumb. And it goes without saying that some could teach and some could not. After dealing with all these teachers, I've come to the conclusion that students should be allowed to evaluate their teachers so that those who cannot teach can be removed.

2   Admittedly, an evaluation by itself may not be grounds to remove a teacher, but it can show that there is a problem. It's also true that an evaluation may be flawed to a degree because it involves one person's evaluation of another, which makes it subjective. But if enough students give a negative evaluation of the same teacher, maybe the administration would look at the results and consider replacing the teacher who cannot teach. It's also possible that students, knowing about the evaluation, could gang up on a hard teacher; however, this wouldn't always be the case. Even then, the administration or faculty senate would be aware that there is a problem.

3   While it is possible to have a flawed evaluation, students should be able to evaluate their teachers to bring to the attention of the administration the ways that some teachers belittle students. I'll never forget Miss Wood, one of my math teachers in middle school. If one of us couldn't get the right answer to a problem after she explained it, she would give us a pacifier and make us suck it the rest of the hour. Another teacher made us stand at the front of the room with our nose in a circle on the blackboard if we talked out of turn. Needless to say, we students had little respect for these teachers and learned little in their classes.

4   Another reason students should evaluate their teachers is to show that some don't have a real interest in students. They're just earning a paycheck, and it shows. They don't care who learns and who does not. For example, Mr. Brassher's method of teaching was to assign a chapter in history to read, questions to be answered at the end, and then the test. He never tried to find out if we comprehended the material. He prided himself on how many students failed his class because he was such a hard teacher. The truth was he couldn't teach. A good teacher makes the material clear enough so students understand it and can pass.

5   Students also need to evaluate their teachers because some are so weak in their subject matter, they can't transmit it to the students. It seems as if they read the material the night before and then try to present it the next day. I had one teacher who was teaching *Canterbury Tales* who never could understand Chaucer's presentation of the pilgrims. We had to explain to her what the story was about because we knew more than she did. When she graded our weekly tests, she didn't catch half the errors; we laughed about it behind her back. I realize teachers can't know everything, but they're supposed to know more than the students they teach. How else can they get the information across so we can learn it?

6   The biggest reason students need to evaluate their teachers, though, is to weed out the ones who can't teach so that those who can teach can do their job. In this way not only will the school system be improved, but

students will also be better prepared for college or for the work world. It makes no difference whatsoever what the teacher looks like or how old he or she is; what matters is whether he can transmit the material so students can learn. Education needs to adopt the same practice as the business world; let those go who cannot do the job. Maybe student evaluations would help determine who can and who can't.

—*Sharon Weston*

Activity 1: Analyze the Model

1. How does the writer get the attention of the reader in the introduction? Is her use of the inverted pyramid successful?

2. Is the writer's thesis arguable? Is it open-ended enough so that you know there can be an opposition?

3. What transition does Sharon use to begin the con paragraph?

4. What are the con points? Is a specific antithesis stated?

5. Are Sharon's pro points stronger than her con points? How does she support her pro points?

6. Does Sharon's conclusion begin with a restated thesis and then broaden out? How does the last statement reflect the introduction?

Guidelines for a Successful Pro-Con Essay

The pro-con paper employs many of the same techniques you use every day in trying to prove a point about something you feel strongly about. An important difference, though, is that in writing you can only make your case once. So you have to be well-organized. The following guidelines can help you.

1. Express your opinion clearly in the thesis or, as it is called in argumentative writing, the position statement. Sharon's thesis or position statement was that students should be allowed to evaluate their teachers so that those who cannot teach can be removed.

2. Build your argument with strong reasons and evidence, and make sure that each point you make is relevant to the thesis or position statement. Sharon's points supporting her position were that students need to evaluate their teachers because (1) some use belittling techniques for discipline causing

students not to learn, (2) some don't have a real interest in their students and present the material in such a way students don't learn, and (3) some don't know enough to teach.

3. Determine what your antithesis would be and include points that support it, but then show why these points don't build a strong argument. Sharon acknowledged several reasons why students' evaluations may be flawed, but then she refuted them by saying flawed or not, at least they would let the administration know that some problem existed.

4. Use transitions especially to move from the thesis to the antithesis. Sharon used *admittedly* to begin her con paragraph, but other transitions can be used just as effectively, such as *it is true, granted, no doubt, nobody denies, on the other hand, the fact remains, undoubtedly,* and *unquestionably.*

5. Develop your paper in a way that will most likely convince your reader. In Sharon's paper the con points are given early, leaving way for the pro points to receive more treatment. By presenting her reader with the strongest pro points at the end, she made it more likely that they would agree with her reasoning.

6. Select an appropriate tone for your essay. For a paper about an issue that involves people or that in some way affects you personally, your tone may be impassioned; for a paper involving community or political issues your tone may be serious but more restrained. A mocking, cynical tone is also possible, if you can carry it off. Sharon's tone was somewhat passionate, especially when she presented her specific examples.

7. Avoid slanting the material so much that it suppresses valuable evidence and causes an imbalance. Sharon argued for evaluation of teachers, but she did not suggest that all teachers were bad—rather, that the bad ones should be weeded out so that good ones would be better able to do their jobs. She also allows room for recognition of the fact that the evaluation could be flawed and that it should not be the only method for determining the ability of the teacher.

8. Never use illogical reasoning in developing your argument. For example, don't reach the conclusion that all students will flunk out of school after being given a second chance just because you know one or two that have. The conclusion is false because it generalizes from too little evidence. Similarly, don't use polarized thinking such as "either/or," saying a person is either a saint or a crook; or circular reasoning, saying that a person is bad because she is not good. The important thing to consider in developing your points is their honesty and authenticity. Sharon developed her paper with logical points that she had observed in her thirteen years of schooling.

9. Choose a title that clearly indicates the subject and suggests the writer's attitude toward it. Sharon's title, "To Evaluate or Not to Evaluate," suggests that there are two sides to evaluating teachers.

10. Have your audience in mind as you write so that you connect with them and see things from their perspective as well as your own. If your argument has no meaning for them, it is unlikely they will agree with your thinking. Sharon's audience is the administration or school board, so she acknowledged possible problems with her proposal but also pointed out specific incidents of poor teaching that they may not have known about.

Working with Your Own Topic

The student model showed how the writer had carefully thought through the topic to argue it convincingly. Your paper will be successful if you follow the same sort of thought processes.

Choosing a Topic

In selecting a topic for your pro-con essay, give some thought to things that concern you and/or that you would like to see changed, and think about how you can persuade others to accept your viewpoint. Keep the following in mind as well.

- **Choose a topic that involves a debatable opinion.** The topic you write about must involve an opinion rather than a fact, because facts are not debatable. And it must be an opinion for which there are arguments for and against. For example, "NASA has sent a spaceship to determine if there is life on Mars" is not an appropriate topic for a pro-con essay; it is a fact, something that can be proved true, and thus nothing that can be debated. But "NASA's sending a spaceship to determine if there is life on Mars is a ridiculous waste of money" would work. Not only is it an opinion, but reasons and evidence can be provided both to support and to refute it.

- **Anticipate if and how you can overcome your audience's resistance.** Of necessity, argument provokes resistance; therefore, you should not expect your audience to agree with you wholly. Since people rarely change their minds without a good reason, you must anticipate some opposition to your position and have a way to overcome it. Knowing who your audience is helps you know whether you will be able to persuade them easily. Put yourself in the position of the audience—see things their way before you argue your way. If you find that your argument is not strong enough for you to believe it, you can rest assured that your audience will never believe it either.

After thinking about the pros and cons, you decide that you have strong feelings about allowing old people the right to die with dignity without life support tubes. You also think you know the arguments on the other side of the issue and how you can refute them, so you decide to use this as your topic.

Prewriting Strategy: Make a Double List

A double list is a good way to see whether you have enough points for your thesis and to make sure that they are more convincing than points supporting the antithesis. Here is one student's double list on the topic of death with dignity. Notice that she headed each list with either her thesis or antithesis, a good way of keeping her ideas focused.

The points for and against life support are recorded below in the order the writer developed them in her paper, but the list does not have to be in that order. The list is primarily a way to determine how much you have to say and whether you have any antithetical points that you can directly refute. Note also that the antithesis does not have to be stated explicitly, as this student did, but writing it down can be a helpful organizing method.

Topic: Let The Old Die Peacefully

Thesis: Old people who are ill and who have no chance of recovery should have the right to die without being put on life support.	Antithesis: Allowing a person to die without using every means possible to keep him or her alive is not morally right.
In most cases, people feel their lives have been lived and they do not want merely to exist.	The family may be unwilling to part with the person and may feel responsible for letting him or her die.
After a full, active life, it is degrading for an old person to deteriorate into a comatose state. (Mrs. Halloran)	
If a person has asked not to be put on life support, why should money and hospital beds be wasted in the effort to keep him/her alive? (Uncle Harry)	A possibility might exist that the person would live.
Even if an elderly person can be kept alive, how much longer can he/she reasonably expect to live anyway?	

Writing Strategy: Develop the Antithesis as well as the Thesis

Before you begin writing, figure out how and where you will develop your antithesis. This writer decided to deal with it right after her introductory paragraph, so she could get it out of the way. Her introductory paragraph uses an anecdote to get to her thesis; her transition to her antithesis comes at the beginning of the second paragraph.

My grandfather celebrated his 101st birthday this year. We had a big birthday party with cake and all of the trimmings. We also watched a video of his 100th birthday last year when over 100 people were invited. Grandpa's mind is still sharp, and he walks without help; he even lives alone in his own home. But one thing he made all of us promise is that we won't put him on life support should he become ill. The more I have thought about it, I believe he is right. Old people who are ill with no chance of recovery should not be put on life support.

Unquestionably, some people feel that denying life support is wrong; they even go so far as to say that it is immoral as well as illegal. They think that no matter the age or health condition, everything possible should be done to keep the person alive. Often the person's family is unwilling to part with the loved one, and they hold on to the last hope that the person might get better and live longer. They do not consider the fact that people who are in their eighties and nineties or even above might be ready to die and prefer dying.

The student developed her paper from this point on by discussing only points supporting her position. She had rid herself of her con points and did not want to bring them up again to weaken her argument. Her final supporting point was developed in the last paragraph before the conclusion, and the conclusion summed up her argument.

Revising Strategy: Keep Anecdotes on Focus

This student undoubtedly had a lot to say about the subject. It wasn't hard for her to put her words down on paper after she started. But she had so many examples and anecdotes supporting her position that she had to leave some out and focus on only those that pertained directly to her thesis. Can you see why she replaced one anecdote that she used in the first draft of her paper?

First Draft

Another reason for not using life support is that often an extremely ill person doesn't want to exist as a totally different person from the way he or she once was. Larry's mother has had Alzheimer's for ten years and is getting progressively worse. For some unexplained reason, she began getting the disease when she was in her late thirties. Larry had to care for the family and take on the household responsibilities when he was twelve. His mother can't do things for herself now and doesn't even know the family when they visit her at the nursing home. Her mind has deteriorated so badly she never makes sense. The family held a conference with the doctor and decided she should not be put on life support if she became physically ill.

Revision

Another reason for not using life support is that often an extremely ill person doesn't want to exist as a totally different person from the way he or she once was. My friend's grandmother had a stroke and lay comatose for four months. She didn't even know when people were in the room. The only way she was kept alive was through a feeding tube. She was such a pretty, lively lady until then; she would never have wanted to look like that. But the family decided, against her written wishes, to keep her on life support.

The following questions can be used to evaluate a pro-con essay. Have a peer reader apply them to your first draft; then do the same yourself. See Chapter Three for additional points to consider.

Revision Questions

- Did the writer choose a topic that had reasonable arguments for both sides?
- Does the thesis statement clearly state the writer's opinion on the topic?
- Are the points supporting the thesis developed by sound reasoning and evidence? Are they all relevant to the thesis?
- Does the writer present points supporting the antithesis? Are transitions between points for the thesis and antithesis made smoothly?
- Are the points for and against the argument organized in a logical, effective manner?
- Do the anecdotes or illustrations add to the support? Are any anecdotes superfluous or not relevant to the thesis?
- Is the tone established in the introduction? Is it used consistently throughout?
- Is it clear who the audience is for the essay? If the essay were for a different audience, how would it be written differently?
- Does the title reflect the stance the writer takes in the paper?
- Are good grammatical techniques and word choice used?
- Is the paper free from punctuation and spelling errors?

A Published Model

The following essay by Lloyd Garver, entitled "No, You Can't Have Nintendo," supports the assertion that electronic games are bad for children. As you read through the essay, pay particular attention to the evidence the writer gives.

No, You Can't Have Nintendo

1   My wife and I are the kind of mean parents whom kids grumble about on the playground. We're among that ever-shrinking group of parents known as Nintendo holdouts. We refuse to buy a Nintendo set. (Nintendo, for those of you who have been living in a cave for the past few years, is something that you hook up to your TV set that enables you to play various games on your home screen.) Around Christmastime, my son made a wish list, and I noticed that Nintendo was No. l. I said, "You know you're not going to get Nintendo." He said, "I know I'm not going to get it from you. But I might get it from *him*." Alas, Santa, too, let him down.

2   I've heard parents' rationalizations about the games: "They're good for hand-eye coordination." (So is playing ball.) "It's something kids can do without an adult watching." (So is—dare I say that word—READING.) "While he's playing at the screen, I can relax for a few minutes." (Who among us hasn't used the electronic babysitter from time to time? But "a few minutes"? Who are we kidding?)

3   I don't think that playing a video game now and then is really harmful to children. But the children I know are so obsessed with these games that they have prompted at least one second-grade teacher (my son's) to ban the word Nintendo from the classroom. When I asked my 7-year-old if the teacher wouldn't let the kids talk about the games because that's all they were *talking* about, he said, "No. That's all we were *thinking* about."

4   Our society is already so computerized and dehumanized that kids don't need one more reason to avoid playing outside or going for a walk or talking with a friend. I'd still feel this way even if there were nothing intrinsically wrong with games whose objectives are to kill and destroy.

5   I know, I know. There are games other than those like Rampage, Robocopy, Motor Cross Maniacs, Bionic Commando, Dr. Doom's Revenge, Guerrilla War, and Super Street Fighter. But aren't the violent

games the ones the kids love to play for hours? And hours. And hours. My son told me he likes the "killing games" the best, hasn't had much experience with "sports games," and likes "learning games" the least because they are "too easy." (Manufacturers take note.) My 5-year-old daughter told me she enjoyed playing Duck Hunt at a friend's house. The beauty of this game is that even very young players can have the fun of vicariously shooting animals. And then there's the game with my favorite title—an obvious attempt to combine a graceful sport with exciting action: Skate or Die.

6   Some might try to convince us that these violent electronic games are good for a child's self-esteem and development. For years psychologists have been telling us how important fairy tales are to help children work out their fears and fantasies about good and evil, life and death. Maybe electronic games are just a modern way of doing this. Maybe, but. . . .

7   Maybe, but I don't remember kids reading and rereading "Hansel and Gretel" instead of playing outdoors when I was a kid. I don't remember hearing about children stealing money so they could go buy copies of "Little Red Riding Hood." I don't remember many of my childhood friends skipping school so they could stay home and read "The Tortoise and the Hare." But this is what's going on with video and computer games.

8   The January (1990) issue of the *Journal of the American Academy of Child and Adolescent Psychiatry* (foreboding enough title for you?) featured an article entitled "Pathological Preoccupation with Video Games." The author believes that some game manufacturers try to develop programs that "deliberately promote habituation," and the goal of some of the people who make up these games is "to induce an altered level of concentration and focus of attention in the gamester."

9   If you have children, or know any, doesn't this "altered level of concentration and focus" sound familiar? If not, try talking to a child while he is staring at the screen, pushing buttons. He won't hear you unless the words you happen to be saying are, "I just bought a new game for you."

10   In case you couldn't tell, I'm worried that electronic games are dominating children's lives. There are games that simulate sports like baseball and basketball, and that's all some kids know about the sports. Someday soon, a young couple will take their children to their first baseball game and hear the kids exclaim, "This is great. It's almost like the *real baseball* we play on our home screen." When I took my son to a recent Lakers basketball game, the thing that seemed to excite him most (in addition to the self-flushing urinal) was a video game in the lobby. You see, if a kid didn't want to be bored watching some of the greatest

athletes in the world play, he could just put a quarter in the machine and watch lifeless electronic images instead.

11 My son's teacher was right. Kids do play and talk about these games too much. They even have books and magazines that kids can study and classes so they can get better at the games. And that's what's got me worried. I'm just concerned that this activity is so absorbing, kids are going to grow up thinking that the first people to fly that airplane at Kitty Hawk were the Super Mario Brothers.

12 I don't like to discourage children from doing something they're good at; in this case, I must. And believe me, my desire to see them play the games less does not diminish how impressed I am by their skill—they seem to be getting better and better at these games at a younger and younger age. If you believe in evolution, you have to assume that right now DNA is coming together in new ways to create a "Nintendo gene" in our children which they'll pass along to their children. So, our grandchildren will be *born* with the ability to play electronic games. And, about the "Nintendo gene"; I've got a feeling it's going to be dominant.

—*Lloyd Garver*

Activity 2: Analyze the Model

1. Is the writer's choice of a title appropriate to the paper?

2. Even though the thesis is not actually stated until paragraph 11, how do the preceding paragraphs point toward the stance his paper will take?

3. Why do you think the writer chose to put his thesis that far into the paper? Is it effective at this point? Why do you think so?

4. What are some of the arguments the author brings up that do not support his position? How does he refute them?

5. Does the writer's use of dialogue add to or subtract from the paper? How effective is his use of parentheses to express his thoughts?

6. Who do you think is the audience for his essay? What is the writer's tone?

Activity 3: Write a Pro-Con Essay

As shown through the sample essays, you must be familiar with the topic you choose so that you can offer convincing arguments to support it and refute those arguments that do not support it. Think of the topics below as possibilities if you have difficulty in deciding what to write about.

↘   **Possible Topics**

- Should insurance be refused to people who build houses in fragile environments?
- Should the police force homeless into shelters during cold weather?
- Should women serve in the military?
- Should everyone go to college?
- Should younger people replace older people in the work force?
- Should there be an honor system for taking exams?
- Should students work full time while carrying a full school load?
- Should there be censorship on television?
- Should elementary school students be required to wear uniforms?
- Should people be allowed to invest their own Social Security money?

The Evaluation Essay

Understanding Evaluation

When you go to a restaurant or to a new coffee shop, you probably rather automatically form opinions of the food or drink, the atmosphere, and the service. In other words, you evaluate them: you judge their value, quality, or worth. You are able to do this because you have been to other similar places and have some idea of what to expect—that is, you have a frame of reference on which to base your thinking. Without such a frame of reference, it would be difficult to make a reasonable evaluation.

Evaluating is something you do every day, from deciding whether a TV episode was good to forming an opinion of your friend's new suede jacket. More often than not, the judgments are not about big things; however, you are now at the point in your life when you are evaluating more serious issues, such as whether a particular university is a good place to continue your education or whether a particular job will be right for you. Since you have no prior experience to fall back on, you will have to judge these cases on other evidence, such as what you have heard or read or seen. The criteria that you will use for evaluating will still have the commonalities of value, quality, importance, or worth.

You may not realize it, but you have a personal standard by which you judge things and people. It is rarely a written standard; it is inherent in your thinking, automatic and natural. Your standard of judgment comes about through your background and experiences. It is based on your convictions and your perspective of things. And it is what helps you make a determination about whether any number of things or places or situations are good or bad.

You actually use two sets of standards in making judgments: internal and external. Internal judgments are based on knowledge, expertise, and experience. External judgments are based on what you can see or observe. For example, the first time you walked in the classroom, you used external judgment in evaluating the instructor—what you saw and what you heard about him or her. After you were in the class for a week or so, you began to form internal judgments—how well the instructor prepared the lesson, how much the instructor knew, how capable he or she was in getting the lesson across.

Usually you evaluate things in your everyday life for your personal information—whether you like something or not, whether a certain decision will be good for you. But sometimes your opinions can help others make evaluations. If someone you knew could not decide, for example, whether a certain mountain bike was worth buying, your evaluative opinions about the bike's weight, construction, and other significant elements might help that person make a decision.

Understanding the Evaluation Essay

The evaluation essay is a written explanation of your judgment of something. Usually it is based both on what you see and observe and on less tangible qualities such as workability, durability, appeal, and value. Though its purpose is not necessarily to persuade the reader to accept your viewpoint, an evaluative essay can often help someone—or even convince him or her—to make a certain decision.

Suppose, for example, you were writing an evaluation of a certain new model 4-door pickup truck for a school publication. You would probably begin with a description of what the truck looked like on the outside, how many seats it had, what the interior looked like, and how large the bed of the truck was; and then you would comment on some or all of those elements. You would go on to discuss the feel of the truck, the way it drove, the prestige in owning one, and so on. Both tangible and intangible qualities would be important to a complete evaluation of the truck, for the reader might then use what you say to decide whether or not to make a purchase.

The exact criteria you use in evaluation are determined by the purpose of the essay. The purpose determines the direction the paper will take and the kind of support that is needed. For example, if you are writing a critique of a movie to determine if it is suitable for small children, you probably would evaluate it in terms of such things as the simplicity of its plot, the appeal of its characters, and the number of frightening or violent scenes it contains. You would not be concerned with things like complex character development or sophistication of camera shots.

Even though they deal with objective criteria up to a point, evaluations are based on judgments, and those will be subjective. In the movie review, for example, you may come to the conclusion that children will like the movie because the furry orange main character is clever and amusing. But that is only your opinion; others may disagree with it. The same is true with most evaluations. Someone else's view of the pickup truck or of an ideal vacation spot may involve different standards or criteria than yours, yet both evaluations can be valid.

The first thing the writer must do, then, is to set the standards of the evaluation. Once those have been determined, the rest of the paper can evaluate the work or product in terms of those standards. Clearly, however, the standards must be appropriate to the audience for which the evaluation is intended. The movie review will be written with one audience in mind, the evaluation of the 4-door truck with another, and the assessment of the vacation spot with still another. Thus audience is a particularly important consideration for this essay.

Student Model

The model that follows was written by a student whose assignment was to choose a community project or service to evaluate. She decided to write on the quality of public transportation in her city. As you read through her essay, note her use of both external and internal standards of evaluation and the way she combined the two.

In Transit

1   Because the mass transit system in our city has been in such deplorable condition, the city council and mayor have just upgraded it by building a new bus terminal and buying a number of new buses. The bus routes, however, are the same, and the buses attract the same people. While the veneer on the outside and the interior of the bus are definitely improved, the quality of public transportation is no different because it does not accommodate more people.

2   It is true the beautiful white buses are more pleasing to the eye than the rickety dingy gray ones our city just discarded. On the other hand, the advertisements painted on the buses are distracting. One that is shown presently is two disk jockeys dressed (or undressed) in an unsightly manner. It's degrading to see such parading through the streets, and there's no way not to see it if you're going the same way. I suppose the bus company must make money by allowing advertisements to be painted on the buses, but I think just plain white buses with some kind of chrome or other trim would be much better. At least it wouldn't be offensive.

3   The interior of the buses has also shown a definite improvement. The seats have seat belts, which is an added safety feature, and the seats are

comfortable. There is one section that also has a place for a wheelchair with straps to keep it stationary. A camera has been installed in each of the buses, as well, to record everything that is going on. In addition, the new buses have a light brown interior that is attractive, yet it won't be easy to show dirt and grime. In the old buses, the seats were bumpy and broken; some of the padding had come out of the cushions, the upholstery was wearing out, and the walls were filthy.

4   It isn't enough, though, to have beautiful buses to transport people; other changes need to be made. One of the biggest needs is to accommodate more people. This means changing routes and adding routes; it also means running buses longer and starting earlier. It is difficult for some people to get to work on time with the schedule as it is now. A friend of mine, Jessie, had a construction job, and he was actually fired because he kept getting to work late. His employer said they couldn't help it if his bus were late; their day started at 6:00 o'clock. The earliest bus came at 6:30, and sometimes it was late. He had to find a job that didn't start as early.

5   Many people also need to catch buses closer to their homes instead of having to walk several blocks to a bus stop. It isn't safe to stand at a bus stop early in the morning before daylight or at night to be put off at a stop three or four blocks from your home. More than once there have been cases of women being abducted and raped because of this. Buses need to be re-routed to accommodate more people and so that those who catch the bus will be safe.

6   Public transportation has had a facelift, it is true, but it needs more than that. The mayor and city council need to be concerned for the welfare and safety of those who ride the bus and to be sensitive to the needs of those who do not have transportation of their own and must use public transportation. When that happens, the quality of mass transportation in our city will be improved, inside and out.

—*Janelle Davis*

Activity 1: Analyze the Model

1.   In the introduction what did the writer use as her standard of judgment or her criteria for evaluating the bus system?

2.   What tone for the paper does she establish in the introduction?

3.   What audiences might be interested in her paper? Do you think she should share her paper with the city council and mayor?

4.   How does the writer judge the buses? How evenhanded is she in her evaluation?

5. What problems does the writer have with the less tangible aspects of the transit system? What are some examples showing why the system needs to change to meet the needs of people?

6. Do you think the writer is qualified to evaluate the transit system based on her facts? Why or why not?

Guidelines for a Successful Evaluation Essay

Evaluation is basic to thinking and learning as well as to writing. As you compose your evaluation essay, keep in mind the standards you use in everyday life and apply those to your essay. In addition, use the following guidelines.

1. In determining the topic for your evaluation essay, choose one on which you have an opinion and on which you can make a good value judgment. Janelle chose public transportation since she saw it as a problem in her city, one that needed to be corrected.

2. Make it clear in the introduction what your standard of judgment will be. Janelle intended to evaluate whether recent upgrades had helped the transportation system by talking about both the buses and the transportation system in general.

3. Determine the purpose for the essay in order to know the slant the paper will take. For example, by criticizing the advertisements on the buses as well as the inadequate routes and schedules, Janelle hoped to effect certain changes.

4. Organize the body of your paper by presenting each criterion in your evaluation and then discussing it. In paragraph 2, Janelle evaluated the exterior of the buses; paragraph 3 discussed the interior; and paragraphs 4 and 5 explained the need for more bus routes and rerouting buses to accommodate more people. Each point was developed with specific examples.

5. Use comparison and/or contrast if that will help support your judgment. Janelle compared the exterior and interior of the old buses to the new buses.

6. Keep in mind the audience for the paper as you write to know how to approach your topic and whether concepts or terms need to be defined. Janelle's audience was the mayor and city council, who were very familiar with her topic. If she wanted to, she could have mentioned specific streets where more buses were needed, since her audience would have known what she was talking about.

7. Make your essay bear the ring of sincerity. Justify your criteria with solid information that convinces the reader you know your topic. Janelle spoke of her friend having to get a different job because of getting to work late and of her personal reaction to the outlandish advertisements on the buses.

8. Make sure that you have presented the criteria you are using clearly and fairly. The student paper gave credit to the mayor and city council for getting new buses and a new bus terminal, but she felt in fairness she should show that those were not enough. The issue of accommodating riders' needs still needed to be addressed.

9. Use the conclusion to sum up the points you've made. Janelle's conclusion summed up her paper by recognizing the changes in the buses but also stressing the need for better schedules and routes.

Working with Your Own Topic

The guidelines should have helped you to understand that an evaluation essay must be based on unbiased reasoning, appropriate criteria, and solid evidence. If you keep these points in mind, you should find writing your paper relatively easy.

Choosing a Topic

Keeping the following points in mind will help you decide what to evaluate.

- **Choose a topic that you know something about and can evaluate in a convincing way.** To determine whether a topic has merit, think of the criteria you might use to evaluate it and see whether you have evidence or examples to support them. If you don't, choose another topic and analyze it in the same way. At the same time, keep in mind that the topic must involve something you have experience with. For example, to evaluate a cruise ship and its facilities and crew would be impossible unless you had been on the ship. On the other hand, if you had just finished taking a cruise, you could probably evaluate the experience effectively.

- **Choose something that you can evaluate impartially.** To make your evaluation seem fair to your audience, you must be able to take a look at your subject in a fair, evenhanded way. For example, if your recent bad experience at a popular restaurant would keep you from remembering your six other great meals there, you will not be able to do a good evaluation of it.

Now that you know the criteria for choosing a topic, perhaps you have decided that one you could work with is the quality of the literature courses offered by your English department. This is a topic you are familiar with and have some definite opinions on.

Prewriting Strategy: Surveying and Synthesizing

Although there is nothing wrong with using only your own opinions in an evaluative essay, sometimes you can get a fairer view of things by seeing what others think as well. One student decided to evaluate the quality of English courses by looking at several specific issues. His general feeling was that there was too much content overlap in the courses and that contemporary writers were ignored, but to see if this standard of judgment had merit, he made up a survey and asked students to respond to it. He also included a place in the survey for other complaints students had concerning the English curriculum.

The student's survey included seventy-five students who had taken at least six semesters of English, since he felt they had had a wide enough exposure to the curriculum to know what could be done to improve it. He tabulated the most common complaints:

- Too much course overlap (sixty students)

- Not enough ethnic courses (fifty-seven students)

- Not enough time allotted for modern writers (fifty-two students)

- More world literature (forty-five students)

- More Shakespeare courses (eighteen students)

With the data the student collected, he could see that his original evaluation of the curriculum was pretty much on target. He also learned of other common complaints, such as not enough ethnic courses. Through synthesizing his information, he found a number of points to support his evaluation and develop his paper.

Writing Strategy: Fairness and Evenhandedness

To give an evaluation essay credibility, as well as to gain audience acceptance, it is wise to be fair in your presentation of information. Few things are all good or all bad, and the exceptions should not be ignored. This student did not want to be entirely negative in presenting his results, even though they did indicate a definite need for a change in the English course offerings. He, therefore, spoke briefly of the curriculum's strengths in his introduction in addition to summarizing all of the complaints his survey had uncovered. His thesis, *A substantial number of students feel that the English course offerings need to be changed to avoid overlap and concentrate more on modern writers as well as include more ethnic literature,* is critical but fair: he is careful not to generalize his information to include *all* students. The first paragraph of the body of his paper also begins in a conciliatory fashion.

> Everyone recognizes what a mammoth task it is to come up with unique, individual courses. But often the same works must be read in two or three required classes. A case in point is Edgar Allan Poe's "The Tell-Tale Heart," which is studied in detail in both Composition I and American Literature. The same is true with the play *Pygmalion* by George Bernard Shaw, a requirement in both Great English Dramas and English Literature. *Othello* is taught in both of these classes too. Because of these overlaps, other writers of equal importance are ignored while these writers are studied twice. A detailed overview of each course would provide insight into the overlapping and show how changes could be made.

Revising Strategy: Tie the Conclusion to the Rest of the Paper

To write an effective conclusion, you have to deal with points you've made so far and avoid introducing new ideas. It is evident from the conclusion of his paper that this student got into a new area, language difficulties with certain writers, which neither his thesis nor the rest of his paper had addressed. In revising the conclusion, he cut out those parts; notice the difference in the two versions.

First Draft

> As the survey results indicate, revamping the English course offerings is in order. According to the students, there is an overlapping of the same writers, which causes other writers to be ignored. It's Shakespeare almost every year; he's not the only great writer who ever lived. His plays have to be interpreted because they were written almost four hundred years ago. We don't talk that way today. Because of so much time spent on the "oldies," there is hardly ever time left for modern writers, who have just as much to say. They speak in today's language, too, and don't have to have interpreters. If changes are made, more time could be given to ethnic writers, who many students feel are currently shortchanged. By making these changes, students could have a more well-rounded picture of the literature that is a part of the heritage of all English speakers.

Revision

> As the survey results indicate, revamping the English course offerings is in order. According to the students, there is an overlapping of the

same writers, which causes other writers to be ignored. Because of so much time spent on the "oldies," there is hardly ever time left for modern writers, who have just as much to say. If changes are made, more time could be given to ethnic writers, who many students feel are currently shortchanged. By making these changes, students could have a more well-rounded picture of the literature that is a part of the heritage of all English speakers.

The questions below can be used in analyzing your own essay. After you have used them to critique your paper, have a peer evaluator do the same. You might also consider additional revision points from Chapter Three.

Revision Questions

- Did the student select a topic that he or she could evaluate knowledgeably?

- Is the purpose for the essay evident in the introduction? Does the introduction offer an insight into why the paper will take the approach it does?

- Are the criteria the writer discusses in the body all valid ones that relate to his or her purpose?

- Is the evaluation fair and impartial, or is it biased? If it is biased, what might the writer add to make it more evenhanded?

- Is the paper organized so that it is easy to follow? What could the writer do to make it clearer?

- Does the writer keep the tone consistent throughout the essay?

- Will the evaluation sound sensible and relevant to its intended audience?

- Does the writer seem sincere in his evaluation? Does he or she give good evidence to support the points made?

- Does the writer's conclusion effectively draw the paper to a close? Has the writer used good sentence structure?

- Is the paper free from errors in spelling and punctuation?

A Published Model

The evaluation essay that follows, "La Vita: Reason to Go On Living," was published in the amusements section of a local newspaper and deals with a restaurant. As you read through the essay, notice the writer's tone and familiarity with the topic, and determine what criteria are used in making the evaluation.

La Vita: Reason to Go On Living

1 "Enjoy the Life" is the upbeat pronouncement scrawled across the La Vita business card, a mauve and white number with stylized stars around the name.

2 The card is the perfect metaphor—intentional or by chance—for this sprightly new restaurant on Taylor Street, where Italian restaurants are *di poco valore,* a dime a dozen. Small and intimate, with most of the left side taken up by a bar and open kitchen, La Vita has been filling its tables—slowly but surely—with repeat customers looking for that special plate of pasta or an interesting risotto del giorno.

3 Which brings me to the menu. While I heartily approve of its brevity—about two dozen dishes (exclusive of the pizza selection), half of which are appetizers—I do not agree with the overall balance. For example, if you want chicken, you have but two choices: pollo limone and pollo Marsala. If you want meat, it's a veal chop or sautéed veal scallops. Yes, some daily specials come into play, but they are not enough to fill in the obvious voids.

4 Also, veal chops are so costly for a restaurant to procure that a higher ticket price is necessary (La Vita's are $21.95), so why bother? Go with a grilled ribeye steak or pork loin.

5 Starters range from a basic house salad to luxurious risotto studded with meaty pieces of portobello mushrooms. However, I would recommend the grilled calamari, two full-bodied squid, slashed (to prevent curling), grilled and settled into a light film of a well-made Cognac sauce. Or the baked clams, a half-dozen littlenecks, beautifully executed, extremely tasty and as pristine as can be.

6 Or start with a pizza. La Vita offers no fewer than seven versions (plus a selection of add-on toppings) of a 9-inch number that, based on the two sampled, are worthy of consideration. The pizza is suggested as an individual serving, but a split is a better idea. Try the *quattro formaggi,* a rousingly cheesy composition (Swiss, mascarpone, mozzarella and blue) that makes me wonder how many permutations there are of a four-cheese pizza. On a more Italian note, the honored pizza Margherita, a simple and delicious combination of tomato sauce, fresh basil and fresh mozzarella, is extremely noteworthy.

7 A pasta special one evening was close to being exquisite. Ten or so medium-size squid ink ravioli ("black ravioli," said our waiter with more

than a bit of exultation) were stuffed with crab meat and layered with a light cream sauce. The effect was dramatic, the taste wonderful and the three little shrimp atop the pasta an unexpected surprise.

8   My tastes leaned toward the simple during another visit, so I passed on the capellini mare (clams, mussels, shrimp and scallops) and the fettuccine with salmon in favor of the penne arrabbiata. (Lately it seems that I have had trouble passing up an arrabbiata sauce, but then a number of years ago I had the same affinity for a carbonara sauce.) It was a most pleasing dish, classic in its interpretation, which is nothing more than pasta in a spicy red sauce with a flavor kick from sautéed pancetta.

9   The two main courses sampled left me feeling reasonably good about the kitchen. The pollo limone was a tender and meaty boneless breast of chicken swathed in a lemon-butter-caper sauce that had almost perfect flavor balance (maybe a touch less lemon the next time?). The chunks of roasted potatoes and thin strips of grilled zucchini arranged around the chicken were nice, too. The only thing I can find to say about the grilled salmon was that it was a nice piece of fish—squeaky fresh, perfectly cooked and pleasantly anointed with a brush of olive oil.

10   Desserts were here and there. A three-layer wedge of squishy white chocolate cake was wedding material. But the chocolate truffle (chocolate-coated ball filled with vanilla and chocolate ice cream and drizzled with chocolate sauce) was excellent. Coconut sorbet was refreshing.

—*Pat Bruno*

Activity 2: Analyze the Model

1. What seem to be the writer's qualifications for writing the evaluation?

2. What kind of assumptions does the writer make about what the audience already knows about Italian food? How well does he clarify the meaning of unfamiliar terms?

3. What criticisms does the writer have of the restaurant? Do you agree with where he positioned them in the evaluation?

4. What kind of specific facts, details, and examples did the writer use to support his evaluation?

5. What did you learn about the writer as you read his evaluation? Does he show he is knowledgeable and is his judgment impartial and fair? Explain.

6. Were you surprised at the abrupt ending of the evaluation? What else would you have wanted the writer to say?

Activity 3: Write an Evaluation Essay

You have been given the guidelines for writing an evaluation essay, and you have seen student models as well as a published model. Now you will write your own, but first you need to think of a topic that you feel qualified to evaluate. You may be able to use one of the suggestions below, or those suggestions may help you think of related topics.

↘ **Possible Topics**

- The "ABS" exercise program
- Your present employer
- The T-factor diet or some other diet program
- A politician who seems wishy-washy
- Service clubs in your school
- One or more restaurants where students hang out
- The athletic program at your school
- A particular vacation spot
- A judge's decision
- A political campaign

The Literary Analysis Essay

Understanding Literary Analysis

How often have you, in talking about a book you have just finished reading, declared, "That's the worst book (or the best) I've ever read." Or you may have said there was no plot or the characters were dull or the setting seemed distant and foreboding. Without realizing it, you were analyzing the book, judging it according to preconceived ideas about what you expected. You do the same thing when you watch a play, but that is as it should be. It shows that you are thinking instead of just absorbing what you read, see, or hear.

You base your analysis on your own past experiences and your background of knowledge. The person who has read widely and enjoys theatrical performances has a wider range of expertise in judging these works than one who seldom cracks a book or goes to the theater. He or she is able to form an analysis from a broader scope.

Of course, just to read a book to analyze it borders on study, and you probably don't do that unless you are required to. It is a lot more fun to read and then look back on the book or story and make an analysis for your own pleasure. You actually do that without thinking. Dependent on whether you liked the work, you might recommend it and encourage others to read it also.

Understanding the Literary Analysis Essay

The literary analysis essay is putting into writing what you observe from reading a book, story, or poem or watching a performance of a play. Since a literary analysis involves truly literary works, movies are not analyzed in quite the same fashion; you would not, for example, look for literary devices in movies. You may, of course, write a review or evaluation of a movie, but that isn't the same thing as writing an analysis of a book or play.

173

A literary analysis is generally based on an examination of the work that looks at it first as a whole and then considers its various parts. If you are reviewing a book, often a fast reading helps to gather an idea of what the book is about and how events and characters relate to each other. The same is also true with a play; it would be difficult to write a critical analysis after having seen or read it only one time. The second time around gives you an insight you could not possibly have the first time.

A literary analysis looks at a work to make a critical judgment of it from one viewpoint or another. Note that *critical* in this sense does not mean trying to find elements to criticize, because that is usually thought of as negative. Instead, it means looking at the work in terms of what's in it, or what it tells you about life, or how it compares with other literary works by the same or different authors. Quite often your instructor will ask you to analyze the work according to a literary technique that is used within it—satire, setting, characterization, imagery, symbolism, conflict, point of view, theme. When that happens, you automatically know how to approach your second, close-up look at the work.

Sometimes, though, your instructor expects you to write a literary analysis without any specific directions. When that happens, the first step you should take is to ask questions. Looking for answers to things like "What is the function of the setting?" "What makes the character/s act as they do?" " How do the characters relate to each other?" "What is the tone?" "What is the theme?" " What do certain symbols mean?" "What is the purpose of the writer?" "How does this work relate to the writer's other works?" is the beginning of the process of analysis. The way that you answer these questions is particular to you. Another person reading the same work may see something entirely different, and that's all right. You are basing your analysis on your own background and insight.

If your instructor asks you to explicate a poem, what he or she usually means is to take the poem line by line to show how each element fits into the general pattern and purpose for the work. This kind of analysis requires a very close reading that looks for meaning in the repetition and interconnectedness of words and images. In this chapter, however, we will concentrate primarily on the analysis of prose works—books, stories, and plays.

After first reading a book for content and general knowledge of characterization and plot, the next thing to do is to decide what you want to emphasize in your essay. One of the things you should avoid doing, which is tempting, is to write a summary of the plot as the bulk of your paper. The summary is never an analysis; it merely tells what is going on. If you decide a summary is needed, it should be very short—no more than one or two paragraphs.

If you are familiar with the author and other books by him or her, you may want to write your analysis by comparing your book with another of the author's, such as Ernest Hemingway's *A Farewell to Arms* and *The Sun Also Rises.* Such a comparison may look at plot, setting, characterization, or a combination of such elements. Or you may want to compare the way a specific technique, such as irony, is used in two works. These may be works by the same author, but they need not be: you might decide to compare the irony in Thomas Hardy's *The Return of the Native* with Charlotte Bronte's use of it in *Jane Eyre.* Or you may want to compare and contrast the independence of women in both books.

A literary analysis often combines expository writing with persuasive writing. Expository techniques are used to explain the details you are focusing on and to show how they fit into the work as a whole. The thesis statement, however, expresses an interpretation that may differ from the interpretation of other readers. You would use persuasive techniques—using your details as evidence—to convince readers that your interpretation is sound.

The organization of a literary analysis essay often follows one of these three patterns:

- **chronological order:** discussing characters or events as they change over time. An essay analyzing Pip's development in *Great Expectations* might use chronological order to show his growth and maturity.

- **order of importance:** presenting the most noteworthy or significant point either first or last. A critique of Ray Bradbury's "All Summer in a Day" might analyze the shy and fearful character of Margo, the little girl, beginning with her not making friends to her finally not even wanting to let water run over her in the shower.

- **comparison-contrast order:** grouping similarities or differences within a work or between two works. An analysis of the imagery of light and darkness in Tennessee Williams's *The Glass Menagerie* might compare and contrast how it is used in the portrayal of Tom, the narrator; Laura, his sister; and Amanda, their mother.

Whichever method you choose for developing the body of the essay should always reflect evidence gathered from your reading. Quotations or examples or other descriptive details should be included as support.

Student Model

The literary analysis essay demands that you look at the work in depth, and after you have decided what you will emphasize, begin gathering information for support. One student, Dave Besse, had read Emily Bronte's *Wuthering Heights* and chose to emphasize tyranny in the novel. As you read, look for his thesis statement and the information he presents to support it.

Tyranny—A Weapon of Harm

1   *Wuthering Heights,* written in Gothic style by Emily Bronte, has a somber tone and dark and evil themes. One of the major themes is tyranny, which contributes to the Gothic style. Tyranny is uniquely used because all of the oppressors are aware of its use and yet while they are capable of

hurting some characters, they also show love toward others. Tyranny, normally thought of as an obsession with power, is used in *Wuthering Heights* as a weapon to hurt specific characters.

2   The two characters who maliciously oppress others are Hindley Earnshaw and Heathcliff. As soon as Hindley's father adopts Heathcliff, Hindley develops hatred for the boy. Hindley is jealous of the love between his father and his foster brother, Heathcliff. This, added to Hindley's worry that he will be cheated out of his inheritance by Heathcliff, causes Hindley to hate his foster brother forever.

3   Years later, when Hindley's father dies, Hindley becomes master of Wuthering Heights, and he becomes a tyrant over Heathcliff. "He drove him from their company to the servants, deprived him of the instructions of the curate, and insisted that he should labour out of doors instead; compelling him to do so as hard as any other hand on the farm" (50). Hindley is also envious of the love that Catherine has for Heathcliff, and he tries to force them to live apart, but Heathcliff and Catherine "forgot everything the minute they were together again" (50). Even so, Hindley's abuse is almost solely directed toward Heathcliff. The only time Hindley abuses anyone else is when he is drunk.

4   Unlike Hindley, whose reason for his abusive power is his hatred for Heathcliff, Heathcliff's abuse is directed at avenging past insults. Through gambling, Heathcliff is able to acquire all of Hindley's assets, but instead of abusing Hindley, Heathcliff waits for Hindley to die as a drunkard and then uses his power to degrade Hareton Earnshaw, Hindley's son, the same way that Hindley degraded him earlier. Nellie Dean, the housekeeper, says, "Hareton was reduced to a state of complete dependence on his father's inveterate enemy; and lived in his own house as a servant, deprived of the advantage of wages: quite unable to right himself, because of his friendlessness, and his ignorance that he had been wronged" (169).

5   In addition to insults from Hindley, Heathcliff is insulted by Linton, the man his foster sister Catherine marries, so he marries Edgar's sister, Isabella, out of revenge. He is cruel to her and causes her to leave. She dies a few years later, leaving their son, who doesn't even know his father, to Heathcliff, who abuses him. Heathcliff is not content with acquiring Hindley's estate in his thrust for revenge; he also wants the Linton property. He goes about getting it by forcing young Catherine Linton to marry his son, so that he can acquire the property when Edgar dies. He tells Nellie, "I shall have that home. Not because I need it, but—" (253).

6   Both tyrannical rulers, Heathcliff and Hindley, have their downfall. Hindley receives poetic justice. The person to whom all his abuses are directed, Heathcliff, eventually takes all of Hindley's property. Hindley lives his last years miserably, dying an alcoholic, and leaves Heathcliff to torment his only son, Hareton. Heathcliff says this about Hareton, "I've a pleasure in him. He has satisfied my expectations. If he were a born fool I should not

enjoy it half so much. But he's no fool; and I can sympathise with all his feelings, having felt them myself. I know what he suffers now, for instance, exactly; it is merely a beginning of what he shall suffer, though" (195–196).

7   Heathcliff's rule ends with death, seeing that there are no more people to be avenged and he has no more reason to live. He starves himself and leaves Wuthering Heights to its true inheritors, Hareton Earnshaw and Catherine Linton, who eventually marry.

8   There is a parallel in the beginning and ending of the novel: Wuthering Heights is in the hands of the proper owner, an Earnshaw. But for the years in between, there is tyrannical rule by its masters and a lack of freedom for its inhabitants. Hindley Earnshaw and Heathcliff both use tyranny as weapons to hurt each other and others they despise. Heathcliff's tyranny is a product of the abuse of Hindley Earnshaw and the insults of Edgar Linton. Hindley's tyranny is the abuse of power out of hatred for Heathcliff.

9   Bronte's novel, Gothic and macabre, effectively shows what happens when hatred becomes a way of life and takes over a person's actions. The hatred takes on anthropomorphic proportions and becomes tyrannical; then, because of its obsession with destroying others, the hatred consumes the person who does the hating as well as those at whom the hatred is aimed.

—*Dave Besse*

Activity 1: Analyze the Model

1. What is the theme that the writer emphasizes throughout the essay?

2. If you haven't or hadn't read the novel, is it possible to understand the essay? Does the writer summarize the book at any point?

3. What are some examples of tyranny shown by Hindley and Heathcliff? Whom do they hurt besides themselves?

4. Do the quotations help you understand the characters and the theme better? Explain.

5. What order did the writer use to develop his paper? Would another order have been more effective?

6. Does the writer's evaluation of the book at the end give added support to his view of the novel? If so, how?

Guidelines for a Successful Literary Analysis Essay

As you think about writing your literary analysis, keep in mind the techniques you use every day when you tell someone about a book you just read; many of the same techniques apply to your written critique. In addition, follow the guidelines below.

1. From the literary work you are analyzing, choose an element that you think best defines or characterizes the book. It might be characterization, point of view, plot, setting, theme, conflict, or style. Dave chose to emphasize the way Bronte depicted the actions of two of the characters in particular and showed by their dialogue how they felt about each other.

2. Determine what your purpose will be in writing the analysis. Usually this will be to explain how the work is written, concentrating on the style or use of literary devices; to determine how the theme is applied in the work; to analyze how the conflict affects the characters and plot; to examine the way the characters act, their motives, and their interactions; or to compare specific elements of the work with other similar works. Dave chose to analyze the theme of tyranny as he saw it in *Wuthering Heights*. He used Heathcliff and Hareton Earnshaw as the focus of his essay and showed how their tyrannical actions affected not only themselves but others.

3. Be aware of your audience as you plan your essay so that you will know exactly how much of a plot summary should be given or how much information you should provide about the characters. It is clear the student felt his audience knew the story and also knew the characters to the extent that he did not feel the need to identify them more.

4. Use the introduction to give the title of the work, the author, the general focus of your paper, and finally the thesis. If you feel that a summary of the work is in order, include it either as a part of the introduction or immediately after the introduction, but be sure to keep it brief. As you saw, Dave chose not to write a summary.

5. Choose a method of organization for the body of the paper that suits your purpose for writing. Dave wanted to show the tyranny of two characters, so he used a comparison of the two as a framework for his analysis.

6. If you observe particular weaknesses or strengths in the work, include them as a part of your overall analysis. Depending on your purpose, these may be either the main focus of the essay and mentioned in your thesis statement, or criticism of specific elements that you bring up where appropriate. Dave made no direct criticisms of *Wuthering Heights,* but could have done so if he thought, for example, that certain actions were implausible or characters' motivations were unclear.

7. To persuade your reader to accept your analysis, support it with examples, direct quotations, or paraphrases from the text. Dave's use of direct quotations in paragraphs 3, 4, 5, and 6 backs up the points he makes about the characters' tyranny. He identifies the source of each quote by putting the page number in parentheses immediately following it. (For correct punctuation of quotations, see Chapter Sixteen.)

8. When describing events in the story, use the same tense—preferably present tense—as much as possible. Quotes from the book may be in past tense, but they need to be worked into the text as smoothly as possible. Notice how Dave does this in paragraph 3 with his second quote, which is in past tense.

9. Use transitional words, phrases, or hooks to help your paper read more smoothly and to tie your thoughts together. The student writer made good use of transitions and transitional hooks by connecting his paragraphs with references to the preceding paragraphs.

10. Use the conclusion to restate the thesis and/or summarize the main points. The first part of Dave's conclusion, in paragraph 8, pulls together his thoughts by saying that Heathcliff's tyranny is a product of the abuse of Hindley and Linton, while Hindley's tyranny is abuse of power caused by his hatred for Heathcliff.

11. Choose a title that is indicative of the work but different from the title of the book. For example, Dave's title was "Tyranny—A Weapon of Harm," not *Wuthering Heights*. (He could, of course, have made the name of the book *part* of his essay title.)

Working with Your Own Topic

Now that you have been given guidelines for writing your literary analysis, the next step is to begin prewriting on your own. This calls for knowing what you will write about first.

Choosing a Topic

Often the work you will be analyzing will be suggested by your instructor. If so, your first step is to decide what aspect of the work you will concentrate on. If you are to pick a book or story of your own, you need to select one you think you can analyze acceptably within the constraints of the assignment.

- **If the work has been selected for you, choose an aspect of it that you feel comfortable with and can make a strong case for.** Quite often this means scanning the book again to get a feel for plot, characters, language, and literary devices. Consider the book as a whole first; then note how elements like descriptive details, foreshadowing, or symbols fit into the work. Try to decide what impressed you most in reading. Was it the continued use of coincidence in bringing the main characters together? Was it the mood the writer established through his descriptions of setting? Or was it the completely unsatisfactory ending? Once you have an angle, make sure you have at least three good examples or points to use in developing it. If you can't come up with that many, you don't have a topic that is strong enough to sustain in an entire essay.

- **If you are selecting your own work, choose one that you can analyze without having to explain too much background.** A book with a convoluted plot or a confusing historical context will be more difficult to work with than one you can summarize quickly. Keep in mind that even if the work you select is not familiar to your audience, you will still want your essay to make sense to them even if you only make reference to events rather than tell the whole story.

Once you have narrowed your choice to one or two works, approach each as you would if your instructor had selected the work—rereading, looking for an angle of approach, checking for adequate examples to support it. In addition, consider other works involving the same author or theme that you might create comparisons with. If you still can't make a selection, choose the work you have the strongest feelings about, positive or negative.

One student who used *Nineteen Eighty-four* by George Orwell as his subject was intrigued by the slogans of INGSOC, the ruling party of Oceania: "War Is Peace," "Freedom Is Slavery," "Ignorance Is Strength." He decided that these might offer him an angle from which to approach his analysis—words used opposite from their true meaning. Suppose that you too have read *Nineteen Eighty-four* and have been assigned to write your critique based on it. You will need to determine the angle from which you will approach your paper.

Prewriting Strategy: Brainstorm to Determine a Focus

Brainstorming is a good way to select an angle from which to approach a literary work. Here is the way this student got to his topic:

The Use of Newspeak in Oceania Society

- Simple vocabulary
- Train people to think positively
- Have no chance for a rebellion to organize because the words don't allow it

The Purpose of War in Society

- War is peace in that a state of constant warfare helps to keep the party in control of the people
- Unifies the country against a single enemy
- Helps take care of surplus labor parks—soldiers, etc.
- Retaining the same level of thought, same level of technology and help from a powerful hierarchical leader
- Destruction of the products of human labor which would make people too civilized
- Keep a general state of scarcity of items

As you can see, the student seemed to ramble; he didn't even put things down in the order he used them in his paper. In fact, you notice he started with one idea, scratched that idea, then changed it to another. From the ideas his brainstorming generated, however, he began to focus on how the government kept the people in control through constant warfare. He made a more organized list of the points his paper would cover and also jotted down a few examples to support his points.

Topic: War Is Control

- unifies the country against a single enemy (Winston talking with old man about past times—how times are better now—propaganda)

- helps by using surplus labor

- controls the population (Winston's sister and mother sent away to die—vaporizing people not longer wanted—hanging those against the Party)

- keeps people from being too comfortable ("War eats up the surplus of consumable goods"—p. 165)

- causes people to be against each other (children/parents, neighbor/neighbor—constant state of suspicion)

- controls people's emotions (people could not marry if they "gave the impression of being physically attracted to one another"—p. 57)

Writing Strategy: Write a Succinct Thesis Statement

Particularly when you have a lot to say about a subject, as this student did, it can be difficult to write a clear and concise thesis statement. It may help to remember that the thesis need not cover every point in the essay; instead, it should simply show the direction of the paper.

The student's first thesis was virtually the whole essay in a nutshell:

> The Party promoted constant warfare to keep the people controlled emotionally, to keep them engaged in military duty, to keep them from becoming to comfortable and intellectual, thus seeing the uselessness of the Party, and to keep the people in a general state of primitiveness.

His second attempt eliminated much of the wordiness and so was much more effective:

> The Party promoted constant warfare to keep the people controlled emotionally, intellectually, physically, and psychologically.

This thesis statement shows where the essay is going and guides the student in the writing, but it leaves the bulk of the material to be covered in the body—which is where it should be handled.

Revising Strategy: Add Specific Examples from the Text

When you write about a literary work, you have a ready source of examples: the text of the work itself. Quote from it freely—both to give life to your paper and to keep yourself on focus. In developing the first two topic sentences in the body of his paper—"One of the reasons for constant warfare is emotional" and "All the countries have a population surplus, thereby creating a need for constant warfare"—the student writer used quotations and other examples from the text as support. By the time he got to the third body paragraph, however, he began to talk in generalities without giving support to his points. Notice how much more specific the revision is than the first draft of this paragraph.

First Draft

War maintains a general state of primitiveness. Valuable resources are used to support the war effort—resources that would otherwise make people more comfortable. The draining of resources by the war effort also impedes the advancement of science and technology. However, to go too primitive would create as much problem as being too advanced. War provides an easy way to keep humanity constant and stagnant.

Revision

War maintains a general state of primitiveness. It uses the natural resources of the country to support the war effort—resources that would otherwise make people more comfortable. The draining of resources by the war effort impedes the advancement of science and technology, thus causing only those things that are connected with war to be designed and manufactured. It overlooks all but the basic needs of man and keeps the population in a state of practical poverty. As one antique shopkeeper says, "You see how it is; an empty shop, you might say. Between you and me, the antique trade's just about finished. No demand any longer, and no stock either. . . . And of course the metal stuff's mostly been melted down" (80). Only the necessities are provided; only the proletariat are considered worthy of being educated and trained; the proles or common people are regarded as nothing. By the constant state of war, humanity remains stagnant and primitive.

As you look back at your paper, use the questions below to help you determine if you are on the right track and have developed your paper according to the guidelines given. Have a peer evaluator apply them to your essay too. For additional points to consider, see Chapter Three.

Revision Questions

- Does the introduction include the title of the book, the author, and the thesis?
- Is the thesis clearly stated, giving the main idea and the elements to be discussed?
- If a summary is included, is it brief and necessary to an understanding of the essay?

- Does the essay identify major points that support the thesis?

- Does the essay give ample supporting evidence? Is the evidence specific and relevant?

- Are quotations used for support? Are they punctuated correctly?

- Does the order used to develop the paper—logical order, chronological order, or order of importance—seem appropriate to make the writer's point?

- If the writer points out strong or weak points in the work, does he or she make a convincing case about them?

- Is the paper written with the audience in mind?

- Does the conclusion reinforce the thesis of the essay?

- Are parallel structure and effective transitions used throughout?

- Are spelling, usage, and punctuation rules adhered to?

A Published Model

The following essay, "Symbolism in *The Glass Menagerie,*" uses the patterns of development discussed throughout this chapter. As you read it, notice how the thesis is expanded on throughout the essay.

Symbolism in
The Glass Menagerie

1   *The Glass Menagerie* introduces an extensive pattern of symbolism that ranges from the clearcut to the subtle. Four elements—glass, light, color, and music—are the dominant symbols and motifs, serving to reveal deeper aspects of characters and underlying themes in the play.

2   The menagerie of glass, Laura's collection of animal figurines, represents the fragile relationships among all the characters. The glass unicorn is most obviously a symbol of Laura—delicate, sadly different, an anomaly in the modern world. But like Laura and like the shining perfume bottles in the lighted shop windows Tom passes, the unicorn is a beautiful object. When the unicorn is broken by Jim's clumsy but well-meant exuberance, Laura is about to be wounded by news of Jim's engagement. After her brief romantic encounter, Laura gives the unicorn—no longer unique—to Jim and retreats emotionally to her glass case. The glass motif recurs throughout the play in other forms. Laura visits the conservatory at the

zoo, a glass house of tropical flowers that are as vulnerable as she is. A glass sphere that hangs from the ceiling of the Paradise Dance Hall reflects rainbow colors and represents the dreams of the dancers. Laura is spoken of as "translucent glass," while the practical and prosaic gentleman caller protests before dancing with Laura, "I'm not made of glass."

3   Lighting in the play is significant for several reasons. Dim and poetic, the lighting, along with the gauze curtains, lends an unreal aura to the set, suggesting that this family functions in a world of dreams. Like the tricks Tom professes to have up his sleeve, lighting gives truth "the pleasant disguise of illusion." In another function, lighting serves to punctuate scenes by focusing on absent characters. Several times through lights we are reminded of the "fifth character" in the play, Mr. Wingfield, who appears only through a photograph. When Tom mentions Malvolio the Magician and his trick of escaping from a coffin, Mr. Wingfield's photograph lights up. Tom too will flee, like his father and the magician, beyond the temporary refuge of the fire escape. A more subtle variation of lighting is seen in the lovely, deformed candelabrum (another symbolic representation of Laura), in which Jim's giant shadow is reflected.

4   There are many references to color in the play, most notably blue, which is associated with Laura, and yellow, commonly linked with Amanda. Jim's nickname for Laura, Blue Roses, suggests a phenomenon that is contrary to nature. There is an opposition between these strange, different flowers ("Blue is—wrong for—roses") and the natural, gay jonquils associated with Amanda. In the original version of the play, Amanda's party dress was described as "a girlish frock of yellow voile" and the light that surrounds her as "lemony." The color comes to suggest Amanda's outgoing and optimistic attitude just as blue connotes the melancholy outlook of Laura.

5   Music is used throughout *The Glass Menagerie* to evoke mood and haunt memory, reinforcing the symbolism of the play. Williams once described the recurring glass menagerie theme as a tune that is light, delicate, and sad, fragile as spun glass. He added, "It is primarily Laura's music and therefore comes upon her and the lovely fragility of glass which is her image."

6   These elements of glass, light, color, and music are drawn together in the ending scenes of the play. The final appearance of Amanda and Laura is played "as though viewed through soundproof glass." Thus the viewer, like Tom, retreats to another world, leaving the women to their fantasies. But like Tom, who is repeatedly lured back by familiar bits of music, by a piece of transparent glass, or by tiny bottles in delicate colors that suggest "bits of a shattered rainbow," we are drawn back to scenes and characters in the play, settings and people who refuse to be left behind.

Activity 2: Analyze the Model

1. Does the writer include the things that are a must in the introduction: title of book and thesis?

2. Is the thesis clear and well supported throughout the essay?

3. Does the writer give a summary? If not, do you think one is needed for better understanding of the analysis?

4. Does the writer give adequate examples and quotes to support the thesis? Which element is best supported of the four?

5. Which order does the writer use for developing the analysis—chronological, order of importance, or comparison-contrast?

6. How does the conclusion tie in with the introduction?

Activity 3: Write a Literary Analysis Essay

The literary work you are to analyze may be given to you by your instructor; however, as you think about narrowing the work to a topic that you can handle, consider working with some of these elements: characterization, plot, setting, conflict, theme, style, flashback, foreshadowing, symbolism, figurative language, and the general framework of the work. Here are some examples of how you might approach these areas in various works, whether you or your instructor selects them.

↘ Possible Topics

*   How the main character in _____ keeps creating roadblocks that impede his own success

*   How the conflict in _____ is more external than internal

*   How the theme of isolation is approached differently in _____ than in _____'s other works

*   How _____ shows the independence of women as opposed to how they are normally portrayed in the novels of that period

*   The importance of setting in _____'s works

*   A look at the world of the future through the eyes of _____ in _____

*   How the satire is more gentle than biting in _____

*   How _____ and _____ handle the theme of death differently

*   Why the symbolism in _____ seems weak and inconsistent

*   The love-hate relationship between the two main characters in _____

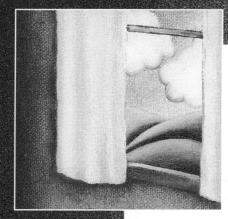

Writing

As you have learned throughout this book, there is a process that writers often follow regardless of the type of essay they are writing. The prewriting, writing, and revising strategies you have learned will be useful to you in nearly every writing situation. However, there are two additional topics that will serve you well in your academic career and beyond: writing essays in test situations and writing with style. These are the focus of Chapters Fifteen and Sixteen.

The further you progress in school, the more likely it is that you will be faced with essay exams in a variety of courses. Whether a history instructor asks you to write about the causes of a specific event or a chemistry instructor asks you to describe a particular process, you will be expected to illustrate your knowledge in an essay that is well organized and well thought out. While writing an essay exam does call for prewriting (or at least prethinking), writing, and revising, it also requires you to make sure you understand the question you are being asked and to learn to allocate your limited time wisely. Part of being a successful student is learning to master essay exams, and Chapter Fifteen will help you do just that.

Aids

Similarly, Chapter Sixteen will help you learn to develop your own unique style in writing. Style has to do with the way you use words. As a writer, you can develop your own voice, which is that aspect of writing that expresses your personality and point-of-view. Whether you are writing an in-class essay, responding to an essay exam question, or writing on the job, you can write with a personal style that says something about who you are. You may even have different styles for different situations: a fairly informal style for letters to friends or e-mail and a more formal style for academic writing.

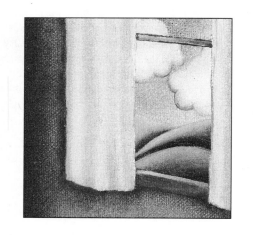

Writing Essays in Test Situations

As you progress in school, one of the givens is having to take tests that require essay answers. Writing quickly and under pressure in this way is also a skill needed in taking certain kinds of standardized examinations and even in applying for some jobs. So it is important to develop good strategies for answering essay questions. Some of these strategies are the same ones you learned to use in writing essays in general; you only need to apply them now on a smaller scope. Others apply strictly to essay tests. It is natural, though, that when you look at a test and see that half or all of it is essay questions, you immediately wish you were somewhere else.

After entering college, one student remembered that every time he took one of his instructor's essay tests in high school, he looked at the instructor and mentally said "I hate you." After he went to college, though, he looked back and said "Thank you." Learning strategies to respond to essay questions stood him in good stead in later studies, and it can do the same for you.

It goes without saying that you can't write a good response to an essay question if you don't have the specific knowledge to answer it. An instructor can always spot a student whose essay "circles the globe" because he or she is trying to bluff an answer. Still, if you have come this far in school, it is assumed that you have acquired some knowledge and have usually studied before you go into a test situation. Even if you go to a test prepared, however, you won't write a good response if you don't answer the right question. Sometimes students will say, "But I studied so hard and I wrote so much; surely that means something." The answer to such a statement is that unless the question has been addressed, it matters not what has been written down. Even if you did study hard and know the answer, if you don't put on paper what the question asked for, it's as if you hadn't studied. Knowing what the question demands and how to respond to it effectively are some of the issues this chapter will address.

Getting Ready

Before taking any test, there are things you can do to get yourself ready. Some of these are physical; some are psychological.

Strategy 1: Study by Composing Possible Questions

You usually don't know the exact questions your instructor will ask in an essay exam, but you have some idea. After all, there is only so much material that has been covered. Assuming that you have been taking notes and have some knowledge of the material for the test, the best way to prepare is to assume the role of teacher and write down questions that demand essay answers. As you review the material in this way, you are actually thinking of the most important points that would be included in the test questions. Once you have come up with several questions, close your book and outline the answers, perhaps even timing yourself to see how long it takes to answer the questions.

Suppose, for example, that you expect a test question on Reginald Rose's drama, *Twelve Angry Men.* If your instructor has emphasized how America's legal system stresses the rights of the accused, he or she will likely ask questions related to the justice system as demonstrated in the play. To get yourself ready, you might pose—and answer—related questions such as these:

- What were the evidences presented to the jury? Were they weak or did they make a good case?

- Do you think the jury system produced a fair outcome, and why?

- Why do you think Juror Eleven's statement, "We have nothing to gain or lose by our verdict. This is one of the reasons we are strong." is important to the way the jurors voted?

- Why did Juror Number Three finally change his verdict?

- Do you think the jurors were objective, or did their knowledge of the circumstances of the young man enter into their decision?

- How did the jurors' own backgrounds influence their decisions?

Though you could ask yourself numerous other questions as well, these questions give you an overall view of the play and provide thoughts for what the instructor might ask.

Activity 1: Write Down Questions

Take a book you are reading and follow the questioning procedure given above. Make sure your questions cover the scope of the book, but pay particular attention to areas your instructor has emphasized.

Strategy 2: Get Physically and Mentally Ready

After you have prepared for the test by studying, the next thing to do is to get your mind and body set. Psyche yourself into taking the test; be mentally prepared and physically ready. Bring at least two pencils to class or, better yet, an erasable pen so that you can erase and start over as needed. Bring plenty of paper and a dictionary and thesaurus to help if you suddenly can't spell a word or need another word with a more exact meaning. Electronic pocket spellers are easy to use and can be helpful as well.

If you can move to a part of the classroom where it is quieter, that might also help. One student, David, always moved to a corner of the room with his back to the class when he took his tests so that he could concentrate. If you can't move, however, mentally close yourself in to keep distractions to a minimum.

The point of these suggestions is that the more prepared you are, the more confident and relaxed you will be. And being more relaxed will help you to concentrate on the task at hand.

Activity 2: Get Ready, Get Set, GO!

Write a brief explanation of what you can do to prepare yourself to take a test. Think about the problems you have in test-taking situations and how you might overcome them. If you wish, you can include the suggestions given under Strategy 2.

Taking the Test

Taking the test is more than just sitting down and starting to write. For best results, you need to approach the task analytically.

Strategy 3: Allocate Your Time

After you get the test, the first thing to do is to scan it. Don't just start answering the first question without looking over the whole test. Once you know how many questions you have, then you can apportion planning, writing, and revising time to each question. One rule of thumb with essay questions is to set aside about two minutes planning and one minute revising for each five minutes that you schedule for actual writing.

The first time or two you use this schedule, you may think it is hard to do, but after adjusting yourself to a time limit, you will be better able to complete the whole test. Many times students know the answers to all the questions but because they spend too much time on the first part of the test, they never get to the end—or they write hurried, one-or-two-sentence answers to the last few questions. The unanswered or barely answered questions count off as if the students didn't know the answers. That can be tough to deal with, but the whole test is to be answered thoroughly; not just the part you have time for.

Strategy 4: Understand What the Question Asks

After you have scanned the test and have scheduled your time, the next thing to do is to analyze each question before you start to answer it. This may sound difficult, but it really isn't. You will be looking for two things in particular: (1) specific aspects of the question and (2) key words that indicate the organizational pattern. Your ability to reason logically, to argue persuasively, to organize ideas, and to analyze problems clearly now comes into play.

Identify Each Aspect of the Question.   The typical essay question asks you to do two or three specific things. To make sure you address each of these, you must read the question carefully in order to understand what is required. To illustrate, look at the examples and discussion below.

- From your knowledge of Horatian and Juvenalian satire, show how the eighteenth-century writers, Jonathan Swift, Alexander Pope, Joseph Addison, and Richard Steele used these kinds of satire in their writings.
- Analyze the short story "Leningen Versus the Ants" by Carl Stephenson by discussing the external and internal conflict of the main character. Then show how the conflict was resolved.
- Evaluate George Bernard Shaw's play *Pygmalion* in terms of its being a social satire commenting on class distinctions. Give examples from the play of the different classes, showing how Shaw makes fun of them.

Now, what do you have to work with? Let's see what each of the questions requires.

To answer the first question, you would need to know what is meant by Horatian and Juvenalian satire; then you would show how the four writers used the two kinds of satire in their writings. Your examples from each writer would have to demonstrate that you understood the difference between the two types.

The second question involves an analysis of the external and internal conflicts in "Leningen Versus the Ants." Without telling the whole story, you would describe both conflicts and show how they were resolved. The key word in this question is *analyze,* which demands breaking the story down into the two kinds of conflict and discussing them. You would have to make sure not only that you explained the conflicts thoroughly, but also that you discussed their resolution, as mentioned in the last part of the question.

To write the third essay, you must look at the play from the standpoint of its being a social commentary on class distinction. You would begin by stating that Shaw criticized the social classes in England in *Pygmalion,* and then go on to discuss the different classes and how Shaw portrays each through the characters and the situations he puts them in. You would not retell the whole story, but would refer to it as needed for incidents and other examples that supported your answer. You would be careful, too, that the examples you chose clearly showed Shaw making fun of society.

Knowing, then, that essay questions almost always have different parts and remembering to address all of them is a key strategy in writing good answers. Another is to look for key words or terms.

Know What the Key Term Asks For.   If you miss what the key term in the question tells you to do, you will not answer the question correctly. With a question asking you to *contrast* two poems, for example, you would receive no credit for pointing out their similarities. The terms that follow are those that are most frequently used in essay questions; sample questions using the terms are also provided. Be sure you know what each term means.

- *Analyze:* Break the question down into parts.
  > EXAMPLE: Analyze the effect of Dr. Martin Luther King's "I Have a Dream" speech on the civil rights movement today.

- *Categorize* or *classify:* Explain according to types.
  > EXAMPLE: Categorize or classify the major writers of the Elizabethan period according to the types of writing they did.

- *Compare:* Point out likenesses.
  > EXAMPLE: Compare Mel Gibson and Laurence Olivier in their presentations of Hamlet in the two movie versions of the play.

- *Contrast:* Point out differences.
  > EXAMPLE: Contrast the writing styles of E. E. Cummings and A. E. Housman.

- *Criticize:* Judge the significance of the topic.
  > EXAMPLE: Critique Newt Gingrich's term as Speaker of the House according to the way he was able to work with Congress and the president.

- *Define:* Give brief, clear meanings of words or concepts.
  > EXAMPLE: Define what a hero is according to the Old English epic *Beowulf.*

- *Demonstrate* or *show:* Provide examples to support your opinion.
  > EXAMPLE: Demonstrate the way that Poe used the arabesque in his short stories.

- *Describe:* Discuss the topic in accurate detail, giving facts, not opinions.
  > EXAMPLE: Describe the Rwandan refugees' return to their homes.

- *Diagram:* Make a drawing to show how something works.
  > EXAMPLE: Make a diagram of the state of Texas and show where the major writers were born.

- *Discuss:* Examine in detail.
  > EXAMPLE: Discuss the impact the program MADD (Mothers Against Drunk Drivers) has in your community.

- *Enumerate:* Make a list of topics, points, or items.
  > EXAMPLE: Enumerate the causes of the French Revolution.

- *Evaluate:* Judge the value or worth of something in terms of certain guidelines.
  > EXAMPLE: Evaluate talk shows on television according to audience appeal, charisma of hosts, and topics chosen for airing.

- *Explain:* Give the significance or the meaning of something.
  - **EXAMPLE:**   Explain the effect the Oklahoma bombing of the Federal Building had on the FBI's conception of militia groups.
- *Illustrate:* Explain a concept or topic with examples or drawings.
  - **EXAMPLE:**   Illustrate how the loss of ozone layers in the atmosphere poses problems to humanity.
- *Interpret:* Provide a meaning for or explanation of something.
  - **EXAMPLE:**   Interpret Senator Simon's decision not to run for another term.
- *Justify:* Present arguments or sound explanations in support of something.
  - **EXAMPLE:**   Justify judges' decisions to allow hung juries to stop negotiating.
- *Outline:* Briefly present the key factors or divisions of the topic, often in chronological order.
  - **EXAMPLE:**   Outline the way you plan to organize your time in answering essay questions.
- *Project* or *predict:* Make a predetermination of what might happen.
  - **EXAMPLE:**   Project the way that space travel will affect people in the twenty-first century.
- *Prove:* Back up your answer with definitive facts.
  - **EXAMPLE:**   Prove that Tess in *Tess of the D'Urbervilles* by Thomas Hardy was a victim of circumstances.
- *Relate:* Show the connections or associations between or among topics.
  - **EXAMPLE:**   Relate the procedures in the O. J. Simpson civil trial to those in less publicized civil trials.
- *Review:* Analyze with discussion the major points of a topic or movie.
  - **EXAMPLE:**   Review the technique of irony as shown by Emily Bronte in *Jane Eyre.*
  - **EXAMPLE:**   Review the film *One Hundred and One Dalmatians* in terms of audience appeal, theme, and story line.
- *State:* Present the main points related to a topic without description.
  - **EXAMPLE:**   State the kinds of writing most prevalent in the Middle Ages.
- *Summarize:* Give a brief overview of the main points.
  - **EXAMPLE:**   Summarize the way the outbreak of the E coli virus has affected medical science.
- *Trace:* Describe the development of something from one point to another, in more detail than an outline.
  - **EXAMPLE:**   Trace the development of the third party system in American politics from its inception to the present.

Activity 3: Study the Questions

From the three essay questions below, choose one and do the following: (a) identify the points to cover the answer to the questions completely, and (b) tell what procedure the key terms require you to use in dealing with the facts.

- Explain the conflicts between fathers and sons in Chinua Achebe's *Things Fall Apart.*
- Compare the way that Nathaniel Hawthorne in *The Scarlet Letter* handled Hester Prynn's act of adultery and the way that adultery is regarded today.
- Analyze how each supernatural occurrence in the play affects Macbeth.

Strategy 5: Briefly Outline Your Answer

After you have identified the key words, briefly outline your answer so that you will include all parts to the question. This outline does not have to be formal or even very detailed; but it should include the main points you want to cover, an example or two for each, and an indication of how you will follow the question's directive of analyzing, comparing, or the like. Prepare your outline in no more than the length of planning time you've given yourself; if other points or examples occur to you while you're writing, jot them down then.

Here is a rough outline based on one of the sample essay questions above.

Shakespeare's Uses of the Supernatural in Macbeth

- Witches (make him ambitious and cunning)
- Floating dagger (makes him think about his motives)
- Banquo's ghost (frightens him; makes him crazy)
- Child apparitions (give warnings—Macduff, Birnam Wood—which he misinterprets)
- Parade of kings (enrages him)

Activity 4: Outline an Essay Question

Choose another of the sample essay questions covered in this chapter, or one your instructor provides for you, and write a brief outline for it.

Strategy 6: Write a Thesis Statement Based on the Question

One easy way to make sure you are answering the right question is to turn the question around into a statement that is, in effect, like a thesis statement in an essay or a topic sentence in a paragraph. For example, for the essay question on *Macbeth,* the thesis statement should be something like this.

Each incident of the supernatural that Macbeth encounters—the appearance of witches, a floating dagger, Banquo's ghost, the child apparitions, and the parade of kings—has a decided effect on how he reacts.

Now begin to write your answer. Write on every other line of your paper so that you have space to make changes or corrections. Follow the plan you outlined, using details or evidence to support your answer. Finally, conclude the question with a statement that sums up the main ideas. Then check your answer for grammar, spelling, and punctuation errors and to see if you have answered each part of the question.

Activity 5: Write a Thesis Statement

Write a thesis statement and an introductory paragraph for the topic you outlined in Activity 4.

Strategy 7: Review Your Answer

Because of the time constraints of an essay test, most instructors will not mark off too heavily for small errors or wording problems. Still, you should allow yourself enough time at the end to review your response and to correct as many errors as possible. Assuming that you made sure in advance that you answered the right question using the right development process, you should still have time to do the following:

- See that your essay is organized with a thesis or topic sentence leading into your answer.
- Check for supporting points to back up each assertion you make.
- Make sure that you have complete sentences and your paper is well written.
- Look for errors in spelling, punctuation, and grammar.

Activity 6: Analyze Your Answers

Find copies of an old essay test you took and analyze your responses according to the information in this chapter. Determine how you did on each of the questions. How would you improve your essay if you had a chance to do it over again?

A Final Word about Grading

Essays are always hand-scored, which means that the instructor *will* grade your paper. Usually if the question has several parts to it, the instructor will give you points based on what you have answered correctly. In other words, you will get part credit rather than no credit at all.

Note also that in a multi-itemed test, many instructors will put the point value beside each question, indicating that some questions will receive more points than others. Plan your answering strategy accordingly. It is smarter, for example, to answer three 10-point questions that you feel very confident about than spend a lot of time on one 25-point question that you find quite difficult. Save that difficult question until the end, and then write as much about it as you can in the time available.

Saying It with Style—Correctly

Style—just what is it? On certain levels it might mean the kinds of clothing people are wearing, or the way they cut their hair. It might also refer to a person's way of speaking. Sometimes a speaker will put on an affected air, which will make him or her sound superficial. At other times a speaker may imitate a particular person—sometimes to amuse, sometimes to impress others. In both cases, the speakers are changing their normal way of speaking to accommodate their surroundings. They are changing their style, adapting their language for a particular occasion.

Style is also a part of writing. As we noted earlier, it has to do with your choice of words, your use of things like dialogue and repetition, and the rhythm of your sentences. Just as people can change their speech to suit the situation, so may writers change their style according to their audience. For example, if you were writing a persuasive essay, you would use language appealing to the group or person to whom you were writing. If you were writing in your journal, you would be using language that only you would read, so it would be very informal. That is as it should be. You write depending on your audience and your aim or purpose.

Activity 1: Create Different Styles

Choose a nursery rhyme and change it so that it is written in at least three different styles: (1) formal, (2) colloquial (language that sounds like the speech in your area of the country), and (3) Elizabethan style with flowery language. Share these with classmates to see how they have changed the same nursery rhymes.

Strategies for Developing a Strong Style

Even the most boring writers have some sort of style to their writing. It's just that their style doesn't compel the audience to get involved with what they have written. There are certain things that all writers can do, however, to improve their style.

Use Your Personal Voice

One element of your style to work on is your "voice"—the unique way that you make your writing sound like you. If a student's voice is truly distinct, most instructors will know how that student's writing will sound after they have read just a few of his or her papers. It's the same way that someone can tell who is speaking without seeing the other person: by recognizing the speaker's voice.

Many students eliminate their real voice from their writing in an attempt to produce something that they think their instructor will like. Unfortunately, writing like this loses its distinctive qualities and comes to sound like all the other voiceless students' papers.

As with speaking, your voice in writing may take on many different tones as you express different attitudes—happiness, anger, sadness, exuberance, gloom. You show these attitudes by the words that you use and how you put them together.

In the following passage from "The Yellow Cat" by Evans Wall, see how the voice is shown.

> She caught her breath as the thought came. It wasn't *him* that got shot! Maybe Mac came back to—!
>
> She turned and ran around the cabin.
>
> A body lay just outside the kitchen door: but not that of the blond boy. A lithe, tawny animal. Seeming, in death, twice his natural size.
>
> Voices drew nearer. The crowd was coming from the front of the cabin. She couldn't face them and answer questions.
>
> Bending down, she took up the body of her dead pet, held it cradled in her arms and walked stumblingly away. Away through the silvery moonlight, away among the tall stalks of dew-drenched tasseling corn.

The writer chooses his words carefully to show the anxiety of the girl who was afraid she had shot someone. Notice then the change when she realizes it was her pet instead, and she carries it "stumblingly away."

Now look at a different example of voice, from the short story "Encounter" by Thomas S. Smith. Notice the difference in tone, wording, and sentence structure from the previous example.

> It had been only a dream. I hadn't thought too much of it. I had even dismissed it from my thoughts. It had been nothing but a nonsensical dream.
>
> Not even after Brother John had spoken of the reality of the devil in one of his sermons had I given much thought to it. Yes, I believe evil exists in today's world—evil personified in Satan or Lucifer or whatever

his label. But as the minister often says, thoughts concerning wickedness are with us but often pushed into the background. Meeting the devil seems out of the question in this day and age.

As you do different types of writing, you will want to vary your voice to fit the circumstances. In the first account above, it's easy to feel with the character what is happening to her. In the second account, the writer is remembering a dream and there is little action. The voice varies because of the different circumstances being described.

Activity 2: Create Voice and Tone

Write two descriptions of a favorite hangout. In the first description, use neutral language that doesn't reveal your feelings about the subject. In the second description, use words and expressions that reflect your feelings. Share the descriptions with a classmate. Ask him or her to describe the tone of each and to examine the two accounts for evidences of the same "voice."

Use Specific, Well-Chosen Words

In writing as in speaking, using the right word helps the reader visualize the intended meaning. For example, it is correct to say "chase" the ball, "run after" the ball, and "go get" the ball because they all mean the same, but "chase" is more descriptive than "go get." It carries with it the picture of running fast, and you can see what is happening.

Using the right word is a way to appeal to the senses so that the reader can see, hear, feel, touch, or taste what you are describing. Look at the sentences below to see the difference that descriptive words make in painting a picture of the two fighters.

1. At the end of the count, the two fighters came to center ring.
2. At the end of the count, the two fighters advanced ferociously to center ring.
3. At the end of the count, the two fighters merged at center ring.
4. At the end of the count, the two fighters approached center ring with fire in their eyes.

As with the example about the ball, sentences 2 and 4 carry a much more vivid picture than sentences 1 and 3, yet all four say essentially the same thing. It's the choice of words that makes the difference and helps you to visualize the two fighters.

Activity 3: Use Vivid Words

Change the lifeless sentences below in at least three ways to create a more vivid picture.

1.   The girls cooked dinner for their father.
2.   The stadium was filled with fans.
3.   I could hear the siren last night when I lay down.
4.   Mary called to tell us the news about Juanita.
5.   The bell rang for school to begin.

Make Your Writing Concrete Rather Than Abstract

Abstract words are those that name qualities, ideas, or characteristics—things that cannot be seen; concrete words are those that name things that can be perceived by the senses. Abstract writing is similar to abstract words. It lacks specific details and is filled with vague, indefinite words and broad, general statements. Abstract writing is not incorrect, but it lacks the excitement that concrete writing gives. Look at these examples to see the difference that concrete writing makes.

ABSTRACT: Mrs. Smith grades hard.
CONCRETE: Mrs. Smith flunked half the class and didn't give a grade above a C.

ABSTRACT: John Gunther's book *Death Be Not Proud* is sad.
CONCRETE: John Gunther's book *Death Be Not Proud* is a moving account of his son's losing bout with leukemia.

As you can see, neither abstract example conveys the whole story. The impact is much less than that of the concrete examples, which, by replacing the abstract terms *hard* and *sad* with specific explanations that define them, make the sentences really say something.

Using specific details is the best way to avoid abstract writing, and the more specific, the better. When you learn to use specific details in your writing, you are giving yourself another tool in creating an individual style.

Activity 4: Use Concrete Writing

In the five sentences below, change the abstract writing to concrete writing. Replace vague or abstract words with words and phrases that convey a more vivid image.

1.   The story he told was funny.
2.   The happy clown joined the circus.
3.   Dogs bark when they see cats.
4.   *Mary Poppins* was the best movie I saw when I was a child.
5.   The fire was very hot.

Avoid Loaded Words

Loaded words are those that have strong connotations, either positive or negative. They appeal to the emotions and therefore can easily bias people in one way or another. Loaded words are often found in political campaigns as politicians try to convince voters to vote for them. The candidate who describes himself or herself as *issue-oriented,* as one who will stand up for *family values* and *fight organized crime,* as one who will spend *every working moment* engaged in activities which will *benefit his or her constituents* is suspect at the beginning. He or she is using emotion-loaded words to appeal to the feelings of people who don't think through campaign promises.

Often you see loaded accounts of trials in the newspapers; that is, language is used that is meant to sway reaction toward one side or the other, depending on who wrote the story. Look at the example below to see the same account written by two different reporters.

ACCOUNT 1: In the courtroom this morning, attentive jurors listened to Janice Hopkins tell the story of how she had been attacked in the stairwell of her apartment by a man carrying a knife. Everyone in the courtroom listened carefully to the details of the brutal attack.

ACCOUNT 2: In the courtroom this morning, enthralled jurors listened while Janice Hopkins told every detail of how she had been viciously assaulted in the stairwell of her apartment by a man wielding a knife. Everyone in the courtroom strained to hear every word of her exhaustive and vivid testimony.

Both newspaper accounts give essentially the same information, but the second account is definitely more biased. In the first account, the jurors are "attentive," a neutral term, whereas in the second, they are "enthralled." In the first, Janice "tell[s] the story," the man is "carrying a knife," and everyone in the courtroom "listened carefully." The only clue to the kind of attack is the word "brutal." In the second account, however, the words change to "told every detail of the vicious assault," "wielding a knife," and "strained to hear every word of her exhaustive and vivid testimony." While the second account paints a more vivid picture, the writer has clearly chosen words that make his audience see things in a certain way. Because few people know the whole story, the words are powerful.

While it may seem that loaded words only come up in political or legal situations, you often use them unconsciously in your descriptions of things. For example, you are writing a personal narrative that involves a dinner given in your father's honor. If you describe the dinner as a gourmet feast with all of the trimmings fit for a king, your description is loaded in favor of the meal. On the other hand, if you describe the same dinner by saying that you would have done as well eating at a fast-food joint, then you are conveying a negative image. Unless you have a specific point to make—for example, you want to present someone in a particular way in a character sketch—it is generally better to use an accurate description rather than one involving loaded, emotionally charged words.

Activity 5: Find Examples of Loaded Words

Find five newspaper or newsmagazine clippings that use loaded language—either in advertisements, editorials, or other parts of the paper—and bring them to class. Analyze the emotional impact of the words and present your findings to the class.

Avoid Clichés

People use clichés in speaking as well as writing, but many clichés have been used so often that they have very little value. Clichés are often called tired words because of their overuse; they have become vague and have little meaning. To be effective in writing, it is best to avoid using clichés because they are dull and lifeless. Look at the paragraph below to see how ineffective clichés are and then note the revision of the same paragraph.

First Draft

It was a cold winter night that was as clear as a bell. I was so hungry I felt I could eat a horse, so I stopped at Chan's Diner. The server, who looked as old as the hills, was slower than molasses, but I tried to remain cool and collected while he took my order. The restaurant actually was a beehive of activity so I tried not to fly off the handle while waiting for the food. When I finally ate, I felt like a dead pig in the sunshine because I was so stuffed.

Revision

It was a cold, clear winter night with the stars shining. I was very hungry, so I stopped at Chan's Diner. The server was elderly and rather slow but, though I was irritated, I tried to be patient while he took my order. The restaurant was exceptionally busy, so I held my temper while waiting for the food. When I finally ate, I ate so much that I was stuffed.

Activity 6: Rewrite Cliché-Filled Sentences

Explain the clichés below and then write a sentence expressing the same idea but with fresh, new language.

1. He wouldn't harm a fly.
2. What goes around comes around.
3. A bird in the hand is worth two in the bush.
4. Birds of a feather flock together.
5. What's good for the goose is good for the gander.

Vary Sentence Structure

While the normal sentence pattern is subject-verb-object, a whole paper written in this order can get pretty dull. It is much better to vary your sentences to avoid monotony and to achieve greater variety and interest. Varying sentence structure can be as simple as placing a modifier at the beginning of a sentence or using subordination to combine sentences. The examples below show the subject-verb-object pattern and then the variation.

The building was enormous and elegant and was an impressive sight.

Enormous and elegant, the building was an impressive sight.

An ice hockey team was formed this year for the first time in the history of the city.

For the first time in the history of the city, an ice hockey team was formed.

Sue and Kimble arrived at the commencement late. It rained so hard they were afraid to travel fast.

Because the heavy rain made them afraid to travel fast, Sue and Kimble arrived at the commencement late.

Too much sunshine can cause heatstroke. It is good to know the symptoms of too much sun.

Since too much sunshine can cause heatstroke, it is good to know the symptoms of too much sun.

Activity 7: Vary Your Sentence Structure

Rewrite the paragraph below to get some variation in sentence pattern. Combine sentences when necessary.

Holidays are a big time for children. They like to celebrate everything from birthdays to special days of the year. Valentine's Day is a big time for them. They enjoy sending and receiving Valentines in school. They watch fireworks at Fourth of July celebrations. Thanksgiving is special too. Children learn about pilgrims. They enjoy Christmas most. They like to decorate Christmas trees and get presents from Santa Claus. Holidays are fun for them all year.

Create Your Own Style

You may have heard that writers are born rather than made, but that is not true. Some people may have a propensity for writing, but they are not necessarily born with the desire to write. It is created in them as they observe their surroundings and find a need to express in words what they see and hear and feel. They become sensitive to sounds and to the feelings of others. But they learn the techniques of writing just as you are doing—by studying and by trial and error. They see what works and what doesn't, and they learn to use language to create their own style.

The end result of studying the techniques in this chapter and others in this book should be that you too learn to develop your own style, your individual way of expressing yourself in writing. For just as no two people have the same fingerprints, no two people write the same. You may learn to write by imitating another person's style, but that doesn't mean you will write in the same way he or she does. It means that you will take some of the person's techniques and make them work for you, but you will never be able to write exactly the same. You have your own voice, and that is as it should be.

Improve Your Sentences

In this last part of the chapter, you will learn about some ways to improve the structure of your sentences by eliminating common weaknesses and errors. Let this be your guide to good essays.

Use Parallelism

Parallelism means that all sentence elements that are alike in importance should be expressed in the same way. Parallelism should be used with words in a series, such as nouns, verbs, prepositional phrases, adjectives, infinitives, participles, and clauses. Usually the first word sets the pattern for the rest in a series. Here are some examples:

POOR: He liked to fish, hunting, and to golf.

BETTER: He liked to fish, to hunt, and to golf. [Parallel infinitives]

POOR: The baby was kicking, crying, and threw a fit.

BETTER: The baby was kicking, crying, and throwing a fit. [Parallel verb forms]

POOR: The lawyer gave specific instructions about when they should arrive, how they should dress, and the exact things to say.

BETTER: The lawyer gave specific instructions about when they should arrive, how they should dress, and what exactly they should say.

POOR: Her favorites are desserts, eating fresh fruit, and to drink hot chocolate.

BETTER: Her favorites are desserts, fresh fruit, and hot chocolate. [Parallel nouns]

POOR: By the people and giving the people free reign is the way our government should be run.

BETTER: By the people and for the people is the way our government should be run.

Avoid Wordiness

You have already looked at using the right words in making your sentences interesting and meaningful. But you also have to be careful not to use too many words, particularly "deadwood"—words that don't really say anything. After you have completed an essay, think about what you meant to say and then look at how you said it. Often you are redundant, saying the same thing in more than one way. For example, if you say you are "looking forward toward the future," you are being redundant. Since *forward* means future, a better wording would be "looking toward the future." Many common expressions are redundant, but people aren't aware of it because they hear others use the expressions. Here are some more examples.

past history [*history* is sufficient]

huge throng [*throng* is sufficient]

requirements needed for [*requirements for* is sufficient]

Besides watching for common redundant expressions in your writing, other ways to avoid wordiness are (1) to delete words or groups of words that repeat ideas and (2) to compress or substitute single words for groups of words. See the examples below.

DELETION: The horse threw the rider over the fence, making him wary of riding a horse again, and he decided this was the end of horseback riding. (The sentence could end after *again* because the next part is saying the same thing.)

COMPRESSION: We walked through the place where they grew their flowers and took in through our noses the sweet air that smelled like perfume. (This sentence could be compressed by saying, "We walked through the garden and smelled the perfumed air.")

In both examples, the two sentences say the same thing, but words are left out or substituted in the improved version. Wordiness can destroy the meaning of what you are trying to say because the reader can get bogged down in all the unnecessary details.

Activity 8: Cut Out Deadwood

Copy each phrase below. Cross out any words that make it redundant.

1. still and all
2. combined together
3. hopeful optimism
4. connect up
5. throughout the whole night
6. one and only
7. exact same
8. circle around
9. numerous in number
10. true facts
11. fatal death
12. small in size
13. advance planning
14. meet up with
15. join together
16. each and every
17. young in age
18. long length of time

Activity 9: Compress and Delete

Compress or delete words from the following sentences to eliminate redundancies.

1. The trailer was knocked over by the high winds and horrible gusts and nothing was left standing except the stones on which it stood.
2. The Boy Scout leader called all of the scouts and asked all of the scouts to bring their cars to run in the soap box derby race.
3. Flowers that are ornamental are often fragile and do not stand cold weather well, which means they must be cared for gently so they will weather cold weather.
4. *The Complete Gardener* is a book which should be given to all neophyte gardeners. It helps first-timers know when to plant and gives them tips about taking care of plants.
5. Warming by a fireplace is wonderful in cold weather; nothing is better than being able to sit in front of a fireplace and get warm.

Avoid Fragments and Run-ons

There is nothing more distracting than reading a paragraph with fragments or run-on sentences. A fragment is a group of words that does not express a complete thought. It does not have either a subject or a verb and therefore cannot stand alone. A run-on sentence combines two sentences by using a comma—or no punctuation—instead of a period or semicolon or conjunction. Look at the examples below of fragments and run-on sentences and note how they can be corrected.

FRAGMENT: Making jelly out of muscadines in the summer when we visited our grandmother.

CORRECTED: We made jelly out of muscadines in the summer when we visited our grandmother. [Subject added]

FRAGMENT: In the newspaper were pictures of the plane crash. Showing the wings breaking off on impact.

CORRECTED: In the newspaper were pictures of the plane crash showing the wings breaking off on impact. [Fragment connected to complete sentence]

RUN-ON SENTENCE: The boys gathered firewood for the camp after they got back they made a huge bonfire.

CORRECTED: The boys gathered firewood for the camp. After they got back, they made a huge bonfire.

RUN-ON SENTENCE: The swans were the most beautiful creatures I had ever seen, they were as white as snow.

CORRECTED: The swans were the most beautiful creatures I had ever seen. They were as white as snow.

Activity 10: Write Sentences Correctly

Rewrite the sentences below to eliminate fragments and run-ons.

1. The toucan she brought me from Costa Rica as a part of a wood chime.
2. Marrying cousins is against the law in some states having a baby that might be deformed is one reason.
3. Recycled paper, recycled glass, and recycled plastics picked up every Tuesday in our city.
4. When she won three gold medals in the Olympics in Atlanta.
5. Jasper and Nan got all of the supplies together ahead of time. To make the canoeing trip go smoothly.
6. After the collision with the train that made me sick to even think about. I decided I would always stop at every railroad crossing and look both ways.
7. Working my way through college, I had little money to spare, the tuition was more than I expected.
8. To do the right thing every time mother called.

9. You will not receive remuneration for the time you spent at the away from the office you said you enjoyed the work more than you would have working at your desk.

10. Listen to that woman, she will never tell you the wrong thing, she is always right because she goes by the rule book, which is parliamentary procedure.

Use Pronouns Correctly

Too often students use pronouns incorrectly because they aren't sure how to handle them. Incorrect pronouns make sentences ambiguous because the reader is not quite sure what is intended. The most common pronoun errors are (1) ambiguous reference, (2) implied reference, (3) buried reference, and (4) double reference. As with redundancies in speaking and writing, knowing how to recognize these errors will help you avoid them.

Look at the following sentences to see how the pronouns are used incorrectly and then how the sentences can be corrected.

AMBIGUOUS REFERENCE: Missy told Claudine that she could visit her anytime. [Who does *she* refer to?]

CLEAR: Missy said to Claudine, "You can visit me anytime."

IMPLIED REFERENCE: The Speaker of the House promised the president he would do what he could to pass the bill and he kept it.

CLEAR: The Speaker of the House promised the president he would do what he could to pass the bill and he kept his promise. [*promise* clarifies the implied meaning of *it*]

BURIED REFERENCE: What's the boy's name that got the highest points on the exam?

CLEAR: What's the name of the boy that got the highest points on the exam? [The boy, not the name, got the points.]

DOUBLE REFERENCE: Angela told Ann that she was going to use her name as a reference when she applied for the job. [Same pronoun is used to refer to two different antecedents]

CLEAR: Angela told Ann, "I am going to use your name as a reference when I apply for the job."

Activity 11: Correct Pronoun Errors

Correct the pronoun errors in the sentences below so that the pronouns are not ambiguous.

1. As soon as the office workers left their offices, the custodians cleaned them.

2. Bill did a beautiful painting for our home and then sprayed it with a mixture to keep it from fading.

3. All of the students in the classroom must have studied for their tests if they want it to do any good when they take them.

4. Max rode to New Mexico with Bill, but he didn't think he would ever ride with him again.

5. After reading the woman's statement, she spoke directly to the audience without notes.

Use Quotations Correctly

Quotations always indicate that you are recording exactly what someone has said or you are taking material directly from a particular source. Indirect quotations are those that do not give a person's exact words and therefore are not set off by quotation marks.

> **DIRECT QUOTATION:** My brother said, "Won't you please come to see me this weekend?"
>
> **INDIRECT QUOTATION:** My brother asked that I come to see him this weekend.

A direct quotation is set off from the rest of the sentence by commas or by a question mark or an exclamation point.

> John said, "We can make the next feature if you hurry."

> "What do you think of your new teacher?" she asked.

Commas and periods are always placed *within* quotation marks. Semicolons and colons are always placed *outside* the quotation marks.

> "I'm happy," said Missy, "that you can go with me."

> "Janice," Mary said, "you should never stay out too late when you have a major test"; then Mary told her to wait for her at the mall.

> The books you are reading are called "escape fiction": those by Grace Livingston Hill and the Harlequin romances.

When you write dialogue, begin a new paragraph every time the speaker changes.

"How's my little kitty?" Gail said on seeing her pet. She took him from Peter and hugged and kissed the still groggy animal.

"Why didn't you tell me you were going to have him declawed?" Peter asked.

"I did."

When quoting more than four lines from a source, indent five spaces on the left and then begin the quote *without* using quotation marks. The indention shows that the material is quoted. Continue with the indention throughout the quote. If the first line is the beginning of a paragraph, indent an additional five spaces. Do not indent on the right side of the page. Always either introduce the quote by saying where it is taken from or put the reference at the end of the quoted material.

Activity 12:   Punctuate Quotations Correctly

Correct the errors with quotation marks in the sentences below.

1.   Sheila said that "she needed a new home for her pet hamster.
2.   "I'll call my friend Ted and see if he can help", offered Luis.
3.   Sheila said, "There must be children in the neighborhood who like hamsters.
4.   Ted said that "his little brother might want one."
5.   Sheila exclaimed, "Tell him I'll throw in a huge bag of hamster food"!

A Few Last Words

In this chapter, you have looked at developing a personal style by creating a voice and tone of your own and using words that express the way that you feel. You have had exercises that have stressed using specific and vivid words, avoiding abstract terms for more concrete terms, and avoiding loaded words and clichés.

You have also been made aware of the importance of sentence structure by using parallelism, avoiding wordiness, writing complete sentences, and using pronouns and punctuating quotations correctly. Although there are other grammatical errors to be avoided, these are ones which are most pronounced. By studying the correct way to write so that your sentences are clear and understandable, you are able to help your reader appreciate what you have written.

Keep this book with you in your studies as a ready reference to good usage in writing and for knowing how to write essays correctly.

Acknowledgments

Bruno, Pat: "La Vita: Reason to Go On Living," by Pat Bruno. Pat Bruno is the restaurant critic for the *Chicago Sun-Times* and the author of five cookbooks. Reprinted by permission of the author.

Collins, Catherine and Douglas Frantz: "Let Us Prey," by Catherine Collins and Douglas Frantz. From *Modern Maturity* magazine (June 1994).

Fredman, Catherine: "The Ultimate Outdoor Workout," by Catherine Fredman. From *Fitness* magazine (September 1996).

Garver, Lloyd: "No, You Can't Have Nintendo," by Lloyd Garver. Reprinted by permission of the author.

Hurston, Zora Neale: Excerpt from *Dust Tracks on a Road* by Zora Neale Hurston. Copyright © 1942 by Zora Neale Hurston. Copyright renewed 1970 by John C. Hurston. Reprinted by permission of HarperCollins Publishers.

Martinez, Al: "A Vision of Daffodils," by Al Martinez. From *Modern Maturity* magazine (January/February 1997). Reprinted by permission of the author.

McInnis, Doug: "Reservoirs Speed Up Earth's Spin," by Doug McInnis. © Earth, Kalmbach Publishing Co. Reproduced with permission. To subscribe, call 800-533-6644 weekdays.

Scott, Foresman: From *Scott Foresman, The United States in Literature: America Reads,* Classic Edition edited by James E. Miller, Jr., Kerry M. Wood and Carlota Cardenas de Dwyer. Copyright © 1991, 1989, Scott, Foresman and Company, Glenview, Illinois. Reprinted by permission of Scott, Foresman/Addison Wesley.

Sheridan, James E.: "The Gall of the Wild," reprinted courtesy of James E. Sheridan, Professor Emeritus of History, Northwestern University.

White, E. B.: From *The Wild Flag* (Houghton Mifflin). © 1943 E. B. White. Originally in *The New Yorker.* All rights reserved.

The publisher has made every effort to contact copyright holders. Any omissions or errors will be corrected upon notification.

Index